Personal Finance and the Bible

Hidden lessons no matter what you believe

Neil Coleman Bridge

Copyright © 2018 by Neil C. Bridge. All Rights Reserved.

No portion of this publication may be reproduced in any form, stored in any retrieval system, or transmitted in any form by any means—electronic, mechanical, photocopy, recording, or otherwise—without prior written permission of the author, except as provided by United States of America copyright law.

The author has made every effort to ensure the accuracy of the information within this book at time of publication. The author does not assume, and expressly disclaims, any liability to any party for any loss, damage, or disruption caused by errors or omissions, whether such errors or omissions result from accident, negligence, or any other cause.

ISBN: 978-1-9806-6550-2

Imprint: Independently published

For Mother Bridge, who ensured I made it to the library and church. Not in that order.

Contents

Preface 9
Chapter 1: Start with a Good Foundation 12
    Parable Summary 12
    Where you can find it 12
    The Religious Lesson 12
    The Financial Lesson: Start with a Good Foundation 12
        Financial Education 15
        Formal Education 16
        Health 20
        Assets and Investments 22
        Leverage (Debt) 24
        Cash on Hand (or "Emergency Fund") 27
        Insurance 29
        Wills, Trusts, and Estates 35
        Get Professional Help 39
        Conclusion 42
Chapter 2: Compounding – of Money and Mustard 44
    Parable Summary 44
    Where you can find it 44
    The Religious Lesson 44
    The Financial Lesson: The Power of Compounding 44
Chapter 3: Eight Bags of Gold and Three Servants 49
    Parable Summary 49
    Where you can find it 49
    The Religious Lesson 50
    Financial Lesson 1: Returns – Percentage, Absolute, Relative, and Compound Annual 50

- Percentage Returns 51
- Absolute Returns: Size Matters 52
- Relative Returns 55
- Compound Annual Growth Rate (CAGR) 58
- Return Wrap-Up 61
- In Defense of the Third Servant: Negative Returns 62
- Financial Lesson 2: Inflation – the Sneaky, Silent Enemy 65
- Bonus Career Lesson: Respect the Boss 69

Chapter 4: Diversify by Sowing Far and Wide 71
- Parable Summary 71
- Where you can find it 71
- The Religious Lesson 71
- The Financial Lesson: Diversify your Investments, Income Streams, and Managers 71
  - Counterpoint: The Case for Concentration 77

Chapter 5: Grapes don't grow on Thorn Bushes 79
- Parable Summary 79
- Where you can find it 79
- The Religious Lesson 79
- The Financial Lesson: What you see is usually what you get 79

Chapter 6: The Tax Man Cometh 84
- Parable Summary 84
- Where you can find it 84
- The Religious Lesson 84
- A bit of Background 84
- Financial Lesson 1: Pay, and Pay Attention to, your Taxes… 85
- Financial Lesson 2: … But Don't Overpay 90
- Bonus Financial Lesson 1: Tax Brackets, or, Life on the Margin 91

Bonus Financial Lesson 2: Watch out for Flattery.................................94
Chapter 7: So you want to be a Landlord?..97
    Parable Summary..97
    Where you can find it 97
    The Religious Lesson 97
    Financial Lesson 1: (Mis)adventures in Landlording 98
        So you DON'T want to be a Landlord (but still like Real Estate)? 103
    Financial Lesson 2: Don't Throw Good Money after Bad....................104
Chapter 8: The Prodigal Son 110
    Parable Summary..110
    Where you can find it 111
    The Religious Lesson 111
    The Financial Lessons...111
    Financial Lesson 1: Don't Squander your Money................................111
        How Prodigal are You?...112
        Don't be fooled by Large Numbers 114
        The Principle of not spending the Principal 118
    Financial Lesson 2: Trust in a Trust 121
    Corollary Lesson: The Importance of Safety Nets...............................124
        Youth..125
        Health..127
        Family that can (and will) Help 128
Chapter 9: Good Times, Bad Times (You Know You'll have your Share)..131
    Story Summary..131
    Where you can find it 133
    The Religious Significance 133
    Financial Lesson 1: Get while the Getting's Good................................133
    Financial Lesson 2: Don't Forget to Enjoy Yourself.............................136

Financial Lesson 3: Keep some Powder Dry 137
Aesop: Of Grasshoppers and Ants (and Diapause) 139
Chapter 10: The Rich Fool, or How much is enough? 140
Parable Summary 140
Where you can find it 141
The Religious Lesson 141
Financial Lesson: Money isn't Everything 141
Appendix: Investments and Where to Put Them 145
Introduction: Investment and Accounts – Liquids and Containers 145
Part One: The Liquid you pour in – Investments 146
Certificates of Deposit: The CD you can't listen to 146
Bonds, Government Bonds 150
Bonds, Corporate Bonds 159
Taking Stock: Investing in Company Stock 164
Joining Together: Mutual Funds 177
'Til Death (maybe) do we Part: Annuities 194
Variable Annuities 202
The Hybrid: Indexed Annuities 206
A "Real" Investment: Real Estate 209
Things: Investing in Commodities 214
Collectibles 217
Mind your own Business 222
Cash is King 227
Part Two: The Container – Accounts 231
Deposit Accounts 231
Employer-Sponsored Plans: Defined-Benefits 233
Numbers and Letters: Employer-Sponsored Retirement Plans 237
IRAs: The Do-it-Yourself Retirement Plan 254

Health Savings Accounts: Stealth-Mode, Tax-Free Retirement Accounts 259

More Number-Names: 529 Plans 266

Taxable Accounts 276

Conclusion.. 281

Preface

You don't have to be a Christian, or even religious, to benefit from this book. In fact, you will be disappointed if you are looking for deep theological insights. Instead, this is a book about personal finance, and the Bible happens to contain a lot of financial lessons hidden beneath the primary spiritual lessons.

People who aren't exposed to, or interested in, the Bible never get a chance to hear those financial lessons. People familiar with the Bible might never even think about the financial lessons in the stories they read because they only hear about the spiritual side.

Schools almost never teach personal finance lessons that students will need every day of their lives, focusing instead on Hamlet's dying words or the quadratic equation. Graduates often never learn basic personal finance concepts, much less how retirement accounts work, or what investment options will be available to them.

When I was growing up, I attended church every Sunday and listened to sermons expounding on spiritual lessons from biblical passages. I was a very attentive listener because my mother sat beside me and she was not one to tolerate nonsense.

In addition to my biblical education, I was always fascinated with financial matters, and had read just about every financial book the local had on its shelves before I graduated from high school.

I couldn't help but draw connections between the stories in the Bible and the financial lessons in the books from the library. In particular, the parables used by Jesus (the principal character of the second half of the Bible) to explain religious principles very often parallel financial lessons that are extremely important and relevant today.

Parables are stories designed to teach a simple lesson in a roundabout way. For instance, I could say:

"Take care of your health."

But where's the fun in that? Instead, imagine I said the same thing in parable form:

"There once was a man who had a boat that he never sanded or painted, and which he left outside in the sun, rain, ice, and wind. The man neglected his boat in this way for many years, and the boat deteriorated with each passing season. One day, the man went out fishing in the boat, and when he was a long way from shore, the boat fell apart and sank and the man drowned. And a shark bit his leg off."

After you looked at me with a perplexed look on your face and asked me what I was talking about, and if I was feeling particularly expansive, I might say:

"In my story, the boat represents your body, and the lack of maintenance represents your bad habits like smoking crack, only sleeping three hours each night, and eating only deep-fried foods. Just as the boat sank, your body will eventually give out and you'll die terribly. And probably alone."

Parables are not the most direct way of teaching, but they are interesting and you're more likely to remember them. Parables also happened to be Jesus' preferred teaching method. Jesus traveled around with 12 followers (his "disciples") and was always trying to teach them spiritual lessons via parables. The usually didn't understand the message, leaving an exasperated Jesus to explain what he meant.

Jesus' parables are recorded in the first four books of the second part of the Bible. The books – Matthew, Mark, Luke, and John – are the names of four of Jesus' disciples who wrote them down as they remembered them. The parables were designed to convey spiritual lessons. But they very often double as financial lessons if you're paying attention.

Each chapter of this book discusses a selected passage from the Bible – usually a parable – focusing on the financial lesson. Each chapter summarizes the parable, notes where you can find it (in case you want to verify that I'm not making it up), briefly notes the religious lesson (one or two sentences in case you're curious; skip over this part if you don't want to be contaminated by religion in any way), and then discusses the financial lesson in detail.

There is also a large Appendix that almost functions like a second book. The Appendix reviews some common investments and investment account types, explaining how they work and their advantages and disadvantages. The Appendix is designed to serve as a reference you can look back to, and is more "nuts-and-bolts" than the main book, which focuses on general financial principles.

One interesting point about parables is that Jesus did not present them as actual events; he explicitly invented them to illustrate a point. Even to the original listeners, the parables were presented as stories and not as actual events. Thus, you can take the parables as they were originally intended – illustrations – and focus on the hidden financial lessons contained within.

If you already know the stories, hopefully the financial tie-in will let you see them in a different light. If you didn't already know the stories, even better: you'll learn the financial lesson and get a snippet of something that's in the Bible as well. Either way, it should easier to keep the financial lesson in mind if you connect it to the parable.

Finally, nothing in this book or its Appendix is intended as legal, investment, or tax advice. Seriously. That isn't just a boilerplate disclaimer. Every person's situation is different, which implies that perfectly good advice for you might be terrible advice for someone else. The point of this book is to provide you with some basic ideas and concepts to arm you with enough knowledge to help make better sense of the financial world and be able to ask smart questions when you talk to professionals (investment advisors, accountants, lawyers, etc.). This book is a starting point, not a destination.

Chapter 1: Start with a Good Foundation

Parable Summary

A wise man built his house on a foundation of rock. It rained, rivers rose, and the wind blew. But the wise man's house was fine because its foundation was on solid rock. Meanwhile, a foolish man built his house on sand. It rained, rivers rose, and the wind blew. And the foolish man's house fell apart. The story is silent on whether the foolish man and his family were inside when the house collapsed or whether the house floated down the swollen river, but the reader is free to imagine those details.

Where you can find it

Matthew 7:24 – 26 and Luke 6:46 – 49.

By the way, the parables often appear in multiple places in the Bible since they were written down by different people. They sometimes differ in minor details, as you'd expect from independently-recorded recollections, but are essentially identical.

The Religious Lesson

Jesus' teachings are the spiritual foundation and listeners should put those teachings into practice.

The Financial Lesson: Start with a Good Foundation

One could argue whether the "wise man" was actually wise, or whether he just seemed wise compared to the idiot who built his house on sand. You don't need an engineering degree to know that sand makes a poor foundation for a house. Any five-year-old who has built a sand castle at the beach could have told Mr. Foolish that his housing endeavor was doomed.

The important financial lesson from this parable is not about houses. Obviously, you don't build a house on sand. Modern building code requirements would prevent you from doing so anyway.

Instead, the lesson here relates to the importance of creating a strong financial foundation for yourself in order to increase your odds of being financially successful. Or, said differently, to decrease your odds of financial failure.

The "house" in the parable is your life. The wind and rain are the bad things that happen – job loss, stock market crashes, identity theft, illness, your husband draining your bank account and running away to Mexico with the shifty-eyed babysitter you never trusted, and so forth. The "rock" and the "sand" represent decisions you make that determine how financially stable your life will be.

The fact that this parable is about foundations is why we'll look at it first. See what I did there? Pretty clever, eh?

"Success" and "failure" are relative terms, but the parable does a nice job of bypassing such semantics by creating a clear and vivid dichotomy: the successful Mr. Wise is sitting safely in his rock-foundation house, perhaps enjoying a nice glass of wine, while Mr. Foolish is flailing around for a sofa cushion to hold onto as he gets washed down a raging river.

Whatever you call "success," you can improve your odds of achieving it by establishing your life on a solid foundation.

What is the financial equivalent of a foundation of "rock?" The parable presented a simple choice of where to build the house: rock or sand. But financial life isn't that straightforward. After all, Mr. Wise only made one decision – where to build – with only two options – rock or sand – and he was finished. Then he could sit back and relax.

We face hundreds of decisions in our financial lives. And each decision requires a choice among far more than two options. And those options are more complex than simply "rock or sand." And the answer isn't nearly as obvious.

For example, Instead of choosing between rock and sand, we have to decide which of 10 mutual funds to invest in, each with its own 500-page prospectus detailing complicated fees, penalties, dates, ages, and tax consequences. Of course, that's just the decision tree we face *after* we choose among various competing investments. And which type of account to keep them in.

There's no way this book could spell out in detail every situation that might arise and what to do in every one. First, I don't know. Second, even if I did, I couldn't fit everything in one book. Third, everyone's financial situation is unique, which means that the right decision for any particular individual must be unique. Fourth, specifics would quickly become obsolete, as the financial world is ever-changing, with new developments every year.

Rather, let's talk about the broad categories of decisions that will lead to a stronger foundation if you can get them right. Or at least avoid getting them too wrong. If you simply recognize that you are facing a decision affecting one of these areas of your life, you will be at a huge advantage because you will know to slow down, think, and do some research before making a decision.

When I was in law school, we had to take the "character and fitness exam" (I passed, so you can rest easy knowing that I am of good moral character – or at least I was at one time). The professor teaching the exam review course said that ethical rules were always changing and that the goal was not remember a particular rule. Instead, the goal was to recognize when you were in a situation with ethical connotations. Once you recognize that you're in an ethical situation, you can go research the rules to make the right decision.

In the parable that started this section, note that Mr. Wise's house was not indestructible. A powerful enough storm could have destroyed his house, regardless of its foundation. Mr. Wise didn't *guarantee* his house's safety by building on rock; he just improved its chances.

That's what this chapter is about: identifying areas to focus on that will improve your odds of not being blown away. This chapter covers basic concepts; if you find it too simplistic, feel free to skip on over to Chapter Two. But everything starts with a foundation, and if there is a reader of this book like the middle-school version of me at the library, he'll appreciate this chapter.

So, what are some broad areas that make up the financial foundation?

Financial Education

First, you should take some time to educate yourself on financial matters. Note that the previous sentence said "educate yourself." That implies proactivity on your part – learning the rules of the game. And by "educating yourself," I do *not* mean sitting down in front of the TV in the evenings to watch a bunch of talking heads opine on the likely direction of the latest market trend and what you should do to get ready for the next day of trading.

Financial self-education involves learning how finances work. Do you know what a 401(k) is, whether you have access to one, and the maximum amount you can contribute to one? Do you know the difference between a Traditional IRA and a Roth IRA, and circumstances where one might be superior to another? Are you familiar with idea of a "1031 Exchange" and what type of real estate transaction that applies to? Do you know the difference between capital gains and dividends, and how each is taxed? Do you know how much you pay each year in taxes and fees?

If not, good news! The answers to these questions and thousands more are readily available. Usually for free. There is no excuse for not learning about this area of your life. It is incredibly important, and the information is there for the taking.

Think back over the last month and add up the number of hours you spent entertaining yourself with mindless TV. Then tally up the amount of time you spent learning something new about your finances. Then consider which one is more important in the long run.

You're already on the right track. You bought (or borrowed, or stole) this book, so you are clearly someone who reads and is interested in your finances. So finish reading this book to familiarize yourself with some basic financial principles, and read over the Appendix to get an overview of some common investments and investment accounts.

Then, go to the library, find quality online resources, and/ or listen to people who actually know what they're talking about to learn some more. Be careful about that last one; a lot of people sound like they know what they're talking about, but are actually morons.

What do you read? Start in the financial section. Section 332 of the Dewey Decimal System is a good place to start if you still enjoy going to an actual library like I do (the Bible is in section 200 if you want to read the parables this book is based on).

As mentioned in the Preface, schools don't teach these things. They should, but they don't. You are probably the only one looking out for your own financial future, so start building your foundation by figuring out the basic workings of the world in which you live.

Focus on facts, not opinions:

Fact: "Gold, silver, and oil are commodities that can be bought and sold by regular people on exchanges."

Opinion: "You should sell everything you own, buy as much gold as possible, and wait for the coming [fill in the blank with doomsday scenario *du jour*]."

You don't have to know every nuance of every possible situation, but you work to learn the basics. The point of self-education isn't to do everything yourself. You will still employ professionals like accountants, attorneys, and financial advisors.

In fact, you will probably be *more* likely to employ professionals as you educate yourself because you will be familiar with more financial options and potential pitfalls. You should know enough to be able to ask those professionals the right questions and be less likely to do something stupid or be taken advantage of.

A world of possibilities will open up to you as you learn about financial rules, investments, accounts, tax breaks, and so forth. Spending some time learning about those things is a good way to start putting your financial foundation on rock.

Formal Education

Formal education is another important aspect of your financial foundation. By formal education, we are talking about education in a school or university setting. This includes what type of, and how much, formal education you pursue.

Formal education is a huge component of your financial foundation. It can be helpful or set you back. For many people reading this book, the bulk of formal education – high school, college, graduate school, professional schools – will be in the past. Others might have major scholastic decisions looming ahead, or even be in the process of making them. Still others might be in a position of providing education-related advice (or funding) to someone else.

In general, think of education as an investment of two precious resources: time and money. With the first one being almost infinitely more valuable than the second one.

The fact that *money* is involved is obvious – you pay schools for access to educational resources like professors. In the United States, formal education gets very expensive very quickly after high school. For those who attend private schools before college, it gets expensive even more quickly.

The idea that education is an *investment* is not obvious. At least it doesn't seem to be obvious, given some of the nightmarish stories about people with six-digit student loans, but limited income prospects.

An "investment" is simply when you put your money into something with an expectation of future income. With that working definition in mind, education obviously fits. People put money into an education in order to get a good job or develop skills that will bring in more money later.

Education as an investment was not always so clear. Hard as it may be to believe, there was a time when people largely pursued education for its own benefit (money and standing were inherited, skills were learned on the job, and formal education was largely for the elite to round themselves out). That time has long since passed for the vast majority of people, though, and in the world we live in, education generally looks like an investment.

Unless the prospective student is independently wealthy and has no need for an income, formal education works like a financial investment. And it should be treated that way. For example, that means making an informed decision about what to study, and taking it seriously. If the "future income" in the previous paragraph is coming from a future job, then it is probably worthwhile to think through which courses of study will improve the odds of finding employment after school. It is also worth thinking about which courses do not improve those odds.

What if the hapless student is not interested in a lucrative field, but is passionate about something else? There are several options. One is to study a lucrative field anyway. As nice as it may sound to "follow your passion," if that passion lies in the same direction as abject poverty, you might regret it.

A second option is to study more than one thing. Study your passion alongside something your research says will lead to a better return on your investment. Then, you at least have more than one option upon graduation. So, if a college major in comparative pre-Columbian cave art doesn't pay the bills for some reason, you can always fall back on the major you didn't like, but earns you income.

A third option is to use formal education to study something that is more likely to pay off, and study a less-lucrative passion on your own. If you really like cave art, then by all means study it. Just don't pay a huge amount to be formally educated in it if you don't expect it to be a wise financial investment. We live in an age of knowledge accessibility that the librarians of Alexandria could never dream of. There are readily-available videos on the Internet for any available subject. Or go to the library (cave art is section 709 of the Dewey Decimal System).

A final option is to avoid expensive formal education altogether. If you don't plan to work at a job requiring a college degree, don't go to college. Otherwise, you're essentially paying a huge amount to spend four years partying or hiding from the world or drifting aimlessly from one course of study to another. If you're interested in a subject you don't plan to pursue as a career, you can always study it on your own (see above paragraph).

The bottom line: don't turn what should be an investment into an expensive luxury purchase that you'll being paying off for years or decades to come.

I mentioned that formal education is also a huge investment of time. That's not just a figure of speech; time is literally an investment. Economics even has a term for it – "opportunity cost." In other words, the *cost* of your time is the value of the *opportunity* you give up by not doing something else.

Suppose you spend four years in college and could have been making minimum wage somewhere. The opportunity cost of going to college is four years' worth of minimum wage. Not a huge amount, but a very real cost.

It pays to actually think about the opportunity cost. Bill Gates, who was creating software while attending college, actually dropped out of school after realizing that the opportunity cost of his time attending class was simply too great. His time spent building what became Microsoft was worth far more than the minimum wage cited in the previous paragraph, and the calculation led him to wisely drop out. He ended up doing all right.

In extreme cases (albeit very real – I have read multiple articles about just such scenarios), a student goes to college and multiple rounds of graduate school, pursuing a low-return course of study. Upon graduation, the student goes to work making only slightly more (or no more) than he or she could have made upon graduation from high school. The poor (literally and figuratively) student now has a couple hundred thousand dollars in student loan debt (which cannot easily be discharged, even in bankruptcy, as of this writing) *and* has foregone eight or more years of potential earnings. It's a lose-lose situation and not the way to build a solid financial foundation.

Of course, there is no guarantee that the student who pursues the supposedly wiser course of study will actually land a lucrative job and have a better return on investment. Just as Mr. Wise could not guarantee that his house would not wash away. It is simply about improving the odds.

Even after you "finish school," you're not finished. A common mistake people make is to think of education as having a finish line. "Once I get a degree in such-and-such or graduate from Thus and So University, I'll be done" is the mental refrain. You're smarter than that. You can stop learning when the world stops changing and when you know everything. Even if you are an expert in a particular field, your knowledge starts to erode the moment you stop keeping up with it, because the knowledge within that field continues to change.

Continuing your education could be as simple as reading articles about the field, attending courses and conferences, or even returning to school. Be alert for opportunities and take advantage of them. Find out whether you can get additional training through your job, join an association related to the field you want to work in, investigate evening courses at local schools or online.

I have seen people make this mistake over the course of long careers, and the results aren't pretty. Someone who was at the top of his or her game at one time, but who thinks of education as a one-time deal, is like someone who sits complacently on a rock while floodwaters rise around him. It's incremental; skills become outdated one year at a time. Eventually, the person who never bothered to improve his skillset is left behind. And guess which people are the easiest for companies to fire when times get lean.

Don't be that person. Make an effort to maintain and improve skills within your chosen profession, or even to build up skills outside your profession so you have more options. Like your initial investment in formal education, an investment in ongoing education is one that can have a big return.

By the way, calculating the actual rate of return on an investment in education is possible, and interesting, though it is sadly beyond the scope of this book. Except to say that knowing how rates of return on investments are calculated is a valuable financial skill that you may want to learn. You can find books about it in the Economics or Mathematics sections of the library (section 330). Or go online.

The bottom line is to think of education as an important component of the financial foundation you are building.

Health

Health may seem like a strange topic for a personal finance book, but the two are tightly connected. A strong financial foundation is of little value if your health is too poor to enjoy it. Some health problems are not preventable, and there's nothing you can do about that.

But other health problems are pretty clearly correlated with lifestyle choices. If your lifestyle consists of chain smoking cigarettes between fast food restaurant drive-ins and spending every evening cuddled up with a bottle of sweet, sweet bottle of whisky, your health will likely suffer. There are always cases to the contrary (i.e. the Rolling Stones), but the odds are not on your side.

Poor health is expensive. As of this writing, the United States is one of the most expensive places to buy medical services. If your health fails, things can get very bad very fast. Even those fortunate enough to have health insurance through work can find themselves paying for medical procedures out of pocket if they become too sick to work and maintain the insurance. Not only can poor health drain you financial reserves, it can prevent you from earning income as well.

Start thinking of maintaining good health in terms of building your financial foundation. As my mother likes to point out, medical advice changes constantly. Coffee is good for you today, the news reports, but tomorrow it kills you. Foods go from dangerous to healthy overnight.

Even so, it is a logical fallacy to say "medical advice changes; therefore I shouldn't worry about what I eat and drink." The second part does not naturally flow from the first (this is the logical error of a *"non sequitur"* – read more about logic in sections 150 and 160 of the library). Just because portions of health advice change does not mean you should throw up your hands and grab a cheeseburger with them. There is broad consistency among medical professionals about what is generally good for you (exercise; clean air; unprocessed food; diets heavy in vegetables, fruits, nuts, and berries; etc.) and things that are bad (smoking, excessive alcohol, a sedentary lifestyle, crystal meth).

Make smart choices about your health so you can not only maintain the strong financial foundation you are building, but so you can live longer to enjoy it.

Assets and Investments

Assets and investments might be the first thing you think of when you hear "financial foundation." Indeed, this area is extremely important. But I did not start the chapter with this discussion to put it in perspective and promote the idea that assets and investments are simply *part of* a firm financial foundation.

Note: this section only discusses investments in broad terms. For a more detailed discussion, see the "Investments" section of the Appendix to this book.

"Assets and investments" is sort of a redundant phrase since investments are generally assets. The title is designed to help clarify what "assets" actually are, since many people are confused about the term. Think of a financial asset in terms of something valuable you own that generates income at some point. The income could be recurring (like a monthly payment) or a one-time thing (like if you sell at a profit).

A bank account that earns interest is an asset because it has value (the account balance) and generates income (the interest). A house you own and rent out to someone else is an asset because the house has a value and generates rental income.

In general, you build a strong financial foundation by investing some of your income and building up a base of assets that generate future income. If your strategy from the "Formal Education" section above pays off, you will hopefully have a sufficient income to allow you to put money aside. Recall that, in the "Formal Education" section we described education itself as an "investment" because it is something you own that generates a stream of income (i.e. from a salary) in the future.

It's not the income itself that builds the foundation. The income is a tool that you use to invest in assets along the way so you have resources available when you need them (i.e. for retirement, unexpected medical expenses, or if you have to go on the run from the law). Income is important because the more you have, the more you can potentially put away, but it's only part of the picture. Expenses are hugely important as well.

If you earn $1,000,000 per year, but spend it all on frivolous nonsense, your financial foundation is no stronger. You probably *are* better off from an experience perspective since all that "frivolous nonsense" would leave you with great memories. But you can't pay for your retirement with memories.

Hopefully you don't need a book to tell you the importance of living below your means – spending less than you earn. Everyone knows that spending more than you make is a bad idea. By keeping your spending lower than your income, you create positive cash flow. Once you achieve positive cash flow, the key is to connect that with the idea of making smart investments and solidifying your financial foundation.

So, what investments should you make with income stream generated by your formal education? This is where the "Financial Education" section at the beginning of this chapter comes in – educate yourself on the options available to you and decide what works best for your situation. This book is not designed to give specific advice about where specifically to put your money, and a comprehensive rundown of every type of investment vehicle is well beyond its scope.

Having said that, the Appendix of this book is a good place to start the process of self-education. The Appendix discusses basic investments and investment account types. It includes a basic overview of some common investments and accounts, along with pros and cons of each. The Appendix certainly won't make you an expert, but it will definitely improve your knowledge if you don't know much about this area.

People often refer to things that don't really fit the criteria as "assets." Cars are a great example. A car you own has a value (you could sell it), but doesn't generate an income unless you are a professional driver. Rather than generating income for you, your car actually requires you to spend income from your job to maintain it. It is really the opposite of an asset (the opposite of an asset is a *liability*).

Similarly, if you own a house that you do not rent out, it has a value but does not generate income. Instead, you spend money each year in things like taxes, maintenance, loan interest, and so forth. It is really a liability masquerading as an asset. It might be a nice liability since it prevents you from living out on the streets in a cardboard box, but don't confuse it with an investment asset.

Build your financial foundation on rock by investing your income into assets that grow and generate returns in the form of future income and increasing value.

Leverage (Debt)

The flip side of investing in assets over time is to avoid excessive debt through borrowing. The word "leverage" is sometimes used to mean "debt." That comes from the idea that you can use a little bit of your own money in order to borrow a lot more from someone else. It is sort of like how a weakling can push down with a little bit of force on one side of a lever and lift up an object that he otherwise couldn't. If you're interested in the physics behind levers and other mechanical features, by the way, you can look in the Physics section of your library (section 530).

For example, you might buy a $200,000 house by putting down 20% of your own money and borrowing the rest. That means you have to pay $40,000 up front, which isn't a small amount, but is easier to get your hands on than $200,000. Then, the bank lets you borrow the other $160,000, which you pay back over the next 30 years (other timeframes are available, but 30 years is the most common).

The first sentence in this paragraph said "*you* might buy," but if you borrow the money from the bank (also called getting a *mortgage*), then *the bank* is actually the one buying the house. The house isn't yours; you just have a right to live in it until you pay the bank back. Note how your $40,000 acted as a *lever* to let you live in a house that cost $200,000.

You don't *just* pay back the $160,000 you borrowed. That $160,000 is called the *principal*, and you obviously end up paying that back. In addition to paying back some of principal each month, you also pay the bank some *interest*. Interest is like the fee you pay the bank in exchange for it letting you use its money.

You will end up paying much more than the $160,000 over the course of your loan. How much more depends on the interest rate and how many years the loan is for, but it can be a big difference. A 30-year loan for

$160,000 at 5% interest means you end up paying $309,209 by the end of the 30 years. If the interest rate were 6%, you'd pay $345,341. Like I said, a lot more than the $160,000 you borrowed.

You may be more than willing to pay quite a bit more over time so you can have a place to call your own (though we know that it's not really yours until it's paid off; don't worry, we'll keep that between us). But, you should at least know how much you'll actually end up paying over the course of the loan so you are making an educated, conscious decision and not just signing papers and hoping for the best.

If you don't make your monthly payments, the bank comes and takes your house. Well, the bank doesn't come; it sends the sheriff to kick you out and sells the house to someone else.

Loans for other things – cars, boats, etc. – work the same way. You pay principal and interest for a given period of time and then the thing is yours free and clear. If you don't pay, the lender repossesses it. The types of loans we have discussed so far are called *secured loans* because the lender's security that you will repay is its ability to repossess the thing itself.

Credit card debt is a little different. They are *unsecured* loans. Even though you bought things with your credit card, the credit card company isn't going to waste its time trying to repossess every tube of lip balm and bottle of Chardonnay you bought. Much of what you bought on the credit card is likely already used up and un-repossess-able anyway (going out to eat, concerts, gas for your car). So, if you don't pay them back, they just send debt collectors to hound you day and night until you either pay them back or declare bankruptcy.

Bankruptcy is a legal process that lets you get rid of your debts, but at a cost. It becomes much harder to do things like get another loan, rent an apartment, or even get a job. It also comes with an actual dollar cost. Bankruptcy isn't free, and it is possible to be unable to afford to go bankrupt.

We are discussing some of the details of how debt works and some of its consequences to make it clear why it is so important to your financial foundation. Taking on too much debt can erode the financial foundation you are building by reducing the income that you would otherwise have available to invest in assets like we discussed in the previous section.

The key goes back to educating yourself and asking smart questions. Such as: Do I need this item enough to borrow money to own it? Is there a cheaper version that requires less (or no) debt for? Should I wait a while and buy it when I can pay for it outright? How much will it actually cost in the long run, after factoring in interest?

Every dollar you pay in interest is essentially a fee you pay to have something now instead of later. Sort of like an impatience tax. You are paying someone (i.e. a bank) for the right to use its money so you can buy something right now that you can't really afford.

Think these decisions through. If you're getting your hair done and putting the bill on your credit card, and you're not paying the credit card balance off in full every month, you are essentially taking out a loan to your hair done and agreeing to pay for it over the next several months or years.

Good Debt: Fact or Fiction?

Let's talk about the idea of "good debt" before ending this section. You might hear people refer to various types of loans as "good debt." Someone will say that student loans are "good debt" because you're funding your future or that a home loan is "good debt."

Often, the people making these claims are either trying to convince you to take out a loan to buy something they're selling, or are trying to convince themselves that they made the right decision by taking out a loan for something themselves.

The reality is that there's no such thing as "good debt," just as there's no such thing as "bad debt." Debt is debt. It is what it is – a contractual agreement to pay certain amounts of money at certain times over a certain period in exchange for the right to own or experience something.

Modifying the word "debt" with subjective words like "good" or "bad" to describe an entire class of loan, regardless of a person's individual circumstances, is misleading at best. The question is simply whether that contractual debt arrangement is worth it *to you, given your circumstances*. "Good" and "bad" are meaningless, sweeping modifiers that make value judgments about the debt and cloud your decision.

A student might be a great idea if it provides you an education leading to employment that gives you a positive return on your investment. Even if it doesn't lead to meaningful income, the student might still think the education itself was worth the debt load. The idea of "good" or "bad" is a subjective modifier that hides a lot of danger.

Of *course* universities will push the message that student loans are "good" debt and those in the real estate industry will claim that mortgages on homes are "good." They're not unbiased observers. Just because someone claims a particular type of debt is "good" or "bad," or repeats some other, intelligent-sounding person's claims, doesn't mean it's true.

The only way you can make a good decision about whether to take on debt is if you understand the implications of what you're agreeing to. And the only way to understand what you're doing is to educate yourself on the agreement's terms. Read and understand the terms, think it through, and consider the implications on your overall financial foundation before you make a decision.

Cash on Hand (or "Emergency Fund")

Having cash on hand is a relatively straightforward concept, though it is worth discussing in a chapter about building a strong financial foundation. Sometimes "cash on hand" is referred to as building up an "emergency fund."

The latter might be a better term, since this money is not necessarily physical cash currency. It is usually money in a savings account so it is easy to access. Whatever you call it, the idea is to keep some readily-available money around to deal with unexpected expenses that crop up.

I mention emergency funds immediately after the section on investing and building up assets because you might get so excited about putting all of your money into assets for the future that you forget about emergencies that could require large spending right now.

By "emergencies," I'm not talking about a last-minute deal on a flight to Monaco. I'm talking about a broken furnace in the winter that you have to replace, or the loss of your job for an extended time. This is important; an emergency fund is not just a juicy stack of money sitting around for you to raid whenever you want to buy something that you don't have quite enough money for. It is a fund for a specific purpose. In fact, it is a good idea to keep it in a separate bank account so you are less tempted to spend it on nonsense.

This money doesn't just magically appear, of course. You have to save it over time. The best way to put aside an emergency fund is to choose an amount you can afford and put it aside each month as if it's a regular bill. Each month, just like you pay the electric bill to the electric company, pay your emergency fund "bill" into a separate account. It is probably a good idea to prioritize putting this money aside early on, and add to it over time as your requirements increase.

One reason it is a good to set the money aside early is that you never know when an emergency will strike. Another reason is that a side benefit to having some easily-accessible money in the bank is peace of mind. You will literally sleep better knowing that you are no longer one unexpected car problem away from running out of money.

How much do you need? That's a good question. Having too much can be almost as bad as having too little. With too little money put aside, you can't deal with the emergency. Which sort of defeats the purpose. If your emergency fund is too large, you are missing out on opportunities to invest in the assets that will help ensure your financial future. You have to strike a balance.

Some sources will recommend that you keep a certain number of months' worth of living expenses in your emergency fund. I have seen advice ranging from three months to twelve months. During scary economic times, you will inevitably see the number of months suggested by experts start to creep upward, as fear takes over.

Choosing a number of months' worth of living expenses isn't bad advice. For one thing, it ties your savings goal to a meaningful number (essentially an amount of time you could support yourself without an income). It is also very easy to calculate. You just add up your core monthly spending (rent, car payment, average grocery bill, utilities, etc.) and multiply it by however many months' worth of expenses you want to put aside.

If you currently eat lobster with a side of saffron-topped, truffle-infused mashed potatoes at a five-star restaurant every night, you probably want to assume you will scale back on that when calculating the amount. But don't assume you will cut out all non-core spending. Be realistic and add a reasonable amount into your monthly numbers.

There are other methods of calculating an appropriate emergency fund. An easier way than the one described above is to just pick a nice round number to save. A more complicated way is to think through detailed scenarios of what might happen (what if all my appliances and car fall apart at the same time?) and plan based on the likelihood of them occurring.

For purposes of building a strong financial foundation, just keep in mind that you want to minimize your chances of getting stuck with an expense you didn't plan for and can't pay for. That inevitably leads to taking on debt to tide you over, which leads to the erosion of your financial foundation as discussed in the last section.

As a final note about emergency funds: many "emergencies" are the result of a simple lack of planning. For instance, if you buy a house that has a 15 year-old washing machine, you should know that it probably won't last much longer. So, when the washing machine suffers catastrophic failure the year after you buy the house and you have to replace it, it's an "emergency," but not "unexpected." Things break; plan accordingly. By the way, if you don't know how long various appliances tend to last, you can easily find life expectancy information online.

The bottom line is that emergency expenses will inevitably come up. A key rock in your financial foundation is money to deal with them. A smart plan is to start putting money aside now, such that over time you end up with enough money to deal with real emergencies.

Insurance

Insurance is another important component of a firm financial foundation. The more assets you have and the more things you own (even if they're liabilities), the more you should consider how much, and what kind of, insurance you have. The point of insurance is to lower your financial risk from negative events.

Insurance is pretty simple in theory. You pay a fee and someone else (usually a company) agrees to pay you a determined amount if a specified event happens. Most people are familiar with car insurance. You pay the insurance company a fee every month (called a "premium"). Then, if something bad happens, like someone rear-ends your car, the insurance company will pay to have it fixed.

Insurance is available for all sorts of negative events that can happen to a person or property: death, injury, accidents, hurricanes, floods, fires, theft, lost income from a job loss, losing a lawsuit, and so on. There are even specialized insurance policies available. If you are a professional quarterback, for instance (good for you), you can insure your throwing arm.

The key to insurance is to think about what is important to your financial life and what could go wrong. Then, educate yourself on what kind of insurance is available to if those things happen, whether you need it, and how much you need.

It is no accident (heh, heh – a little insurance joke there) that the idea of educating yourself keeps coming up. That was the first thing we discussed in the context of a financial foundation. It is extremely important to spend some time and energy researching areas of your financial life so you know the basics of how things work and what questions to ask. The alternative is to just walk into the insurance salesman's office and say, "what kind of insurance should I get, and how much?"

In some instances, you may find that you need more insurance. If you run over someone in your car, your insurance generally pays not only for their hospital bills, but for their lost income as well. So, if you live in a neighborhood full of highly-paid surgeons, or, God forbid, highly-paid personal injury attorneys, you might want to pay for more car insurance.

Your research might indicate that you don't have insurance for some risks at all. This is important to identify – it means that if some bad events come to pass, you are completely on your own. Suppose you buy a vacation house to get away from the stress of modern life. You enjoy the house, but realize you don't go very often. So, you start renting it out for a few months of the year and sit back, impressed with your financial savvy as the rental income rolls in.

But, you never bothered to update your insurance policy to reflect that it is a rental property. Then a tenant accidentally sets the place on fire or is injured when the deck collapses. Your insurance company may very well say you're out of luck because your insurance policy didn't cover the house if it was rented out.

It is actually fairly common to find people taking on a huge risk for which they are completely uninsured because they don't bother doing the research to find out what they need, or are too cheap to pay for it. The phrase "penny wise and pound foolish" comes to mind. I used the rental house example above because I have seen many landlords whose insurance policies were insufficient to protect them.

You can end up totally uninsured for things you think are covered by insurance if you don't do your research. And doing the research isn't that hard. Your insurance policy itself will tell you what is covered, what is specifically *not* covered, and how much you're paying for it. The insurance agent from whom you buy insurance can also answer your questions. When you buy the policy, ask them specific questions and have them point out where the policy covers (or excludes) the item you're interested in.

Let's go over some useful insurance terminology. The "deductible" is an amount you pay on your own before the insurance kicks in. If you have a $500 deductible and suffer $5,000 in damages, you pay $500. You can usually change the deductible. The higher the deductible, the less you pay for insurance each year (because the insurance company is taking on less risk).

An "exclusion" is a specific item or event that the insurance policy does not cover. This is an important thing to watch out for. Common events (like floods) can be excluded from your coverage. A closely related term is a "rider." A rider is simply a specific event or item you specify in your insurance contract. If your policy does not cover floods, for instance, you might be able to purchase a rider that adds floods insurance. Or, if you have a valuable piece of property that you want to specifically insure – like an original Monet – you might be able to purchase a rider instead of getting a separate policy.

They key word is "purchase." The insurance company won't take on the additional risk of loss without compensation.

Again, the lesson is to think about the things that are important to your financial life and what could go wrong. Then, educate yourself about whether insurance is a good idea to offset your financial responsibility if those things happen.

A good rule of thumb is to rethink your insurance any time you embark on a new venture or make a major decision. At those times, think about new risks and whether you can (and should) insure some of them away. Examples include buying or selling a major piece of property like a house or a car, getting married, getting divorced, having a child, changing jobs, and so on.

Remember: your research might reveal that you have *too much* insurance. This comes in two forms. First, you have unnecessary insurance. Second, you are insuring for a risk far greater than what you are likely to encounter.

A good example of insuring for something unnecessary is a parent taking out a large life insurance policy on a child. "But I care about my child so much," the parents say. Right, but consider what life insurance for. What financial risk are you paying to offset?

Life insurance is for the benefit of the living, not the deceased. The primary point of life insurance is to replace the income of a person who has died on behalf of someone who depends on it. So, it makes no sense to have a large life insurance policy on an income-less child.

On the other hand, it makes perfect sense for parents to have life insurance policies on themselves for the benefit of the child. The income-less child can't support herself on her own. A good way parents can continue supporting the child in the event of their death is to take out insurance policies on themselves for the child's benefit. Essentially, the insurance policy replaces the income the parents would have earned and spent on the child. Taking out a life insurance policy on a child might make sense to pay for burial expenses (which can be quite high), but many people needlessly pay insurance premiums for very large policies on children.

An example of the second type of over-insurance – insuring against more risk than you are likely to encounter – might be a married couple, each with steady incomes, insuring their lives for twenty million dollars apiece. It sounds nice, maybe even romantic, in theory: if you die, you know that your beloved spouse never has to work again and can live out the remainder of her days on a beach, sipping margaritas and applauding your foresight. Or (less romantically), thinking about how you'll be on easy street if your spouse comes to a bad end before you.

But remember what life insurance is for – to replace the foregone income. The value of the future income of each spouse is not twenty million dollars. It is expensive to use insurance to replicate winning the lottery and putting someone on easy street in the event of death. Why is that? Because insurance isn't free. You have to *pay* for it. And even if you are young and healthy, you are going to pay a lot more for twenty million dollars' worth of life insurance than you would for, say two million dollars' worth. The extra money you'd pay for insurance premiums is money you could better allocate to investment assets.

A final type of "insurance" that bears mentioning is "self-insurance." I put the term in quotes because self-insurance is really choosing not to buy insurance, but instead to take on the risk of paying for a negative event yourself.

Suppose you buy your wife a $10,000 engagement ring and do not insure it against loss. You are choosing to self-insure. If the diamond falls out and you have to buy a new one (and you *will* have to buy a new one), you have to buy the replacement with your own money. There will be no insurance company to cover the loss, so you're taking the risk on yourself.

In the previous paragraph, I said that you are "choosing" to self-insure. Maybe you say, "But I didn't make a choice – I just didn't buy insurance." I can't say it any better than the band Rush: "If you choose not to decide, you still have made a choice." If you chose not to think about or research whether you could or should buy insurance on the ring, you have made a decision to insure the loss on your own.

Self-insurance is a perfectly valid thing to do; just make sure you do it intentionally. Make sure that you *decide* to self-insure and don't just end up self-insuring because you were too lazy to do a few hours of research.

Remember my example about people who start renting a house out without updating their insurance? By choosing to become landlords and choosing not to research whether their current insurance policy was adequate for their new endeavor, they might have inadvertently taken on massive risks for which they are personally responsible.

Insurance affects your foundation differently than other foundational elements we discuss in this chapter. Failure to address the other elements leads to an erosion of the foundation over time. For example, if you don't educate yourself appropriately, you might not know about a good financial move you could make, or might not be eligible for a better job. If you fail to build a portfolio of assets, you eventually end up with insufficient financial assets.

But if you get insurance wrong, your financial foundation can fail suddenly and catastrophically. One day you are happily collecting rent on a rental property, and the next day you find yourself standing in its charred remains, with no insurance to cover the loss. Important stuff.

Getting back to the parable of Mr. Wise, who built his house on rock and Mr. Foolish, who built his house on the sand, wise people recognize that insurance is an important part of a solid financial foundation.

In the context of the parable, note that it rained in both cases. The storms were inevitable; bad things are going to happen. They may not happen today. They may not happen tomorrow. But they will happen. The parable is silent as to how much time passed between the time Mr. Wise and Mr. Foolish finished their houses and the storm. Maybe it didn't rain for 20 years and both of them felt safe and secure.

But in the end, only Mr. Wise's house remained, because he had prepared.

Wills, Trusts, and Estates

Another important part of a strong financial foundation relates to the idea of Wills, Trusts, and Estates. These terms represent a very large area. In keeping with this book's overview format, I will only discuss them in broad terms. This area can get very complicated – many people dedicate entire careers to it – but it is important to understand.

Wills, Trusts, and Estates are legal constructions related what you own and how you determine what happens to what you own in various situations. This topic pertains to not only your physical possessions (house, car, furniture, doomsday device, etc.), but also to your financial possessions (bank accounts, investment accounts) and even your intangible rights and obligations (the obligation to pay for your car, or your right to live in your house, for instance).

Most people are generally familiar with a "Will" – a document that explains what happens to a decedent's assets. "Decedent" means "dead person." In finance and the law, you will find that many things are called by delicate names in order not to offend tender sensibilities. When someone dies, a Will's main job is to explain how the person's possessions are divided up among the living.

A "Trust" is like an account that holds assets for someone else's benefit. You might think of a stereotypical "trust fund kid" whose parents or grandparents set aside a great sum of money, such that the child can live the life of leisure, above the mundane cares of the world. More interesting examples exist, too, where people have left vast fortunes in Trusts for the care of a treasured cat or dog or other such creature.

Most Trusts are not so exotic. Trusts can hold all kinds of assets other than money (houses, cars, jewels, art, etc.).

If you're interested in some terminology, Trusts actually require that three people be involved: the person who puts the assets into the Trust (the "Trustor"), the person who gets to actually have the Trust's contents (the "Beneficiary"), and the "Trustee" – a person who holds the Trust's contents for legal purposes on behalf of the Beneficiary and makes sure the Trustor's wishes are carried out.

"Estates" in our context are not sprawling plots of land with a mansion in the center. I introduced Wills, Trusts, and Estates by saying they were "legal constructions." That is to say that they are not *things*, so much as they are *ideas*. Even if they are created with physical paper and relate to physical things, their actual substance is the legal thing that comes into being.

I apologize for the metaphysical nature of this discussion, but it is important to understand that an "Estate" is everything you have, including legal rights and obligations. An "Estate" can also refer to particular property rights, but that area is a bit too detailed for this book.

When someone dies, they leave behind an Estate. This is not only for wealthy people. Everyone leaves behind an Estate, even if they don't have any money. Indeed, even if they die owing money and have a negative net worth, they still leave an Estate (recall that an Estate includes obligations – including the obligation to pay debts). So, a sprawling plot of land with a mansion in the center certainly *can* be part of an estate, but so can an old pair of sneakers, a bank account with three dollars in it, a broken tennis racket, and a debt to a credit card company.

As mentioned, Wills, Trusts, and Estates make up a huge area of finance, and even a cursory overview of the various types of Trusts and Wills and how they interact for estate planning would be well beyond the scope of this book. There is significant interplay between these things (a Will can refer to a Trust that is part of the overall Estate) that would also get us into far more complicated territory than is appropriate for this book. Similarly, other areas of this chapter can factor heavily into planning related to Wills, Trusts, and Estates. For example, insurance can be an integral part of planning.

Rather than try to explain this area in any detail, the goal is simply to explain what this area is, discuss some key concepts, point out why it is important to your financial foundation, and give you enough information that you can follow up on it, as it relates to your situation.

This particular part of the financial foundation is both very important and often neglected. Not a good combination. It is very important to most people that, upon their death, their possessions and assets be distributed to the people or organizations that they wish. Many of those very people do not have a Will, which is instrumental in carrying out those wishes. Perhaps this is because they get nervous thinking about how the icy hand of death is stalking them at every twist and turn. Or maybe they are lazy or don't want to spend the money to have these matters attended to.

Whatever the reason, that is the situation. Fortunately, every state in the United States has default laws for "intestacy." Laws of intestacy spell out what happens to the estate of a person who dies without a Will. These laws are generally designed to reproduce the wishes that most people would have if they had bothered to make a will. And in general they do a good job.

One problem is that "in general" may be good for society as a whole, but not good for you as an individual. For instance, maybe your blood curdles at the thought that your hateful sister who hasn't spoken to you in 20 years would ever lay a hand on any of your possessions. But, if she happens to be the closest relative you have when you die, she might very well get everything you had. You can take comfort in the fact that you won't be alive to see it. But that is cold comfort.

A second problem is that the court system generally steps in to handle situations where people die without a will. That often requires appointing someone to oversee the case. Family members who seemed to like each other just fine when you were alive might suddenly turn against each other and start clawing for their piece of the pie.

This process can cost a lot of time and money as it winds through the courts and cause significant hardship on everyone involved. Again, you'll be cold and dead, so you won't be around to see it. But if you like those people, you presumably won't want to cause them hardship after you're dead. Of course, if you *don't* like them … well, there might be some grim satisfaction of lying on your death bed thinking, "Look at all these vultures standing around me, thinking they're going to get my stuff when I die, but when they will actually spend years in court, paying lawyers to sort through the mess I leave behind. Heh, heh, heh."

A final problem is that the default rules of intestacy only handle the big things, only come into play after you're dead, and are not designed to maximize the value of your estate. They are like a meat cleaver rather than a scalpel. You probably want the scalpel. After all, you spent a lifetime building up your assets; it's only logical to distribute them with the same care you used to build them up.

An "estate plan" is a well-thought-out, intentional strategy that uses a Will and maybe a Trust or two to carry out your specific wishes. Done correctly, an estate plan will address your specific desires, can benefit you while you are still alive, and can maximize the value of your estate. This is your scalpel.

One of the largest benefits of an estate plan is its ability to help you legally minimize taxes. It almost seems like magic that simply drafting up one document and signing it can save you or your family thousands (or hundreds of thousands, depending on your estate) of dollars. But it is absolutely possible with a well-designed estate plan.

Both a cleaver and a scalpel will cut up a chicken, but the second one does it with more precision and gets more meat off the bone.

Wills and Trusts can be used in very clever ways by those who know what they're doing. Attorneys who specialize in them can help you tailor a plan to get as close as possible to what you actually want. More importantly, they can help you think of issues that you might have never thought about on your own.

For example, your state's intestacy laws will almost always ensure that your relatives get your things before a stranger gets them. For most people, that's a good thing. But it is not very specific. Maybe you'd like to leave some money to an animal shelter, or have a tree planted in your honor at the university you attended (where your course of study was guided by careful research, thanks to a previous section of this chapter). Maybe you have some particular items that you want certain people to get after you die, but want the ability to change those items later. An estate plan can help you do all of these things and more.

Don't like your relatives? You can even use estate planning for malicious purposes, if you're that sort of person. Remember the discussion of you lying on your deathbed, grimly happy at the idea that your lack of estate planning would put your despicable relatives' lives in chaos? That's a good way to stick it to them, but they might think you just forgot to make a will, and not realize that you're giving them an intentional posthumous smack in the face.

With an estate plan, you can remove all doubt. You can specifically note that you don't want Cousin Eunice to get anything because she always took the choicest pieces of turkey at Thanksgiving. Or, you can have some of your estate set aside for a charity that your obnoxious Uncle Bernard absolutely despises; you can even have the donation made in his name! The hateful possibilities are endless.

Of course, as before, you won't be around to see your deviousness play out, but if you make the estate plan well before death comes for you, you can enjoy its benefits while you're alive. Think of how much sweeter family gathering will be for you: every time Cousin Eunice reaches for the turkey or Uncle Bernard spouts his odious views, you can smile with cold satisfaction knowing what's in store for them.

In case it isn't obvious, you should revisit these documents every so often, especially after major life events, to make sure they still reflect your wishes. You might soften your views on Cousin Eunice at some point, after all.

The main takeaway in this section is to educate yourself enough to understand the general concepts related to Wills, Trusts, and Estates. You will likely never become an expert, even in a relatively narrow section of this area, but that's okay. If you take the time to at least understand the main ideas, you can hire someone to help you with the specifics. Speaking of hiring people to help you…

Get Professional Help

Our talk of financial self-education doesn't imply that you can do everything yourself. On the contrary, getting the right professionals to help you at the right time is a great way to help you build a solid financial foundation.

Seeking professional advice can apply to many sections of this chapter. It is especially important for the areas of Investments; Insurance; and Wills, Trusts, and Estates. For instance, you probably want to hire an experienced attorney to draft your Will. Even though it is perfectly legal to make your own Will in every state, there are a lot of ways to make a mistake and accidentally invalidate it. Legal textbooks are full of examples of Wills and parts of Wills rendered invalid because little requirements weren't met.

Since you're paying to have your Will made out, why not pay extra for some advice as well. Maybe you want to hire a tax attorney to review your plans and let you know if you could do things a little differently and save your heirs some money on taxes. Every situation is different and this is can be a complicated area. Those who specialize in it can be worth every penny.

I have seen too many situations where someone chose not to hire an expert to help them with complicated matters because it was "too expensive," and ended up much worse off because of it. Those who focus only on price (what you pay) and not on value (what you get) generally shortchange themselves in every area of life.

This is an insidious mistake because it is one of *omission*. You may never know how much better off you would have been if you had paid for advice. My distinction between price and value, by the way, comes from a quote by Warren Buffett, one of the richest people in the world, who said "price is what you pay; value is what you get." I have personally seen people leave tens of thousands of dollars on the table because paying an accountant or an attorney $300 per hour was "too expensive."

Here's a specific example. Years ago, after a real-estate-related market collapse, the government wanted to sweet-talk people into buying houses. So, it set up a program for first-time homebuyers. If you bought your first home between certain dates, and met a few other criteria, the government would give you $7,500. But, the government didn't send a letter to people who qualified; you had to apply for it yourself.

The program was well-reported, but many eligible people never applied. Why? Reasons varied, but at least some of them assumed it was too complicated to do on their own, and either threw up their hands at that point or figured it was too time consuming or expensive to hire an accountant to help them. So they missed out on the $7,500 in free money because they didn't know about it and chose not to hire someone who did.

Even a mediocre tax professional would have known about this program. In fact, anyone who bothered to educate themselves in the slightest about major changes in the tax law that year would have known about it; a link to details about the program was on the IRS' website for months.

Scenarios like the one above play out all the time in various aspects of people's financial lives. Note that many people who missed out on the $7,500 never even knew about it. And consider the real cost of not hiring a professional. An accountant would have charged, say, $250 to look into whether someone qualified and fill out the paperwork. That pales in comparison to the $7,500 value of the service.

Do you know who tends to be industrious and have plenty of time for self-education? Prisoners. In a funny postscript to the above story, I read later about an audit of the tax-credit program that found a large number of payments had been made to "first-time home-buyers" with prison addresses. It turned out there was quite a bit of fraud on the program. It was funny that many prisoners educated themselves enough on the program to trick the government into giving them $7,500, while many legitimate first-time homebuyers never bothered to look into it or apply.

Those who are lazy or price-obsessed will almost always fail to hire experts when it is smart to do so. Focusing on price when you're choosing which can of soup to buy might be smart; being similarly price-focused when it comes to professional advice can be very foolish.

This isn't to say you should hire an accountant to review your finances once per month, or hire an attorney to review your Will every week. Professionals are helpful when something in your life changes, or is about to change. If you are moving to a new state, or are about to sell an inherited house, plan to have a baby, or are thinking of getting married or divorced, for example, those are good times to consult a professional.

This also isn't to suggest that you should just hire the first name in the phone book. Just as you should educate yourself on financial matters, you should research professionals you are thinking about hiring. That isn't very hard in our modern age. In addition to asking for references, you have access to free and low-cost reviews, ratings, and reports about those providing services. With a few clicks of the mouse, or a couple of phone calls, you can usually access a professional association to which a potential advisor belongs and find out if he or she is in good standing or has any outstanding complaints.

Not only is self-education not always a substitute for hiring professional help, sometimes it leads you to seek help in the first place, and it can help you get more out of your experience. By educating yourself about matters related to your financial picture, you will come up with ideas and questions to follow up on with a professional. Does this program apply to me? Can I write that off on my taxes? If I leave such and such to my nephew in my Will, does he have to pay taxes on it?

When chosen wisely and employed at the right time, professionals can help you build and protect your financial foundation.

Conclusion

This introductory chapter is relatively long and covers a lot of concepts. It is also very basic. That is befitting a discussion of a financial foundation.

In our introductory parable, Mr. Wise built his house on a foundation of solid rock, and then enjoyed the security of not having his house wash away. Mr. Foolish did not pay attention to building a solid foundation, choosing sand instead. His house was probably easier and cheaper to build. It probably looked just as good as Mr. Wise's house. It might have even looked better, if he used his foundation money for decorations. But, his house was not equipped to withstand the storm.

The main theme throughout this chapter is to educate yourself on basic matters affecting your own financial foundation, and then act upon what you learn. You will put yourself ahead of the vast majority of people by simply and thinking through matters like your formal education, health, assets and investments, debt, emergency fund, insurance, and estate planning. You will still need professional help, but when you reach out to professional advisors, your research will make you better-positioned to ask smart questions and make good decisions.

The remaining chapters of this book discuss additional financial principles that relate to other parables in the Bible. The themes we developed in this chapter will carry through, and you will see them pop up in the background of the lessons to come. As a good foundational discussion should.

Chapter 2: Compounding – of Money and Mustard

Parable Summary

A man planted a super-tiny mustard seed in his garden. It grew to be the biggest tree in the garden. It became so big, in fact, that birds could land on the mustard tree's branches and sit in its shade.

Where you can find it

Matthew 13:31-32, Mark 4:30-32, and Luke 13:18-19

The Religious Lesson

God's kingdom starts out with a few followers, but grows into a large kingdom.

Jesus only had a few followers at the time of this parable, and now there are a couple of billion, so the parable was onto something.

The Financial Lesson: The Power of Compounding

First, mustard seeds are indeed very tiny. They are a couple of millimeters long – smaller than an apple seed, for instance. Despite what the parable may lead you to believe, mustard *trees* aren't really that big. They're more like large shrubs, really. A particularly big one might be 20 feet tall, but they're certainly not majestic oaks. It also seems odd that the man in the parable planted them in a "garden," which in the Mediterranean you would expect to contain things like sage, rosemary, thyme, oregano, and so on.

But, to carry our garden theme forward, don't get lost in the weeds here. Just keep in mind the main point that an itsy bitsy mustard seed grows into a much larger-than-expected tree. It grows large enough, in fact, that birds (that would presumably have eaten it when it was in seed form) can actually sit on it and in its shade.

This parable is an excellent representation of the financial concept of *compounding interest* and *compounding returns*. Think back to the previous chapter's discussion of the importance of investing in assets. There, we saw that building up a base of assets was a key part of a strong financial foundation. You put money aside while working and then have money available to you when you retire. But our previous discussion glossed over the mechanics of how, exactly, your money turns into more money.

Those mechanics hinge on the idea of compounding. Let's use a simple example of a savings account at a bank. The account has $1,000 in it and carries a 1% interest rate. For simplicity, we'll say your interest compounds every year. What does it mean that your money *compounds* every year?

It means that the interest rate is applied each year to however much money you have. *Interest* is what the bank pays you to keep your money in it. By the way, the bank pays you to let it keep your money because it lends your money to other people at a higher interest rate. It gives you 1% on your savings account and then lends your brother money for a car at 3%. The bank does this over and over with lots of people, and makes money on the difference.

Back to compounding. At the end of the first year, the bank pays you 1% of your $1,000 balance. Because 1% of $1,000 is $10, you now have $1,010 (your original $1,000 plus the $10 in interest).

Now fast forward to the end of the *second* year. How much do you have? You still have your $1,010 from last year. And you still get 1% interest. But now, you get 1% interest on $1,010, which is $10.10. Your new balance is $1,020.10. Note that your interest was ten cents higher in the second year than in the first year, even though you didn't do anything.

That process continues on, such that with each passing year the bank pays you interest on a larger and larger base amount. This is the compounding process. If you are underwhelmed at the rate at which your money is growing, that's because you're paying attention. After all, in the second year, this magical compounding only generates ten cents more than the year before. Don't spend it all in one place.

The small amount in the example is due to several things. The interest rate is low by historical standards and the starting value of $1,000 is relatively low. Also, the example assumed you didn't add any money to the account. And, banks can compound money more frequently than once per year. I won't go into detail to avoid the mathematics, but the more frequently the bank compounds your money, the more you will end up with.

The previous example discusses compound *interest* because interest is what banks pay you. Astute readers will recall that this section mentioned both compound interest and compound *returns*. What is the difference? Bank accounts are just one place you can invest your money. There are other types of investments as well. Other investments (such as company stock) do not earn interest. Instead, their price can increase over time. When the market value (price) of your investment in these kinds of assets increases, the gains are called "returns." As the value continues to grow over time, building on itself, it is referred to as compounding *returns*.

A generic term for the percentage at which your money increases is the *rate of return*.

The Appendix of this book will discuss investing in stocks and other common assets in more detail, along with the pros and cons of each type. For now, just keep in mind that historic returns from stocks have been greater than those of bank accounts. In practice, you probably won't end up investing as much of your money in bank accounts as you will in stock-based accounts.

The good news is that the math behind compounding returns and compounding interest is the same. Many non-interest-bearing investments that you invest in for their higher returns do not generate a guaranteed return. They can be high or low (or even negative). Here's a simplified example of compounding returns:

Suppose you invest $1,000 into the stock market and earn a 5% return the first year. You'd have $1,050 at the end of the year (the original $1,000 plus a $50 return). Then assume you earned a return of 10% the second year. At the end of the second year, you'd have $1,155 (the $1,050 plus a $105 return).

In this example, you can start to see how compounding might be useful. After only two years, your original $1,000 has grown to a meaningfully larger amount. Over time, this can really add up. For instance, if your $1,000 compounded at 5% each year for 20 years instead of just two, you'd end up with a little over $2,712 (assuming your money compounded every month).

If you periodically added money to the investment, as you will probably want to do with your investments, then it would grow even more because each additional investment you made would compound for however much of the 20 years was left.

For example, if you started with $1,000 that compounded at 5% each year for 20 years, and you also added $10 to it every month, you'd end up with over $6,840. That's almost $4,200 more than if you hadn't added money to it.

The extra $4,200 from your $10-per-month additions are obviously not just because of the extra $10 per month itself. After all, $10 per month for 20 years only adds up to $2,400 – quite a bit lower than the extra $4,200 you end up with. The rest of that money is because each of those $10 monthly contributions *also* compounds at 5% until the 20 years is up.

The first $10 contribution compounds for 19 years and 11 months. The second monthly $10 contribution compounds for 19 years and 10 months. And so on.

The mathematics behind compounding aren't complicated, but are beyond the scope of this book. Though it might be useful to know how to do these calculations for yourself, you can find countless compound interest/ return calculators online. It's worth finding one to play around with so you can see how compounding can really work in your favor.

Here's something fun. Well, as fun as anything can be when it involves a compound interest calculator. Calculate how much money you'd end up with, given some assumptions about a starting amount, monthly additions, an interest rate, and some number of years. Then imagine you stopped buying some nonsense you currently buy every month, and instead invested it into your investment. Maybe imagine you got a slightly-less-expensive cable package.

Redo your original calculation, but increase the monthly contribution by the amount you "saved" by not buying some nonsense and see how much more you'd have. Then ask yourself whether the thing you hypothetically gave up is worth the difference.

The crucial point about compounding is that your money earns money, the earned money is added back into what you already had, and then that combined amount earns even more money than before. This cycle continues and has a compounding effect. It doesn't grow by the same amount every year; it grows by more and more.

It's like rolling a snowball down a hill. The snowball starts out small, but gathers more and more snow as it goes. By the time it gets to the bottom of the hill, it's large enough to crush your unsuspecting enemies below. Or to build a snowman with your friends. Whichever.

Just as snowballs can get big, your investments can grow to be quite large, depending on the amount of money you invest (and continue to invest), the rate of return, and the length of time you invest. From our examples, it may seem like the key is a higher rate of return. That certainly matters. But the length of time you invest is *hugely* important.

Using our previous example, a $1,000 investment compounded at 5% for 20 years with no additions grows to $2,712. What if you left it in for 30 years instead of 20? You'd end up with $4,468. Think about that. After the first *20 years*, your total return is $1,712 ($2,712 minus the original $1,000). But, the return *from the last 10 years alone* is $1,756 ($4,468 minus $2,712). You earn more from the last 10 years than you did from the entire first 20 years.

Tying this back in with the parable, the two-millimeter mustard seed grows into the 6,096-millimeter (20-foot) mustard tree via the magic of compounding growth. As the seed grows and the plant develops roots and leaves, those roots and leaves use the sun, water, and nutrients to grow more roots and leaves. Those new roots and leaves, along with the old ones, use the sun, water, and nutrients to grow still more roots and leaves. This compounding effect leads to an impressive final result, especially compared with the seedy beginnings.

Compounding works magic for both mustard seeds and investments.

Chapter 3: Eight Bags of Gold and Three Servants

Parable Summary

A man was going on a long trip. Before he left, he entrusted eight bags of gold to three of his servants. Dividing the money up based on their abilities, he gave the first servant five bags of gold. The second servant got two bags of gold. The third servant got one bag.

When the boss came back from his trip, he asked the servants how they did with the money. The first servant – let's call him Frank – said, "I invested your five bags of gold, and doubled it to 10 bags of gold." The boss said, "All right – great job! Since you did so well with this small amount, I'm going to put you in charge of all sorts of important stuff. You have a solid future with me."

The second servant – let's call him Sam – said, "I also invested the gold you gave me, and the two bags you left with me have since doubled to four bags." The boss said, "Well, now, this is excellent news indeed! Since you did well with that small amount, I'll give you more responsibilities and you'll have a good future with me."

Then the boss turned to the third servant – let's call him Tom.

Tom said, "Everybody knows you're a mean tightwad who squeezes every penny until it squeals. I dug a hole and put your gold in it. Here it is – take it." The boss was super-furious and said, "You worthless servant! If you knew I was so mean and tight, you should have known I'd want you to at least go put my money in the bank and earn some interest!"

The boss was so angry that he told his other minions, "Take the one bag of gold away from Tom and give it to Frank so he can add it to the 10 he already has. Because those who have a lot will get even more, while those who don't have much will lose what little they have."

Then, in case there was someone within earshot who didn't realize how mad he was, the boss said told his minions to toss Tom outside into the darkness where there was crying and gnashing of teeth.

Where you can find it
Matthew 25:14-30

The Religious Lesson

Jesus' followers should spread the message of what they are learning, such that when Jesus returns to earth the message will have spread and the number of believers will have increased. If not, they'll end up being tormented in Hell.

Financial Lesson 1: Returns – Percentage, Absolute, Relative, and Compound Annual

There are all sorts of lessons hiding inside this fun parable. The first one relates to four different ways to think about the rate of return you earn on your investments. This lesson follows naturally from our discussion of compound returns in the Chapter Two (look – it's almost like I put some thought into how to organize these chapters).

Recall from before that the *rate of return* is a measures of how much you earn on your money, expressed as a percentage, whether it is in the form of bank interest or a return from some other investment. The rate of return is nice and simple and is a mathematical certainty. A 5% rate of return for one year will always turn $100 into $105. Period.

However, the ideas of "Percentage Returns," "Absolute Returns," "Relative Returns," and "Compound Annual Growth Rate" are useful to know. First, they give you different perspectives on how well your investments are really doing. Second, they will help you think critically about what financial advisors are telling you. The parable of the boss and his three servants is well-suited to illustrate this lesson.

A word of caution: as you educate yourself more on the financial industry, you will learn that it has many different types of "returns," each with its own nuanced definition. This is useful if you are a company trying to explain to investors how much money they made – or stand to make – if they give you their money to invest. Just remember to look into how they are calculating their returns (usually in the fine print). Some types of returns can explain away poor performance, or try to explain that your investment performance was better than it seems.

Here, we will only talk about four types of returns, and they are designed to help you think about your own performance. I will define exactly what I mean by each one – it's more important that you understand the concept than the word. In at least one instance (Absolute Returns), the financial industry generally uses the word for a different concept than the one I will explain.

Let's look at these four useful types of returns, along with what they tell. And what it *doesn't* tell you.

Percentage Returns

This one is the simplest to understand because we have already talked about it. This is simply the percentage by which your money grew. If your $100 grows to $105, that is a 5% rate of return.

If you don't know much about math, but are interested in where the 5% comes from, just subtract the beginning number from the ending number and divide by the beginning number (105 - 100 = 5, and 5 divided by 100 is .05, or 5%).

Percentage returns are important to understand for several reasons. First, this is the way most investment performance is reported. Your yearly (or monthly, or quarterly) investment account statement will tell you the percentage you earned over that period of time. Or, if you're thinking about putting your money into something with a fixed return, like a bond or a savings account, you will know up front how much you can expect back, in percentage terms.

Another important aspect of percentage returns is that they are independent of the amount of money you invest. Suppose I invest $1,000 and you invest $5,000, and we both earn 5% over the course of a year. You would end up with $1,050 and I would end up with $5,250. You earned more money, but we both had the same percentage return of 5%.

Going back to the parable, both the first and second servants doubled the boss' money. The first one –Frank – started with five bags, and ended up with 10. The second one – Sam – started with two bags and ended up with four.

What percentage return did Frank earn? He earned 100% (using our simple formula from earlier, 10 - 5 = 5, and 5 divided by 5 = 1, or 100%). That's a very impressive rate of return.

What about Sam? He *also* earned a 100% return (4 - 2 = 2, and 2 divided by 2 = 1, or 100%).

That makes sense, and shows how percentages let you compare performance when you have different starting amounts. Both Frank and Sam doubled the boss' money. So you already know intuitive that they did equally well. And the numbers bear that out – they both earned 100%. Doubling your money is always 100%. Whether you double $1 to $2 or $1,000,000 to $2,000,000, you have earned 100%.

But what about the third servant – Tom? He started with one bag of gold and ended up with one bag of gold. What percentage rate did he earn for the boss? Well, going through our formula, we see that he earned 0% (1 - 1 = 0, and 0 divided by 1 = 0, or 0%). That also makes sense. If you don't have any more money at the end of than you had when you started, it stands to reason that your percentage should be zero.

This is fairly basic – that's why it's the first type of return discussed here – but it's important. The percentage return is one way of putting your performance in perspective, regardless of how much you invested.

By the way, if you feel bad for poor old Tom, we aren't finished with him yet. Things don't go well for him in the parable: he gets verbally abused in front of his peers before being fired and physically tossed out onto the street. But, after discussing the other types of returns, I will finish up this section with a defense of Tom.

Until then, let's move on to another important type of return to think about.

Absolute Returns: Size Matters

The *absolute return* is simply the amount of money you earn over a period of time. Here, I are talking about a specific amount of money, not a percentage. This is a question of magnitude, and is very important from a practical point of view.

Returning to Frank and Sam from the parable, recall from the previous section that they both earned a 100% return on the boss' money. On a percentage basis, Frank and Sam were equal. And the boss treats them the same. He praises both of them the same and promises them both promotions. And that makes sense since they both managed to double his money.

But, while Frank and Sam earned the same *percentage*, they certainly didn't earn the same *amount*. Namely, Frank earned an additional *five* bags of gold for the boss while Sam only earned *two*. That's a huge difference and underscores why percentage returns don't tell the whole story. This isn't just a theoretical math lesson; it's very practically important to understand how much you actually made – in terms of absolute dollars and not just percentages.

Why is that important? Because you buy things with dollars, not percentages. You don't go to the grocery store and say, "I'd like this grocery cart full of food, please; here's 5%." You pay with a dollar amount. So, it's important to know the dollar amount you earn, or stand to earn, from your investments. This will underscore our previous discussions about the importance of building up your investment portfolio.

Imagine two people who have each retired. They invest in the same thing and each earn 5% over the course of a year. Based on the "percentage return" discussion in the previous section, they are equal. But, now imagine that the first one had $100,000 invested, while the second one had $1,000,000 invested. The first retiree's 5% gets him $5,000 that year. The second retiree's same 5% earns her $50,000. All else equal, the second retiree is living a much more comfortable life. The first retiree's investments give him the equivalent of $417 per month ($5,000 divided by 12); the second retiree's investments give her $4,167 per month ($50,000 divided by 12).

The fact that they had the same *percentage* return is probably of little comfort to the first retiree.

For the first retiree's portfolio to generate the same amount of money (*absolute* return) as the second retiree, he'd have to earn a 50% return (50% of $100,000 is $50,000). Which isn't going to happen. Or, looked at differently, the second retiree would only need a 0.5% return to generate the same $5,000 absolute return that the first retiree needed a 5% return to achieve.

Those numbers underscore how important portfolio size is, and why it is important to focus on building that up. While the rate of return (percentage return) on your investments is important, it is also important to build up a portfolio of investments large enough to generate a meaningful amount of income for you.

Of course, the percentage return and the size of the investment portfolio are linked. As the parable about the mustard seed in the previous chapter explained, if you start early and invest long enough, even relatively small investments at modest rates of return can compound into large amounts.

What about the hapless Tom? Well, he looks just as bad from an absolute return point of view as he did in the percentage return discussion. He earned zero bags of gold for his boss, while his colleagues Frank and Sam were out earning five and two bags, respectively. Pretty pitiful stuff, and it looks more and more like he deserved to be tossed out on his ear. But recall that I will put up a defense for him at the end of this chapter.

As a side note, I use the term "absolute return" here to mean something different from the financial industry. I use it to mean the amount of money – in dollars – that you actually make from your investments. It is easy for you to remember because you can think, "This is absolutely how much I made."

The financial industry, as is its habit, turned the word "absolute" into a marketing term to describe a type of investment that it wants to sell you. So, if you see something called an "absolute return mutual fund," it will likely be something that claims it can make money regardless of what the stock market is doing. It's a different concept than what I'm talking about.

Why didn't I just call this chapter "Actual Returns," you ask? Because the financial industry has also co-opted the word "actual" to mean something besides what it really means in order to sell products. Like I said, focus on the concept and what it means for you, not the term itself.

Back to the bottom line of this chapter: size definitely matters when it comes to investing. Thinking of your investment performance in terms of percentage returns is good. In addition, think about your returns in terms of how much money they actually (absolutely) generate for you to add a practical aspect to how you think about how well your investments are doing.

Relative Returns

I was going to make a joke about "Uncle Roger coming back," but couldn't make it work. "Relative Returns" are another important type of return for you to know about and think about. As the name implies, this refers to how well your investments performed, *relative to* something else. What is that "something else?" It can be any number of things.

For example, if you have some money invested in a mutual fund that invests in international companies, you might compare your performance to a generic index (average performance) of international companies. Then you can see how well you performed *relative to* the overall index. Or, suppose you just look at the interest rate on your savings account at the bank and compare it to other banks. This will tell you how much you are earning relative to similar alternatives.

Generally, comparing your investments to similar investment averages, or indexes, is a good practice. It gives you a perspective of how well you're doing, given what you are investing in. You can then identify any big discrepancies and decide whether you need to take action.

Using the simple bank account example, you can easily go online and find the national average for bank savings accounts. If you notice that the national average is always 1% higher than your account offers, you are underperforming relative to the benchmark of the national average. You might want to take action by looking into whether you can get a better deal.

The same is true for other investments you may have. If you own shares in a mutual fund, you can review that fund's performance relative to a comparable benchmark. If it consistently underperforms, that might be a sign to make a change.

To the extent this chapter talks about investments you would like to know more about (index funds, mutual funds, bonds etc.), remember that the Appendix to this book provides a basic overview of various investment types and account types.

Considering relative returns can be helpful when things aren't going well. Suppose you have money in an investment that has lost 15% for the year. But, suppose you discover that similar investments have lost 25% over the same time period. That fact might help put your losses in perspective. On a relative basis, you are doing 10% better than the benchmark, even though you are down 15%.

Thinking about your performance relative to *different* types of investment alternatives can also be a useful exercise. For example, you can always compare your performance to 0%. That is to say, suppose you hadn't invested the money in anything. If, at the end of the year, you earn 5% (or, say, $5,000), then you can say you are 5% (or $5,000) richer than you'd be if you had done nothing. That will give you a sense of how much better off you are for having invested in the first place

Of course, if your investments lose money, you might feel like a dolt. If you lose 5% (or $5,000), you might kick yourself thinking how you'd still have that money if you had just stacked it up on your nightstand instead. For that reason, it's probably a good idea to compare your relative performance over a long period time, and not just over a few months or a couple of years.

Another good exercise is to compare your investment performance to what you would have earned on a very safe investment, like a government bond. Even though this might be like comparing apples to oranges, it is a valuable comparison. Think about the return on a government bond as the highest rate you can earn while taking essentially no risk of losing your money. Then you can ask yourself whether the returns you are getting on your actual investments are worth the risk you are taking on.

For example, suppose you have some money invested in your fast-talking brother-in-law's hedge fund. First it was up 80%, then it was down 50%, before going up 60%, doing the hokey-pokey and turning itself inside out. This went on constantly until it finally ended the year with a 20% gain. You made 20%, which is very impressive, but could barely sleep for worrying about whether you would lose your money and end up sleeping in a cardboard box. And, you notice that you have been breaking out into cold sweats and crying for no reason during the day (more than usual, at least).

Now, imagine you look up the government bond's returns and see that they are hovering around 5%. The difference between your 20%-return investment that is edging you toward a nervous breakdown and the virtually riskless government bond is 15%. You can ask yourself if the 15% in extra returns is worth your emotional health. Maybe it is, maybe it's not. The important thing is that you can use this comparison to think about whether the returns you are making are adequately compensating you for the risk you're taking on.

The above examples were intentionally extreme, by the way. There is a whole spectrum of investment possibilities between a government bond and your brother-in-law's hedge fund, so it's not a choice between those two extremes. And you probably can't build up an adequate investment portfolio by just investing in bonds in any case. The Appendix will discuss various common investments in more detail (it won't even discuss hedge funds, which are out of reach for many people due to restrictions on who can invest).

The point is to understand what relative returns are, and to think about the question, "relative to what?"

As is always the case when dealing with the financial services industry, you have to be vigilant. Companies selling investments are always coming up with clever ways to make their returns look good relative to various benchmarks.

"I lost 30% of my portfolio taking your advice," you exclaim to your investment advisor, "while the stock market indexes were all up for the year!"

"Isn't that great!?" he replies, "The Chilean Diamond Mine Index was down 50% for the year, so it's like you're *up* 20%! Now, let me tell you about this Eritrean desalination company I heard about…"

In the parable, the boss was like the investor, with his three servants managing his investments. From the boss' perspective, Frank and Sam were equally good since they both doubled (i.e. earned a 100% return on) his money.

The parable doesn't mention the benchmark that the boss compared Frank and Sam to, but a 100% return was probably very good a couple of thousand years ago, just as it is today. I have to think that Frank and Sam compared favorably to whatever benchmark the boss had in mind (sheep or grain farming, perhaps, or maybe the mustard business).

The real loser, as always, is poor old sad-sack Tom. It is not hard at all to figure out what benchmark the boss compared Tom to – the dynamic duo of Frank and Sam, with their 100% returns, of course. Frank, Sam, and Tom all presumably live in the same town, and they all worked for the same household, and they presumably had access to similar investment options. The boss' anger really comes from the fact that Tom fell so woefully short of the 100%-return benchmark set by his colleagues.

The order in which they reported their performance didn't help, either. The boss comes home and asks Frank how he did, and finds that he got a 100% return. Then he asks Sam the same thing and again finds that he got a 100% return. It might have gone better if Tom had reported first – then the boss' expectations would have started out low, and there's a chance he'd have been happily surprised at Frank and Sam's report.

But he didn't. So we'll move on to our last type of return to consider before we get to our defense of Tom. For this section, just remember that you can put your returns in perspective by thinking of them in relative terms.

Compound Annual Growth Rate (CAGR)

A final type of useful return to think about is the "Compound Annual Growth Rate," or "CAGR." This one is a bit more complicated than the others, if only in how it's calculated. Fortunately, this is not a math textbook. The goal of this book is to explain how various biblical parables relate to personal finance concepts. I have intentionally kept calculations to a minimum, and only use them where they are simple and help illustrate a point.

How to actually calculate a CAGR is beyond the scope of this book (it's really not that difficult and you can easily look it up, and there are numerous online calculators if you want or need to calculate it). But, the concept is very important because it brings in the idea of time. As discussed in the previous chapters, time is one of the most important factors in investing.

Rather than go into how to calculate a CAGR, let's look at what it is and why it's important. When you invest, you start out with an amount of money and you end up with a different (hopefully larger) amount. The phrase, "and you end up with," implies that some time has passed. The CAGR explicitly takes the "time" aspect of investing into account.

The idea of time is hidden in the parable of the boss and his three servants. The parable says that the boss went on a "long" trip. Where did he go? What did he do? How long was he gone? The answer to the first two questions is, "we don't know, and we don't care for CAGR purposes." But the answer to the third question about how long the boss was gone is, "we don't know – *but it's important.*"

In the first section of this chapter, we talked about the "percentage return," which was very simple. We just talked about the percentage by which money grew from start to finish, without discussing how long it took. That is certainly fine as far as it goes. But, as you think about it, the simple percentage return is less valuable when your investment returns accrue over several years.

Why is it important to think about how long the boss was gone? Because his rate of return is less and less impressive the longer he was away. It is probably intuitively obvious to you that doubling your money over the course of one year is very different from doubling your money over the course of 20 years.

The CAGR addresses the time issue and essentially says, "If your investment had grown (compounded) at a steady rate from the time you made it until the time you took it out, what would the rate of return have been each year?" Many investments don't grow at a steady rate – they might be up 5% one year, up 10% the next, lose 6% the following year, be back up by 2% the next, and so on.

The CAGR ignores all the ups and downs and just calculates what annual return you would have needed to go from your starting number to your ending number, over the number of years in question. It is this last part – "over the number of years in question" – that we're focused on. This is where the CAGR adds its value. You can see how well an investment performed with time accounted for.

The CAGR is expressed as a percentage, but it adds nuance that the regular percentage return we talked about does not. If you invest $1,000 and it grows to $1,500 over one year, your percentage return is the same as if the $1,000 had grown to $1,500 over the course of five years. Or 10. An absolute return doesn't help us, either; it's the same $500 for all scenarios. The CAGR, on the other hand, will be different for each of those scenarios, decreasing as the number of years' increases.

That's why the length of the boss' trip is so important. Let's look at the boss' golden boys Frank and Sam again. Both of them earned a 100% return by doubling the boss' money. But, that 100% is only an annual number if the boss were gone for one year. What if he were gone longer?

Let's suppose the boss was actually gone for two years. How well did Frank and Sam do then? It turns out that the CAGR would only be 41.42%. Still very good, but not quite as impressive.

By the way, some of you might be wondering why the CAGR is not just 50% (just as others might be wondering why they're still reading this book). I steadfastly refuse to explain the mathematics, but the answer lies in the fact that we're talking about a compounded annual growth rate, which is an exponential (not a linear, or straight-line) function. Also, for those wondering, Frank and Sam will have the exact same CAGR, regardless of the time period, just like their percentage return was the same, despite the fact that they started and ended with different amounts.

What if the boss was gone for three years? Now Frank and Sam's CAGR is 26%. Five years? That's a CAGR of under 15% (14.86%).

Just notice that the longer the boss' trip, the less impressive are Frank and Sam's returns become. And so it is for your returns. The longer it takes for your investment portfolio to grow, the lower your return, as calculated by the CAGR.

By the way, anytime someone brags to you about what a great investment their house was, you can think about the CAGR and laugh to yourself. Or out loud – your choice. People usually only think about their houses in absolute terms. You may have heard people say things like, "Yep, my house was the best investment I ever made. Eunice and I bought it for $50,000 back in simpler times and now, 51 years later it's worth $250,000." When I hear such comments, I smile and nod while wondering how dangerous tightly-suppressed laughter is to my health. Any idea what the CAGR for that 51-year investment is? It's 3.21%. Not counting expenses and maintenance costs.

But back to our parable and what we're all thinking. Namely, "what about Tom?" Well, I have some good news and some bad news. The bad news is that he's once again the loser. Regardless of how long the boss was away, Tom's 0% is still a 0%.

The good news is that Tom's performance looks better and better, relative to Frank and Sam's CAGR benchmark, the longer the boss was away. For each additional year the boss was away, Frank and Sam's CAGR gets lower and lower. But Tom's 0% can't get any lower, no matter how many years we're talking about.

A CAGR *can* be negative, but only if you lose money. And Tom didn't lose money; he just didn't earn any. Even if he had lost money, a CAGR actually works the opposite way for losses. If he had lost money, the CAGR (where the "G" for "growth" would be negative growth, or a loss) would actually be a smaller and smaller negative number as time went on.

Also notice that Tom's CAGR looks better, "*relative to Frank and Sam's CAGR benchmark,*" as the boss' trip lengthens. That is an important point. You can combine the lesson from this section and the lesson from the previous "relative return" section and compare the CAGR of different investments.

Return Wrap-Up

Before defending Tom, let's close with a couple of observations.

First, the four types of returns we covered, including the CAGR, are simply four ways of thinking about your investment performance. They will help you think about how well (or poorly) your investments are doing, and will help you ask important questions of your financial advisors. There are other ways of thinking about your returns as well, but the four we have covered are a good start.

Second, no single type of return will tell the whole story. The CAGR sounds pretty good. But it leaves out some important details. For instance, it completely ignores how volatile an investment is (how big the upswings and downswings are).

If you invest $1,000 and have $1,500 five years later, the CAGR will always be 8.45%. That will be true whether the investment went up smoothly by 8.45% each year, or whether it went up to $10,000 in year two, down to $2 in year three, back up to $8,000 in year four, and finally settled back to $1,500 in year five. The CAGR doesn't capture volatility.

Now, then, on to our defense of Tom.

In Defense of the Third Servant: Negative Returns

Ah, Tom. The much-maligned third servant who got a severe tongue-lashing after he buried his boss' money in the ground while his co-workers were busy investing it with great success. Tom gets yelled at, belittled, fired, and tossed out into the streets. He is quite literally a metaphor for someone who will spend eternity sitting on a hot rock in Hell.

But is he really that bad?

I propose that Tom wasn't quite the irredeemable derelict that the parable makes him out to be, at least not from a financial perspective. Consider the following evidence.

First, note that the boss didn't give his servants any guidance on what to do with the money. He didn't say, "Go out and invest my money and make as much profit as you can." Instead, he divided his eight bags of gold up among the three servants (five to Frank, two to Sam, and one to Tom) and left on his long journey. It seems harsh that the boss fired Tom for failing to follow an order he was never given.

In fact, in the absence of explicit instructions, Tom may have been the most trustworthy servant. In the financial world, you can hire various types of representatives to help you, with each type following its own set of rules.

For instance, on one end of the spectrum, there are "brokers" (sometimes called "registered representatives") who are essentially salespeople. It is perfectly legal for a broker (like a traditional "stockbroker") to sell you financial products from which she makes a commission, and there is no requirement that the product be right for you or something that you need.

On the other end of the spectrum, some representatives have a "fiduciary" relationships where the representative is legally-bound to act in your best interest. In fact, depending on the type of relationship, the fiduciary's primary role might be to protect your assets from loss.

By the way, researching the various types of financial representatives and their requirements is an excellent place to start your financial self-education. But back to Tom...

It is very possible that Tom, in the absence of a direct order from his boss to invest the gold, decided assume the most conservative role possible – that of a fiduciary whose goal was to protect the assets. And protect them he did – he buried them in the ground and dutifully returned them to the boss when he got home.

For a fiduciary whose role is to protect assets, it can actually be illegal to make certain investments that put the assets at risk, regardless of whether the fiduciary makes money or not. From that point of view, Frank and Sam may have been out of line, with Tom being the only faithful servant.

Another important thing to note is that Tom's returns look especially bad because we (and the boss) view them as relative to Frank and Sam's 100% gains. We talked about comparing returns to a benchmark in the "Relative Returns" section of this chapter. In this parable, Frank and Sam are the default benchmarks because they are similar to Tom.

But we don't know what Frank and Sam invested in. If the boss' trip was relatively short, Frank and Sam probably made some very risky investments. There are very few low-risk ways to get 100% returns over short time periods. There actually are some (notably, investing in a 401(k) and getting a risk-free company match, which the Appendix will cover), but they didn't exist when Jesus told this parable.

The thing about high-return investments is that they often experience quite a bit of volatility, especially in the short term. The boss returned when Frank and Sam were doing very well, but he could just as easily have returned during a downswing.

Imagine how different the parable would be if the boss had returned when Frank and Sam were down by 50%. In that alternate reality, Tom would have looked like a genius with his 0% gains. Frank's five bags of gold would have turned into 2.5 and Sam's two bags would have turned into one, while Tom held onto the entire bag the boss gave him.

The only difference for Tom in that scenario is that the benchmark has changed. Tom's 0% looks very good compared to a *negative* 50% return. Given how mad the boss was about Tom's 0% return, imagine his fury at a loss.

Finally, the boss knew from the outset that Tom wasn't his best investor. The parable notes that the boss distributed the gold based on the servants' abilities. He didn't divide his eight bags up evenly – he gave five to Frank, two to Sam, and only one to Tom. In other words, the boss had five times as much confidence in Frank as he did in Tom, and twice as much confidence in Sam as he did in Tom. So, he shouldn't have been so surprised to find that Frank outperformed Tom by so much.

We can learn something from how the boss divides up his assets. Most people have heard about the importance of diversifying their investments into different types of assets. This is good investment advice (as you'll see in Chapter Four. If you have too much of your money in one type of investment, you stand to lose a disproportionate amount if that investment does poorly.

But note that the boss employs another kind of diversification – diversification among asset *managers*. He doesn't leave all of his money with one person. There is a lot of wisdom in considering this type of diversification. Modern day investors who had all of their money under Bernie Madoff's control, only to find that he had swindled them out of it, would likely agree. Note that boss' diversification among asset managers ensured that the most of his overall portfolio that he could have lost from any one servant was 62.5% (5/8 of the gold with Frank).

Tom gets a pretty bad rap. It's not clear that the boss explicitly told him to invest the gold. In the absence of guidance, Tom may have been wise to assume the most conservative role for himself. Tom's performance looks especially bad compared to that of the high-performing Frank and Sam. And, the boss didn't expect great things from Tom, which is why he only gave Tom 12.5% (1/8) of his gold in the first place.

In any case, we don't get to hear Tom's side of the story – he was too busy being tossed out into the streets – so I thought it was the least I could do to offer up a defense.

Financial Lesson 2: Inflation – the Sneaky, Silent Enemy

We have discussed the important role of time in previous financial lessons. In the first chapter we noted how investments growing at even modest rates of return can become quite large when given enough time. In the previous section of this chapter, we talked about how the compound annual growth rate (CAGR) takes time into account when calculating investment performance.

The parable of Frank, Sam, and Tom hints at another important aspect of time. Only here, time is your enemy, not your friend. This is the lesson of *Inflation*.

Inflation simply refers to the fact that prices tend to go up over time. It's easy to remember: when you inflate a tire, it gets bigger; when prices inflate, they go up. You are already familiar with this concept if you have ever heard someone say (or said yourself) something along the lines of, "I remember when a movie ticket was ten cents and you could buy a nice suit for two dollars!"

Even if you roll your eyes at such comments, they contain an important truth. The prices of things you buy really do tend to go up over time. My father, for instance, remembers buying gasoline for 25 cents per gallon in his youth. At the time of this writing, 50 years or so later, a gallon of gasoline costs around $3.00. He used to be able to buy 12 gallons for what it costs to buy one gallon now. Or, looked at from another perspective, the same 25 cents that used to buy one gallon now only buys 1/12 of a gallon (that's one-and-one-third of a cup). He's not going very far on that.

Now consider how important the idea of inflation is for your savings and investments. We already talked about how your investments can grow at a compounded rate and you can end up with more money than you started with. But inflation causes the prices of the things you'll need to buy with your money to go up as well.

It's often hard to see inflation – prices sometimes rise so gradually that you don't notice it. But the effect has a very real impact on your well-being. Imagine if my father had put a quarter in a shoebox back when gasoline was 25 cents per gallon. Then, 50 years later, he took that quarter out. The quarter is still a quarter and is still worth 25 cents. But that 25 cents won't buy as much as it did when he first put it in the shoebox, so in a very real sense it is not as valuable.

Imagine you are very risk-averse and can't stand the thought of losing your money. Rather than invest your money, you put it all into a fireproof safe in your basement. You do this for 50 years, watching your stack of money in the safe get bigger and bigger each year. You are impressed with yourself for being so diligent in saving money, and for not risking it in any investments.

When you count it up after fifty years, you find that all your money is indeed there. The problem is that the money is simply not worth what it was when you put it in. The first dollars you stacked away might only be worth a few cents or tens of cents, in terms of what they can now buy.

The sneakiness of inflation is in how it works silently and steadily behind the scenes. In the above scenario, you might not even realize the problem because, in one sense, you haven't lost any money. It's all still there. Its value just quietly eroded away over the years.

Very few people actually stack up their money in a giant safe, but many people invest large portions of their money in assets that simply do not have the potential to appreciate much faster than the rate of inflation.

Think about what it means if you happen to invest your money at exactly the rate of inflation. The amount of money in your account gets larger and larger, but it is no larger "in real terms" (in terms of what you can buy with it). In other words, you can buy the same number of gallons of gas fifty years from now that you can buy today.

Trying to grow your money at the rate of inflation is better than putting your money in a safe where it won't grow at all. A better strategy is to give yourself a chance at growing your money *faster* than inflation erodes it. If you manage to do that, your money will actually be worth more (it buys more gallons of gasoline) than when you first invested it.

This book is not designed to offer specific advice on what to invest in, but the Appendix will cover various investment options available to you, along with account types that might help you keep more of your money by legally avoiding taxes. Avoiding taxes (for a while, at least) can help you improve your returns and fight inflation.

My examples use "gasoline" to represent what your money buys, though of course you buy any number of things, as well as services. By the time you retire, in fact, "gasoline" may simply be something your grandchildren ask you about after learning in history class that people used to travel around in boxes fueled by a liquid instead of teleporting themselves from place to place. "Gasoline" is just a stand-in word for "things you buy," and prices for most things you buy tend to rise over time.

What, exactly, is the rate of inflation? The most commonly used estimate is the "Consumer Price Index," or "CPI." The federal government's Bureau of Labor Statistics (BLS) calculates and publishes the CPI, which tracks the price of an imaginary basket of goods and services you might buy. The rate of change of the price of that basket is the CPI.

The BLS calculates the CPI based on surveys of what people buy for two different groups: one that it calls "All Urban Consumers" and another that it calls "Urban Wage Earners and Clerical Workers." If you happen to live in a rural area, your purchases aren't included. But you're not alone: "institutionalized" people are also excluded, so the price fluctuations of contraband cigarettes, shanks, and "services" you might purchase in prison aren't counted. The BLS uses various statistical techniques to try to avoid letting things like temporary weather conditions or holiday spending skew the CPI.

We don't need to delve much deeper into how the CPI is calculated. It is just worth knowing what it is, because it affects your financial picture. The CPI does a good job of capturing the types of things people buy; if you look over what's included (the BLS website lists what's in the basket), you will nod along, thinking, "Yeah, that covers a lot of what I buy."

Now that you understand what inflation means, if you read that the CPI averaged 2% over the past year, you can translate that to mean that your money now buys about 2% less than it bought a year ago.

Another important takeaway from the CPI relates to your investments. If you read that the CPI averaged 2% over the previous year, and you have an investment that earned 5% during that time, your money actually only buys you 3% more than it did at the beginning of the year. This is the erosion effect we talked about. You have 5% more money, but it buys 2% less, so it's as if you only earned 3%. If you read about the "real rate of return," it's referring to the difference between your rate of return and inflation.

The CPI might also affect you in a very visible way – your paycheck. If you get a "cost of living raise" at your job, it might well be based on the CPI.

The bottom line takeaway of this section is that inflation is the silent march of prices upward that erodes the amount of goods and services your money can buy over time. Thus, it is important to invest your money in such a way that you can at least offset, and hopefully outpace, inflation.

It is easier now to see the role inflation plays in the parable about Frank, Sam, and Tom. The boss gave them each some gold and left for a while. Inflation might help explain why the boss was so angry with Tom. By returning to the boss the same bag of gold he had buried in the ground, Tom returned an amount that could buy less than when the boss left. That's losing money *in real terms*.

Imagine that when the boss left, one bag of gold would buy 10 goats and 100 bottles of wine. But, when he returned, one bag of gold would only buy him eight goats and 90 bottles of wine. He still has one bag of gold. It looks the same, it weighs the same, it's even in the same bag – it just buys less. In a very real and measurable way, Tom lost money for the boss by not investing.

There are a few final points to make about inflation before we move on to another parable. First, prices can go down, resulting in a negative CPI.

When prices are falling it is called "deflation," which is a real thing. That might sound good; after all, with deflation the same amount of investments would buy more and more as time went on. In practice, however, deflation tends to occur when the economy is doing poorly. In times of deflation, things might cost less, but you might not be able to buy them because you don't have a job.

Second, we usually talk about inflation as rising prices, though you may see inflation in hiding in the form of getting less product for your money. My mother often complains about noticing that she is paying the same price for an item that is smaller than it was before. This is definitely a form of price inflation – the price *per ounce* (or yard, or whatever) has risen – but it is sneaky because the overall package is the same price.

Finally, note that inflation only affects you when you buy things, and to some extent you control what you buy. One way to avoid the effects of inflation is to avoid buying a lot of nonsense that you don't need, or cut down on the amount of nonsense you buy. If the price of cigarettes keeps going up, stop smoking. If the price of gasoline keeps going up, move closer to the places you go, ride a bike, or plan your trips to maximize the number of things you do in each trip.

You can't stop buying everything and there are some things you can't even cut back on (lifesaving medicine comes to mind). But, at least keep in mind that the only price changes that affect you are the prices of things you buy. I have yet to complain about steadily-increasing Ferrari prices.

Bonus Career Lesson: Respect the Boss

Let's end this chapter with a bonus career lesson. It fits in a book about personal finance because your career affects your finances.

I previously mounted a defense of Tom for putting his boss' money in the ground, noting that there were some logical reasons why he might have done so. It is harder to defend how he talks to his boss.

If you recall from the parable, the boss, who had just heard about Frank and Sam's 100% returns, asked Tom how he did. Tom answered by saying, "Everybody knows you're a mean tightwad who squeezes every penny until it squeals. I dug a hole and put your gold in it. Here it is – take it." And the boss blew a gasket.

If you're going to deliver bad news to your boss, maybe don't lead by calling him names, alluding to the fact that everyone thinks he's a jerk, and then ending without explanation and without even attempting a positive spin.

Tom might have been wiser to avoid the insults and instead explain why he didn't do as well as his colleagues. He could have said something like, "I didn't want to risk losing the money you worked so hard to earn, and I wasn't sure that I was authorized to invest it, so I found the most remote and secure location I could, and buried your gold in it. I am pleased to report that I am now able to return every piece you gave me."

The boss might still have fired Tom, but I have to think he wouldn't have done so with such relish.

Chapter 4: Diversify by Sowing Far and Wide

Parable Summary

A farmer went out to plant his crop. He scattered the seeds all around. Some seeds landed on a path, some seeds landed on rocky ground, some seeds fell onto ground that also had thorns growing in it, and some seeds fell onto good soil.

Birds came along and ate the seeds that landed in the path. The seeds that landed on the rocky soil sprouted, but they couldn't establish deep roots, so the sun fried them. The seeds that landed in the thorny soil sprouted and grew, but the thorns choked them out. Finally, the seeds that landed in the good soil grew up and did well – multiplying anywhere from 30 to 100 times.

Where you can find it

Matthew 13:3-8, Mark 4:3-8, Luke 8:5-8

The Religious Lesson

Like other parables we have seen, this one is about Jesus' teachings and people's receptivity to them. Seed on the path is like people who hear the teachings, but it goes in one ear and out the other. The rocky soil is like when people hear teachings and get excited, but then lose interest. Seed on the thorny soil is like when people hear teachings and get interested, but then worldly desires get in the way and they lose interest. The seed falling on good soil is like people who hear the teachings, listen, and then live according to them. These people become spiritually "fruitful" (and can presumably multiply Jesus' teachings for future generations).

The Financial Lesson: Diversify your Investments, Income Streams, and Managers

This parable contains an excellent and extremely important financial lesson. Namely, diversify your investments.

This financial lesson initially seems similar to the old saying, "Don't put all your eggs in one basket." The reason you don't put all your eggs in one basket is that, if something happens to a basket containing some eggs (i.e. you drop it, you lose it, someone steals it, etc.), you still have eggs left over in other baskets.

Note the difference between the parable of the farmer sowing seeds and the "eggs in the basket" saying, though. Baskets secure eggs from loss – the eggs aren't going anywhere. In the parable, the farmer literally throws the seeds out into the world, with the hopes that they grow and produce a crop.

This difference is huge and has big implications. The egg-and-basket saying is about *protecting* what you have; the seed parable is about *growing* what you have. Baskets are like insurance; sowing is like investing. Since this is a book about parables, not things your grandmother used to tell you, let's discuss the parable in more detail.

First, note that seeds are themselves a crop. Let's assume the farmer was sowing beans (beans are seeds). A bean is both a crop that you can eat and a seed that you can put in the ground and hope it grows into more beans. A bag of beans represents a choice. You can eat them right now and have a meal, or you can plant them and hope they grow into more beans over the course of a growing season.

Farmers like the one in the parable are in the business of putting seeds in the ground and hoping they multiply into more seeds, some of which can be sold for food and some of which can be put back into the ground as seeds again.

(Note: the previous explanation of how farming works was true for thousands of years, but the advent of multinational agricultural businesses have changed the world to the point that most farmers actually buy seeds each year from a giant company and no longer plant seeds that they grew and harvested themselves. Just ignore that little fact of life for purposes of this parable, which was told long before modern farming techniques, and imagine we're living in simpler times).

Think of yourself as a money farmer and your dollars as your seeds. As we discussed in previous chapters, you want to invest ("plant") your money ("seeds") such that, over time, it compounds ("grows") into a large amount ("crop") that you can retire on ("eat or sell").

We've already discussed the importance of investing, and the Appendix will cover some types of available investments. For now let's focus on why it's important to diversify your portfolio by holding different types of investments.

Although some investments guarantee a particular return, many investments do not come with guarantees. And there are many different things you can invest your money in – big and small companies, bonds issued by various countries, currencies, commodities, real estate, and so on. Some of those investments will pay off big, while others will fall apart at the seams. So, easy enough – just invest your money in the things that will do well, right?

Sadly, you don't know up front which investments will do well. Your financial advisor won't know, either, even one with your best interests at heart. That's just the nature of the game. As soon as you venture out into non-guaranteed investments, which you almost certainly have to do if you want your money to grow into any semblance of an amount that will give you a comfortable retirement, you lose the ability to know how those investments will perform.

Every investor faces the same problem: you know that some investments will do great and others will do terribly, but you don't know which ones are which until it's too late.

Fortunately, there is a solution – diversification. Essentially, if you invest in *everything*, or at least a broad swath of available investments, you can increase your odds of getting positive returns on your investments. You will invest in some things that decrease in value, but you will also invest in things that increase in value. The idea is that, on average, these things will offset each other enough to leave you with a positive return that is acceptably high.

Two things might concern you at this point. First, doesn't investing in everything essentially guarantee that you'll just be average? Second, how are you supposed to invest in everything?

Addressing the first concern, yes, investing in everything essentially ensures that you'll be average. Even if your investment portfolio contains a rock star investment that goes up 1,000% in a year, you'll also have the dud investment that goes bankrupt ends up worth nothing.

But, go back to the idea that you don't know beforehand which ones are which. If you knew the rock stars from the duds in advance, of course you'd invest in the former. But you don't. By investing in everything, you are essentially making a bet that, on average, the investments in your big basket will go up.

As for the second concern, it would indeed be a daunting task to invest in everything if you had to buy a huge portfolio of investments one at a time. First you'd have to find them and then you'd have to buy them. It would take forever. It would also be super-expensive. Buying hundreds of individual investments one-by-one would get very expensive very fast.

Fortunately, the financial services industry has created products like "Index Funds" and "Exchange-Traded Funds" that are your best friend when it comes to low-cost diversification. We will discuss these products in much more detail in the Appendix. For now, understand that you can improve your odds of not losing all your money in any one investment, and ensure average returns, by choosing investments that let you own large numbers of investments at once.

Returning to the parable, the seeds fell on four different types of bad soil: a path, rocky soil, and thorny soil. The seeds that fell on the hard-packed path were easy picking for birds. The rocky soil was too shallow for good roots to develop and the plants dried up in the sun. The seeds that landed in thorny soil grew, but got choked out.

Each of these types of bad soil represent bad investments. Companies you invest in can go out of business due to increased competition, real estate can lose value and tenants can fail to pay rent, commodities like gold and silver can lose value over long periods, and so on. Just as the farmer lost much of his seed investment to birds, the sun, and thorns, you can lose your monetary investment.

But the parable holds out hope. Some of the farmer's seed fell onto good soil. And what happened to that seed? It multiplied. And it didn't just multiply – it multiplied by anywhere from 30 to 100 times (depending on which parable you read). The parable doesn't mention what proportion of the farmer's seeds fell into which kind of soil, but let's assume that the farmer just tossed the seeds willy-nilly and that the seeds fell evenly onto the various soils. So, 25% landed on the path, 25% fell on rocks, 25% fell in with thorns, and 25% landed in good soil. How did the farmer do?

Let's say he started with 1,000 beans. That means 250 beans fell onto each soil and he lost 750 beans (250 lost to birds + 250 lost to rocks + 250 lost to thorns). But, the remaining 250 beans grew by 30 to 100 times. That means the 250 beans that landed in good soil grew into anywhere from 7,500 beans to 25,000 beans (250 x 30 = 7,500; and 250 x 100 = 25,000). And this was over one growing season – let's say one year for simplicity. This means that the farmer's return was anywhere from 650% to 2,400%.

Very cool! It's interesting to see how the math embedded into this parable works out to a positive return.

You won't know at the outset which of your investments are on the equivalent of thorny soil and which are on good soil. But by spreading your money out over lots of investments, you will improve your chances that, overall, you will end up with positive returns.

One word of warning – while this parable is an excellent illustration of how diversification works, the returns are wildly optimistic. You won't get 650% returns and certainly won't get 2,400% returns.

There are a few remaining things to point out. It is important to note that one advantage of investing is that your downside is limited, while your upside is not. Assuming you don't borrow money to invest (called "leveraging" your investment or investing "on the margin"), your downside is limited to how much you invest. If you invest $1,000, you can only lose $1,000. The same is not true of the amount you can make. In theory, there's no limit to how much your $1,000 can grow into.

This disconnect between the upside and the downside (sometimes called "asymmetrical risk") is the investor's friend. It definitely helped the farmer. Imagine that the farmer's upside had been capped at a 100% return (doubling his seed investment). After losing 750 of his seeds to birds, rocks, and thorns, his remaining 250 seeds could only have doubled to 500, leaving him with a 50% loss. By using a very large return (30 to 100 times the initial investment), the parable illustrates the power of a limited downside paired with an unlimited upside.

It is important to point out the value in diversifying your income streams – where your money comes from – as well as your investments. If all of your income is from a job, then your income disappears entirely if you lose your job. How do you diversify your income streams? There are various possibilities.

For instance, you start diversifying your income stream simply by building up a portfolio of diversified investments. Each investment you make is like an untapped stream of potential income in the future. Whether that investment is in stocks, bonds, real estate, or something else we will discuss in the Appendix, it will either produce actual income in the form of interest or dividends, or you can sell it to create income. Owning and renting out property is a very common investment used to produce an income stream separate from job income.

With the above methods, you essentially take income from your job and create alternate income streams (or potential streams) that do not require a job to produce. You will often hear people refer to "passive income" as any income stream that flows in without you having to actively work for it. Just note that the IRS definition of "passive income" is different from the layman's definition. Generally, the IRS talks about "active income," "portfolio income," and "passive income," and each one is specifically defined and has separate tax considerations. Don't assume your income is "passive" just because it seems that way.

Keep in mind, too, that the idea of diversifying your income streams is to have *unrelated* streams of income. This is a very important point for those who invest a large portion of their portfolios in the company they work for, or in companies within the industry they work. In that situation, both your job *and* your investments will be at risk if your company or industry suffers a downturn.

Many employees of a company called Enron learned this lesson the hard way. Enron filed for bankruptcy in 2001, amid a massive fraud and corruption scandal. Quite a few employees had invested most, or all, of their retirement savings in Enron stock, and lost both their jobs and investment portfolios at the same time. It was a jarring lesson for those involved, or even for those (like me) who simply watched the news as employees filed out of the Houston office building carrying boxes, while a plummeting stock chart was superimposed on the screen.

There is one final point to make about diversification before ending this section. In addition to diversification of *investments* and *income*, recall the lesson from the previous chapter about diversification of *investment managers*. In the previous chapter's parable, the boss spread his money among three separate employees to invest. Even though one of those employees did a poor job of investing, the boss still ended up with good returns because he spread some of his money to the other two.

If you plan to entrust your money to the care of a professional investment advisor, it's worth thinking about spreading your money among more than one person. This is true even if you think your manager is very good and above-board, and you recognize that it is simpler to work with one person to handle your investments.

An advisor might not give the best advice, nor is it unheard of for investment advisors to simply abscond with clients' money. Remember the story of Bernie Madoff. Madoff was an extreme case, but outright fraud isn't that rare; it's just that smaller-scale frauds don't make the news.

While writing this book, I had breakfast with some former teachers who told me about a fraud that I later researched. It turned out that a couple of investment advisors had claimed to be investing clients' money, while actually using it to fund their own extravagant lifestyles. They built up a client base of people whose trust they had gained over several years, and who had no reason to question their legitimacy. Over 50 clients, largely made up of public school teachers who invested their retirement savings, lost a total of 10 million dollars.

When I heard that story, I wondered how many of those clients had spread their money out among various advisors.

Counterpoint: The Case for Concentration

There is an important caveat to diversification. People become extremely wealthy through *concentration* of investments, not through diversification. Jeff Bezos became a multibillionaire by starting Amazon and focusing all his time and effort on growing and building that business. Mark Zuckerberg did the same thing with Facebook. Andrew Carnegie, who made a vast fortune in the steel industry, said that it is better to put all your eggs into one basket and then carefully watch that basket than it is to spread your eggs among several baskets.

That makes sense. To end up with above-average wealth, you need above-average investments, and diversification ensures that you're about average. Thus, diversification won't lead to untold riches.

Having said that, before you go out and try to find the next super-investment, just remember that you don't know in advance whether an investment will be a winner or a loser. For every Mark Zuckerberg, there are thousands of other people who lost everything they invested.

If you decide to put all your seeds into one plot of land, you need to look very carefully to make sure there are no hungry birds in the trees, ready to swoop in as soon as you walk away.

Warren Buffett, perhaps the greatest investor who has ever lived, made his fortune by focusing his money into a concentrated group of investments. But, he has publicly said that the average person investing for retirement is better off by putting her money into a low-cost index fund that invests in a broad range of investments (specifically, Buffett recommended a low-cost index fund that tracks the S&P 500 Index). In fact, he has publicly stated that he has instructed that the cash from his estate be placed into index funds.

While concentration is the only that that *possibly* leads to great wealth, diversification ensures that your investments grow as well as the average investment in your portfolio. Historically, even average returns can generate a large (not vast) amount of wealth over time.

Chapter 5: Grapes don't grow on Thorn Bushes

Parable Summary
Good fruit doesn't grow on bad trees, and you can tell what kind of tree it is by what kind of fruit it bears. You can't pick a fig off a thorn bush, or get a delicious grape out of a briar patch. Similarly, good people do and say good things, while bad people do and say bad things.

Where you can find it
Matthew 7:15-20, Luke 6:43-45

The Religious Lesson
Here, Jesus gives advice on how to identify false prophets. He says that you can tell what someone is like by how they live and conduct themselves. You can recognize false prophets by their bad words and deeds.

The Financial Lesson: What you see is usually what you get
This isn't so much a parable as it is an observation, but it's a good observation with implications across your financial life. The financial lesson from this parable is to do your research before making any moves with financial overtones.

Things are what they are. Ignoring genetic engineering, a thorn bush will never produce figs. You'll never pluck a cherry from a cactus. There's a reason farmers don't intentionally grow briars. Similarly, bad people and companies will generally continue to be bad people and companies. More importantly, you can identify bad people and companies by their actions.

Suppose I say you to, "Let's play a guessing game. I just picked a handful of grapes from a plant. What kind of plant was it?" Your answer will hopefully be "a grape vine." Certainly you wouldn't suspect that my grapes came from a Jimsonweed (a weed that produces toxic seeds).

Now, suppose I say, "I just bought a used car from a salesman who said the car was in great shape. When I drove off the lot, the door fell off, the horn started blaring uncontrollably, oil spurted out of the windshield wiper fluid tube, two tires blew out, and there was a dead body in the trunk. When I told the salesman what happened, he slapped me in the face, jumped in his own car, and sped away, never to be seen from again. Was this salesman a good guy or a bad guy?"

That's not a trick question – of course he's terrible. He's a liar and a criminal (still better than some used car salesmen I've come across, though).

The point is that you can tell how good something or someone is by how they behave. Behavior is the "fruit." Although people can change, they tend not to. Have you ever heard the phrase, "once a cheater, always and a cheater?" People who are unfaithful in one romantic relationship tend to be unfaithful in all romantic relationships. It's a phrase where the rare exception proves the rule. It applies much more broadly than just romantic ne'er do wells. It applies to both people and things. And it applies to positive traits as well as negative.

People who give you good advice tend to continue giving good advice. Companies that cheat their customers tend to do so systematically. A shoddy product is a good indication that other products produced by the same company will be shoddy. People who abuse drugs tend to habitually abuse drugs. It's rarely a one-time thing.

How does this relate to your financial life? When you are making financial decisions, you need to conduct research up front to determine the reputation of the people and products you are dealing with. You don't get grapes from briars. You don't get good service from a company or a professional with a history of mistreating its customers.

There is great news in this area. We live in an age of unprecedented access to information about products, professionals, and companies. For almost any service or product you can imagine, there are websites, blogs, consumer advocacy groups, and magazines providing detailed reviews of many products, people, and companies you are thinking about dealing with. Much of this advice is free, and for big decisions, paid services are often well-worth the cost. In addition, you probably know people who have used the types of products or services you are interested in, or who have done business with professionals you are thinking about employing.

These reviews and testimonials are evidence of the past behavior and quality of people, products, and services. That behavior is the "fruit" that Jesus was talking about a couple of thousand years ago.

Before you make a major financial decision involving a person, service, or company, research what kind of fruit it has borne in the past. Major financial decisions can include a large purchase, which investment advisor(s) to entrust with your money, who to hire to renovate your kitchen, which insurance company should cover your new house, what school to attend, or anything affecting one of the foundational elements of your financial foundation from Chapter One.

This hearkens back to Chapter One's advice to "educate yourself." That's not a coincidence. If this book could be condensed into one sentence, it would be "educate yourself." And that's just a two-word sentence (coincidentally, the shortest chapter of the Bible is also two words long ("Jesus wept" in John 11:35)).

Educate yourself. Take it upon yourself to learn about who, and what, you are getting involved with. *Before* you get involved. People have an alarming tendency to spend the majority of their research time on inconsequential things, while devoting little-to-no time researching important things.

You can probably think of a few examples.

Maybe you know people who extensively research purchases of clothing and accessories, including comparisons among styles, fabrics, cuts, colors, vendors, prices, and customer reviews. This research process might span anywhere from several days to several months, requiring a significant emotional investment for a decision about an item that costs a couple hundred dollars on the high end.

I have seen people devote vanishingly-little time and effort to investment decisions related to amounts of money in the range of hundreds of thousands to low millions of dollars. In the instances I am thinking of, people spend anywhere from a few minutes to a couple of hours making decisions that like which person or company to invest their money with, or how they will allocate their money. I have seen people who decide to spend no time whatsoever deciding what to do with their assets, instead letting the money sit idly around, not bothering to look into what to do with it. In most of these cases, the people in question spent untold hours each week watching mindless television.

I have seen people make major purchase decisions about things such as home renovations that will run into tens of thousands of dollars, having conducted almost no research into the contractors and products associated with these decisions. I have seen results that included completed-but-substandard renovations that required significant re-work; contractors who simply took the money and skipped town, never to be seen again; and contractors who caused structural damage to the property before declaring bankruptcy and leaving the homeowner to hire someone else to fix the mess (ironically, again with little research).

Does that make sense? If you spend more time picking out a pair of shoes than you spend on how much insurance you need, you might need to rethink your priorities. If you spend more time on social media researching what your ex-girlfriend is up to than you do finding out whether your investment advisor has a string of complaints from former clients, maybe ask yourself if you should re-allocate your time.

Fifty years ago, we could perhaps forgive someone for a lack of research. It was difficult to find reviews of products, services, companies, contractors, and other professionals. Independent reviews could be hard to find, and you might have to reply on word-of-mouth (which can be suspect because a recommended contractor may turn out to be the brother-in-law of the "mouth" in question).

Now, however, there is no excuse for failure to research. There are scores of websites, blogs, consumer advocacy groups, and magazines dedicated to providing thorough reviews of any product, service, company, advisor, professional, or salesperson you can imagine. And many are free. The only cost is your time. If the investment is large enough, buying a subscription to an impartial review service might turn out to be money well spent. Here's a tip: before you buy a subscription to publication dedicated to reviews (online or in print), check to see if your library has a copy.

Imagine you've started a new job that offers a retirement plan. You have to tell the HR people how you want to take advantage of it. Your decision will help determine the sort of life you have in retirement. Rather than use the scores of resources available to research investment options, companies, and professionals, you decide to spend your time watching "The Absolutely Non-Scripted Pawn-Shop-Owning Housewives of Chop-Shop Voices." Whose fault is it when you retire to a refrigerator box in the alley behind the strip club downtown? Not the nice club, either – the seedy one beside the bar that offers $1 pints from 3:00 PM to 6:00 PM on Thursdays?

That was a rhetorical question; it's your fault!

As the parable says, thorns don't produce grapes. Good trees produce good fruit. Good people do good things. So look for companies and people with good records.

Are you looking for an investment advisor? Trying to find someone to remodel your kitchen or put a new roof on your house? Any time you are about to make a decision that will have a relatively large impact on your finances, take the time to do some research and make sure you are confident that you have chosen wisely.

This advice is helpful when dealing with people in your non-financial life as well. The parable about grapes not growing on thorn bushes is very similar to the old saying, "a zebra doesn't change its stripes." People tend not to change. Cousin Jim, who divides his time between the heroin dealer on the outskirts of town and the county lockup will not suddenly become a trustworthy model citizen. So when he asks to borrow money because *this time* he's going straight, and *this time* he *swears* he'll pay you back, only lend him the money if you don't need it and don't expect it back. Because a zebra doesn't change its stripes and thorn bushes don't suddenly start producing grapes and figs.

Chapter 6: The Tax Man Cometh

Parable Summary
Some of Jesus' enemies came up to him and "Teacher, you're a man of integrity who always tells it like it is and aren't swayed by what other people say. So tell us, should we pay taxes to Caesar [the head of the government at the time]?"

Jesus was smart and saw that his enemies were trying to trap him into saying something damaging, so he said, "You bunch of hypocrites! Why are you trying to trap me? Show me a coin." His enemies brought a coin and Jesus asked, "Who is on this coin?" His enemies said, "Caesar is on it." So, Jesus said, "Give Caesar what is Caesar and give God what is God's."

Jesus' enemies were impressed at his wise answer and couldn't think of any smart-aleck remarks, so they shut up and walked away.

Where you can find it
Matthew 22:15-22, Mark 12:13-17, Luke 20:20-29

The Religious Lesson
Respect the governmental authority under which you live, but be mindful of your obligations to God.

A bit of Background
This chapter, like the last one, is based on a story involving Jesus, and not a parable.

This story features an exchange between Jesus and a group of his natural enemies – religious leaders called the "Pharisees." Throughout his life (right up until the end, unfortunately for him), Jesus and the Pharisees were like cats and dogs. The upstart Jesus was a threat to the Pharisees' established order, so the Pharisees were always trying to get Jesus to say or do something that would get him in trouble. But Jesus was too crafty for them and usually made them look foolish or left them speechless.

In this parable, the Pharisees used a tax imposed by the Roman Empire to try to trap Jesus. When they asked Jesus whether people should pay the tax, the Pharisees hoped he would say, "Absolutely not! No one should pay taxes to this morally bankrupt government. If anything, they should burn it to the ground." Then, the Pharisees could have had Jesus arrested.

Instead of falling into the Pharisees' trap, Jesus gave a characteristically pithy answer that has entered our language as a common phrase – "Give until Caesar what is Caesar's" or "Render until Caesar what is Caesar's" – and shuts them up.

We can glean several worthwhile financial lessons from this story.

Financial Lesson 1: Pay, and Pay Attention to, your Taxes...

The first lesson we get from this parable is to pay, and pay attention to, your taxes. It's actually two lessons, but we will discuss them both in the same section.

This might seem like a fairly obvious lesson, but there is some nuance to it. Unfortunately, a lot of people need to learn this important lesson. If you disregard most of the other lessons in this book, you will probably end up poorer than you otherwise would. If you ignore this advice, you might end up in federal prison in addition to being poorer.

People who fail to pay their taxes tend to fall into one of three categories: those who think they won't get caught, those who are sloppy, and those who believe they have found a loophole allowing them to legally not pay taxes.

The first category of people know they are cheating; they just don't think they'll get caught.

Frankly, the odds are actually on their side. Millions of people are supposed to pay taxes, and the Internal Revenue Service (IRS) has a very limited number of people whose job is to find tax cheats. If your tax situation is simple, the odds are very good that you will never be audited and will fall through the cracks.

But that's a very ill-advised strategy. For one thing, the IRS has several years after you were supposed to pay your taxes to charge you with a crime (how long it has depends on the specifics of what they say you did). So, you have to be nervous for years after you don't pay your taxes, with the black cloud of federal prison hanging over your head. Even if the IRS doesn't accuse you of being a *criminal*, it can still take you to court to make you repay what you owe (plus penalties). And it has as long as it wants to do that, so you're never free of worry.

On top of that, the IRS might get much better in the future at identifying people who don't pay their taxes and improve their odds of finding you. Even if you think there's only a one-in-a-million chance that the IRS would find you right now, what if it improves its processes significantly next year, such that the odds are now one-in-one-thousand? You have worry about your suddenly-improved odds of the IRS coming after you, hoping you don't end up on the wrong side of those odds.

The second type of tax scofflaw is the sloppy person. They keep poor records, or no records, and at tax time are forced to piece together what happened during the year as best they can. These people are not trying to do anything wrong; they are simply disorganized and don't think about taxes until a couple of days before the filing deadline.

The good news for this second group is that it's generally not a crime to be sloppy. The bad news is that it may be difficult to convince the IRS that the "sloppiness" isn't actually a cover for intentionally misrepresenting facts (hint: the first defense most tax cheats try is that they simply kept poor records). Even if the IRS believes you, you still might still end up getting a bad deal if your poor records make it impossible to prove the numbers that you put down on your tax return. So, keep tax records throughout the year, and keep those records for at least seven years in case the IRS comes knocking.

The third basic type of tax scofflaw genuinely believes he has found a tax loophole. Every year around tax time, people crop up with legal arguments about why they are not subject to taxes. Armed with these "brilliant" schemes, they refuse to pay. If these people kept their theories to themselves, they wouldn't be worth discussing in a personal finance book.

Unfortunately, they often actively try to convince other people to join the bandwagon. Sometimes they charge a fee to show others their "system." Sometimes they give it away for free (maybe thinking that the difference between being "crazy" and being "part of a movement" is simply a matter of numbers). These schemes are usually just plausible enough to convince a few otherwise-logical, law-abiding taxpayers to get on the bandwagon and refuse to pay their taxes, too.

It never works.

The good news is that these schemes are easy to recognize. They often cite the Constitution or a law or a treaty or some other actual document, they sometimes say you need to take a few simple steps, and they always conclude that the Internal Revenue Code (the federal tax law) won't apply to you.

Here's how one version works: the "expert" tells you that you can draft up a document declaring yourself to be your own sovereign country and have it notarized. Then, as a sovereign nation, you can declare yourself immune to United States taxes and not pay. The "expert" explains that this is a rock solid plan because, after all, the notary derived power from the government, so the notarization is evidence that the government accepts your sovereignty. Done and done.

Sounds somewhat logical, right? It's absolute nonsense, of course. As are all schemes of this ilk. But they crop up like weeds every year. Even though the IRS puts out announcements every year warning people about this sort of thing, there are always a few people who fall for it.

People who fall victim to these schemes are often trying to do the right thing, thinking that they're hiring clever experts who have an inside track on legal tax strategies. Actor Wesley Snipes ended up spending a few years in federal prison and owing a massive tax bill after getting involved such a scheme. Those who got him entangled in the scheme were people he hired and whom he presumably thought were looking out for his best interests (they also went to prison). There is an obvious connection here with Chapter Five, with its financial advice of being careful who you hire.

Having discussed the fairly obvious advice to pay your taxes, let's turn to the other piece of tax-paying advice found in Jesus' parable. Name, in addition to paying your taxes, you should pay *attention to* your taxes.

Paying attention to your taxes means considering the tax implications of things you do. This will require – you guessed it – some self-education and research on your part. It might also mean hiring tax experts to advise you in some circumstances (keeping the lesson from Chapter Five about hiring good people in mind, of course).

The federal government, along with state and local governments, consider many actions you take to be "taxable events." Some are pretty straightforward. If you buy a $10 sandwich in a locality with a 5% sales tax, your sandwich will cost $10.50. The sandwich purchase is the "taxable event" and the 50 cents is the tax.

Other events are more complicated, such as when you sell real estate, stock investments, or other assets. The amount of taxes you owe might be completely different depending on factors like how long you owned the asset, how much income you made the year you sold it, what sort of account you held the asset in, and so on.

Tax laws change every year, which is why it pays (literally) to keep up with them. Usually these changes are modest, though they can occasionally be sweeping. As I wrote this book, in fact, Congress passed a large-scale tax law that significantly changes certain aspects of the tax law. Even if you rely on an accountant to do your taxes for you, it is worth following tax law updates so you have good questions to ask and things to bring up. The IRS itself puts out quite a few bulletins about changes, making its website a good place to start this research.

This isn't a book about the details of tax law. First, I'm not a tax professional and wouldn't be qualified to give specific tax advice. Second, the advice that's best for you depends on your particular circumstances. Advice that's good for you might be terrible for your brother, and might not even apply to your sister. Third, regardless of what advice you read in a book (or anywhere), you'd still want to verify that it was still applicable when you act on it.

The point of this discussion is to use the parable to illustrate the more general advice that your financial decisions have tax implications, and that you would be wise to research those implications. It would be a shame to kick yourself 20 years down the road for not saving yourself tens of thousands of dollars by filling out form X to open one type of account rather than filling out form Y to open a slightly different type of account (a very possible scenario – see the Appendix's discussion of various account types).

Keep up with news about tax law changes, at least enough to ask your tax advisor smart questions. If you hear about a new type of investment account, research whether it might help you. If you're about to make a large purchase or sale, getting married or divorced, plan to adopt a child, think about moving to a new state, want to start or sell a business, or stand on the edge of any other major decision with financial overtones, do yourself a favor and conduct a little preliminary research on what that might mean from a tax perspective.

Many people will rely heavily (or entirely) on a tax professional. And that's not a bad thing if you have properly vetted the professional. But most people only visit a tax accountant or tax attorney at tax time. Although it's smart to have an accountant review your taxes, consider seeing a tax professional during the non-tax time of the year for general advice, especially when you are facing a big financial decision.

Tax professionals are obviously super-busy at tax time. And good ones (you found a good one because you learned that lesson from the last chapter, right?) have a lot of information that could benefit you beyond simply filling out your required IRS tax forms. But, if you only go at the busiest time of the year, and only ask them to fill out your tax forms, that's exactly what they will do. And no more.

You can go a step further. Get your financial documents together and pay your accountant a visit during August for a tax review. Let them know up front that you want an overall financial review from a tax standpoint, mention any specific concerns, and ask what additional information they need in addition to what you have already put together.

You'll pay for this consultation just as you'd pay for a checkup at the doctor. If you are too cheap to pay for a good tax professional's time, and instead hope to get all your advice from someone offering a "free, one-time consultation," consider the phrase, "penny wise, pound foolish," along with my admonition that I hope you get exactly what you pay for.

Not only does making your trip during the "off season" give your accountant more time to dedicate to your concerns, you will immediately stand out as someone who takes taxes seriously and has specific concerns, and will be treated as such. Also, when you explicitly ask for a tax checkup and mention some specific issues or questions, your accountant will already be thinking about your situation and be better-equipped to give you a thorough answer.

Recall the example in the "Get Professional Help" section of Chapter One about the tax law that provided for $7,500 in free money for certain first-time home purchases. Had someone who met the criteria, but who didn't know about the new law, paid a tax professional a few hundred dollars for a tax review, they would almost certainly have walked out of the office much happier.

The bottom line: First, pay your taxes (obviously). Second, pay attention to your taxes by keeping informed of changes in tax law, noting any changes to your financial situation that might have tax implications, and seeking thorough professional tax advice.

Financial Lesson 2: ... But Don't Overpay

We just learned that you should pay your taxes and pay attention to tax consequences as you make financial decisions. The flip side of the coin (Get it? Because the Pharisees handed Jesus a coin?) is to avoid overpaying your taxes.

Note that Jesus said, "Give unto Caesar what is Caesar's." He did *not* say, "Give unto Caesar a bunch of money above and beyond what you owe."

Let's clarify two terms that are often mistakenly used interchangeably: "tax evasion" and "tax avoidance." They sound similar. After all, if I "evade" a slap in the face, I have also "avoided" a slap in the face. When it comes to taxes, though, the terms have very different meanings.

Tax *evasion* is using *illegal* methods to pay less tax than you owe. Tax *avoidance* is using *legal* methods to reduce the amount of taxes that you owe.

Claiming that you earned $10,000 for a given tax year when you actually earned $100,000 is tax evasion and can land you in federal prison. Putting money into a tax-advantaged account that legally lets you claim that you earned less income than you actually did is tax avoidance.

Side note: many accounts that not only work that way, but the federal government has explicitly created *so that you can legally avoid taxes*. See the Appendix for more information.

You should absolutely employ any legal tax avoidance strategy that helps you out. That's the whole point of educating yourself and hiring tax professionals. On the other hand, you should absolutely avoid any strategy that even dips its toes into the world of tax evasion. Give Caesar exactly what you owe him, not a penny more if you can help it, but *definitely* don't try to shortchange him. He *is* Caesar, after all.

Tax law is complicated. A lot of people complain about that. But think it through a bit more. Complication can certainly lead to headaches, but complication is also what creates a lot of nice, juicy, legal tax avoidance strategies.

Imagine you're a little fish, swimming around in the ocean, surrounded by hungry sharks. Would you rather be swimming around a part of the ocean with clear water, a smooth sandy floor, and no obstructions, or would you rather be swimming in murky water full of seaweed, boots, coral, and various nooks and crannies to hide in? I would take the murky water full of obstacles any day, because to the little fish, every obstacle creates an opportunity to not get eaten.

You didn't create the complicated tax code, so you can't be faulted for taking advantage of it. Jesus had it right with the unspoken ending of his advice: "Give unto Caesar what is Caesar's (but not a penny more)."

Bonus Financial Lesson 1: Tax Brackets, or, Life on the Margin

While we're on the subject of taxes, we might as well throw in a bonus lesson about the United States' marginal tax system and how "tax brackets" work. It really has nothing to do with the story that kicked off this chapter, other than the tax tie-in. But, I so frequently hear people talk about tax brackets in a way that clearly indicates they have no idea what they're talking about, that I might as well clear it up here.

First, the United States has a "marginal tax rate." Specifically, it has a "progressive marginal tax rate."

We know from before that a "rate" is simply a percentage.

The *"marginal"* part is where the idea of "brackets" comes from. This part means that your income is divided up into sections. A "margin" is an edge – like the margin of a paper, or the margin of a section of income.

For example, suppose you earn $40,000. Imagine that $0 to $10,000 is one section of your income. Then, $10,001 to $20,000 is a second section. Then, $20,001 to $30,000 is a third section and $30,001 to $40,000 is the fourth section. Each of these sections is at the edge ("margin") of the section in front of it.

Each of those four sections is also called "bracket," and each one has a different tax rate. Suppose the first section has a 0% tax rate, the second section has a 10% rate, the third section has a 20% rate, and the fourth section has a 30% rate. Imagine there is a final section for anything from $40,001 and up with a 40% rate.

The fact that the tax rate on each successive section gets higher is why it is a *progressive* marginal tax rate: the rate *progresses* upward as you go.

In a marginal tax system like the U.S. has, you calculate the tax you owe by applying each tax rate to the dollars in its respective section (or "bracket") of income.

In our example, you would pay **0%** on the first $10,000 (the $0 to $10,000 section). Then you would pay **10%** on the *second* $10,000 (the $10,001 to $20,000 section). Then you would pay **20%** on the *third* $10,000 (the $20,001 to $30,000 section). Finally, you would pay **30%** on the *fourth* $10,000 (the $30,001 to $40,000 section). You only earn $40,000, so you have no income in the final section, which starts at $40,001.

What is your total tax? Just add up the amount you owe for each section. You owe **$0** on the first section (0% of $10,000), **$1,000** on the second section (10% of $10,000), **$2,000** on the third section (20% of $10,000), and **$3,000** on the fourth section (30% of $10,000), for a total of **$6,000**. You have no income in the $40,001-and-up section, so it doesn't apply.

You might hear people talk about those who get a raise being "pushed into a higher tax bracket." It's often said as a bad thing. The fear seems to be that those unlucky enough to get a raise will suddenly pay a lot more in taxes. That is simply not how it works.

It *would* be true if the marginal (highest) tax rate applied to *all* your income. But it doesn't; it only applies to the *portion* of your income in that bracket.

Returning to our example, imagine you get a $1 raise and your income is now $40,001. It is true that you have entered a higher tax bracket as soon as your income goes from $40,000 to $40,001. Namely, you have gone from the 30% tax bracket to the 40% bracket.

But, now that you understand how marginal tax rates work, you see that the new 40% tax rate only applies to $1. You only pay the 40% tax rate on the *one dollar* at the very end of your new $40,001 income (that forty-thousand-and-first dollar is the marginal dollar – the one on the edge). All of your previous income continues to be taxed at the lower brackets, which remain unchanged.

Many people believe that they pay their highest tax rate *on all of their income*. They think that, as soon as they enter the 40% tax bracket in our example, they suddenly owe 40% on all of the income that came before it. That's simply not the case, as you now know.

In practice, your marginal tax rate isn't as important for you to pay attention to as is your "overall tax rate," or "effective tax rate." That's sort of like the average taxes rate you ended up paying at the end of the day, when all is said and done. You find it by simply dividing the total taxes you pay by your income.

In our example, you paid $6,000 on $40,000, which is an *effective tax rate* of 15% ($6,000/ $40,000 = 15%). Even though you're is in the 30% tax bracket, you effectively pay 15%.

The effective tax rate dispenses with worries about various marginal tax rates and gives you one average rate that you paid on your overall income. It is useful because you can compare what percentage of your income you paid in taxes each year.

Notice from the hypothetical tax brackets in our example that everyone actually pays $0 on the first $10,000 of income, regardless of how much they earn. It so happens that, as of this writing, there actually is a 0% marginal tax rate, and there has been for a long time.

I won't go into the actual tax brackets. First, they are subject to change (they changed while I was writing this book, in fact). Second, they actually vary, depending on how you file your taxes (as a single person versus a married person, for instance), so I'd have to spell out several scenarios. Third, they are very easy to look up for yourself.

Finally, I mentioned that the U.S. has a "progressive" marginal tax rate, which simply refers to the fact that the tax rate gets increasingly higher with each income bracket. A "regressive" tax system would be one where the tax rates actually got *smaller* with higher income brackets. Every so often, someone floats the idea of a "flat tax," which is the idea of not having brackets at all, but instead just choosing an overall tax rate that everyone paid on all of their income. In our example from above, a 15% flat tax on $40,000 would have the exact same effect ($6,000 tax) as the marginal tax brackets I used.

Relatedly, the tax bracket discussion only deals with income taxes and how the marginal tax system works. Other types of income are taxed differently, such as "capital gains" (selling an investment for a profit) and "dividends" (money distributed to company shareholders).

This bonus lesson and my simplified example is designed to illustrate how marginal tax rates work, explain what a "tax bracket" actually is, and cut through the uninformed nonsense that many people spew out related to tax brackets.

Bonus Financial Lesson 2: Watch out for Flattery

There is one more lesson worth pointing out in our story about Jesus and the Pharisees. This lesson is to beware of flatterers and smooth-talkers, and is unrelated to taxes.

Notice how the story starts out. The Pharisees approached Jesus and laid down some sweet-talk. They addressed him as "teacher." They acted like they were asking Jesus for his opinion on the tax issue because he was a man of integrity who wasn't swayed by what other people thought.

But the Pharisees were wolves in sheep's clothing – Jesus' mortal enemies (in the very real sense of the word "mortal" – they ended up literally being the death of him). Fortunately, Jesus saw through the charade and gave them a piece of his mind, while also laying down some wisdom.

Keep in mind that many people you encounter in the financial word are, in essence, salespeople. Real estate agents, investment advisors, insurance agents, university representatives, building contractors, and so on are all capable of providing valuable advice and services. But never forget that they are all in the business of selling you something.

Just because someone sits in a nice office with walnut furniture, wears a nice suit, and went to an Ivy League school doesn't mean he isn't a salesman. Anytime you talk to someone who has something to sell, be alert to sweet-talk and recognize it for what it is – a sales technique.

In my experience, your situation will be better than that of Jesus – most people in the financial services industry are not out to ruin your life (some are, though – see the story of Bernie Madoff). But, many will be willing to sell you something you don't need or that isn't right for you because they are, after all, in the business of selling things.

Look beyond the flattery and smooth-talk and listen to what is actually being promised or sold, and whether it suits your needs. I have known people who developed a personal rapport with flatterers with whom they should have maintained a more professional business relationship. Clouded by the emotional connection that came from confusing flattery with friendship, these people often made poor financial decisions.

There is a lot of money to be made in financial products, and everything you interact with is designed to sell. The office, the business card, the diplomas on the wall, the glossy brochures, the title of the person you're talking to (it's always "Advisor" or "Consultant" or "Manager," never "Sales Rep"), and the conversation are all designed to convince you to turn your money over.

Suppose you hear, "I'm sure a smart, successful person like you will want to invest in this emerging market mutual fund. Here, look at this glossy brochure of how well it has done." Even if you are indeed smart and successful, that is unrelated to the details of the fund or whether it is right for you. Of course the glossy brochure shows investment making money; no one is going to pay to print a brochure showcasing a loser. The important numbers – how much it costs, who runs it, what it contains, and so on will be contained in a decidedly less-glossy document.

Beware of flattery. Even if a product is right for you, separate what you're buying from who is selling it.

Chapter 7: So you want to be a Landlord?

Parable Summary

A man owned some land and decided to make some money by renting it out to winemakers. First, the man planted a vineyard. Then he put a wall around the vineyard, had a winepress installed, and built a watchtower. Having completed his land improvements, he found some winemakers and rented it out to them. Then he moved away.

At the end of the season, the landowner sent some servants to collect the rent from the winemaker tenants. But, the tenants beat up one of the servants, killed another one, and stoned the third (the parable is silent on the difference between "killing" and "stoning" – the victim dies at the end of both activities). The remaining servants went home empty-handed.

The landowner sent servants again (more this time, and presumably tougher) to collect the rent. The tenants gave the second batch of servants got the same treatment, beating and killing some of them, and sending the others back with no rent money.

Finally, the landowner sent his only son to collect the rent, reasoning that surely the tenants would respect his own flesh and blood.

When the tenants saw the owner's son coming, they said to each other, "This is the landowner's only heir; let's kill him and get his inheritance of this land for ourselves." So they dragged the son out into the vineyard and killed him.

Having finished the parable, Jesus asked his listeners what the landowner would do to the tenants. They said, "He'll get his revenge on them, and then rent the land out to some tenants who will pay him."

Where you can find it
Matthew 21:33-45, Mark 12:1-11, Luke 20:9-18

The Religious Lesson
Only worthy people will inherit God's kingdom.

Financial Lesson 1: (Mis)adventures in Landlording

So, this is an interesting parable. Let's look first at the clearest financial lesson – the difficulty in being a landlord and some of the potential pitfalls.

Historically, renting out real property is one of the most common investments one could make ("real" property simply means land and buildings, as opposed to personal property like a car or your shoes). Long before stocks or bonds, people earned money by renting out land and buildings. It is still a very common form of investing.

People become landlords (someone who owns real property and leases it to someone else) in a variety of ways. Some people buy land or houses with the intention of renting them out for income. Other people inherit property and rent it out rather than sell it. Some buy a house, later move to a new place, and rent out the original house. Still others move, have trouble selling their original house, and become reluctant landlords.

Whether you are thinking about buying property as an investment, or deciding whether to keep property you already own, the lesson from this chapter's parable is to think long and hard about whether it's a good idea. Then think about it again.

A lot of people approach real estate investing as if any idiot can make vast amounts of money with little effort. You just rent the property out, sit back, and let the profits roll in. Or so the thinking goes. The parable does a great job of illustrating some real estate pitfalls that make this type of investing harder than it looks.

One mistake people make is failing to consider things like upkeep, maintenance, and how the costs involved to get a property ready to rent out in the first place. Think about what the landlord in the parable had to do to get his land ready to rent to winemakers. First, he planted a vineyard. Then he built a wall around the vineyard. Then he had a winepress installed. Finally, he built a watchtower. After doing all that, he still had to find some winemakers to rent it to.

You're probably not thinking about buying a piece of empty land and trying to build a winery to rent out. But there are strong parallels with the parable's landlord and the efforts you might have to make.

For one thing, when buying rental property, you might be looking at houses in need of repairs. That's because new houses that don't need any work done will come at a premium price. And a premium price cuts into your profits. New or old, houses require a lot of maintenance. Especially when occupied by someone who doesn't own the house and won't maintain it like their own.

Just as the landlord planted a vineyard and made improvements to the land, you might find yourself making improvements like putting in a new countertop or cabinets, buying new appliances, fixing floors, repairing (or replacing) a roof or windows, putting in new plumbing or electric or HVAC systems, and so forth.

The parable doesn't note whether the vineyard's landlord did the work himself or hired people to do it for him (likely the latter), but remodeling a house can get very expensive very quickly if you hire people to do it (assuming you can find reliable contractors, as we discussed in a previous chapter). And doing things yourself might either be infeasible or illegal (some work must be performed by licensed contractors).

After you get the property ready to rent and rent it out, you still have ongoing maintenance. What if the winepress (hot water heater) breaks? What if the foundation of the watchtower (porch) starts to crack? Everything starts to break down as soon as you buy it. It's as if everything in your rental house has a little clock in it, ticking away the moments until it breaks and you have to replace it. Dark, but true. If you own the house, you're on the hook to fix things that break.

Suppose that discussion doesn't dissuade you from being a landlord. Maybe you're handy (or look forward to learning new skills) or think you've found a hidden gem property at a great price.

There is still the matter of tenants.

Tenants are by far the biggest source of problems for landlords. As mentioned before, tenants won't treat your property the way you would treat it, leading to more maintenance. And there's no guarantee that tenants will always pay the rent on time. Experienced landlords can tell you as many tenant-related stories as you have time to listen to. But, less-than-fastidious tenants and tenants who occasionally don't pay the rent is relatively minor on the bad tenant spectrum.

There is a whole subset of tenants that range from horrible to beyond-horrible. There are people, sometimes referred to as "professional tenants," who rent a place with absolutely no intention of paying rent. These tenants are very good at what they do (and by "good," I mean "savvy, in a terrible way").

They move into a place and immediately start plotting against you. They never pay the rent and are experienced in how to stay in your place as long as possible. They know the ins and outs of your state's legal system far, far better than you, and probably the attorney you will inevitably have to hire to help evict them, ever will. They know every motion and document to file with every local court and agency to forestall eviction for another month or two.

It goes like this: your tenants haven't paid rent in several months. You hired an attorney, or filed paperwork yourself in small claims court, and have an eviction hearing. You take a day off work to go to court for the hearing, perhaps with your expensive attorney in tow, thinking your nightmare is almost over.

But when you get to court you find that your tenant has filed a form alleging that you violated a rule of some sort. There's no merit to the claim, but that doesn't matter because your state requires that you respond in writing and stipulates that the tenant gets two weeks to gather evidence to support the claim. While he (and his friends and relatives) lives in your house, of course. Your attorney shrugs (and holds out his hand for the check), "The law's the law." The judge sets another hearing in two weeks, when you anticipate similar shenanigans to transpire.

You spend the rest of the vacation day you took from work at the bar, wondering whether you can just change your name and start a new life somewhere else. Maybe as a professional tenant.

At some point during the process you will find yourself wondering two things. First, why didn't this tenant become a lawyer and use his skills for good instead of evil? Second, why on earth did you think it was a good idea to become a landlord in the first place? You can eventually get even professional tenants evicted, but only after they have stayed in your place for months and months (years, in some instances I have read about) longer than they should have. Not only have you missed out on the rent for that period of time, but you can imagine how well these people tend to take care of the places they "rent."

Fortunately, the professional tenant is a relatively unusual group. The typical tenant problem you'll have is someone who simply doesn't pay the rent on time (or at all) or who damages your property.

Just as the parable in Chapter Five taught us the importance of hiring good people, this parable underscores how crucial it is to screen potential tenants. The landlord in the parable was probably limited in how he could screen potential tenants, so perhaps it wasn't entirely his fault that he leased his property to the worst tenants ever recorded.

You will not have such an excuse because there are quite a few resources available now to help you screen potential tenants. You can check credit scores, call previous landlords for references, verify employment and income, check criminal history, and so forth. There are even services that will do all of this for you (for a fee, of course).

Being a landlord is far more involved than a single chapter of this book could cover. Fortunately for you, there are a lot of resources available on the subject (such as how-to books written by experienced landlords and communities of landlords both online and in-person). This is an area where you absolutely want to conduct a significant amount of research before committing.

Your research should include speaking to professionals about the legal, tax, and insurance implications of your situation long before you advertise a property for rent. Even your advertisement can get you in trouble if you word it wrong.

You should also remember out discussion of "opportunity costs" and strongly consider alternative uses for the money you would otherwise spend on the property. The "cost" of every dollar you invest is the returns you could make through alternate investments. There are good arguments on both sides of whether other investment options offer better after-tax returns on your money, but few will argue that investing in real estate by being a landlord requires a lot more work than, say, owning a mutual fund.

Assuming you decide to decide that real estate investing is for you, your need to research will only increase. For any particular property you think about buying, you will need to estimate your expenses and potential income to get an idea of whether the investment has a chance of paying off. There are various methods of evaluating whether your investment makes sense. Those methods are beyond the scope of this book, but you can quickly learn them by listening people who have been in the business for a while and reading books specializing in real estate investing.

Here is a very rudimentary framework for thinking about how real estate returns can work, focusing on the role that leverage (borrowed money) plays.

Imagine you buy a house that costs $100,000. You make a traditional 20% down payment, which is $20,000. Then, you earn $5,000 in net rent (after taxes, fees, expenses) the first year. Your return on investment would be 25% (the $5,000 profit divided by the $20,000 you actually invested). If you paid the full $100,000 purchase price, on the other hand, your return would have been 5% (the same $5,000 profit divided by $100,000).

Now imagine that the value of the house goes up by $5,000 at the end of the first year, in addition to the $5,000 you earned in rent. The simple return on your $20,000 investment is suddenly 50% (the $10,000 total value divided by $20,000).

Obviously, leverage can be huge boost to your returns in real estate investing (that is true for any type of investing). A little of that thinking and you might suddenly find yourself shopping around for plane tickets to Tahiti, dreaming of running your real estate empire from a beachy paradise.

Just remember that leverage works both ways. If your tenants skip town after a few weeks, not paying rent and damaging your property, you might just as easily find yourself paying out $5,000 in repairs instead of raking it in. And, the value of the property can just as easily go down by $5,000 (or a lot more, as a lot of people discovered, circa 2010). Those $10,000 in losses on a $20,000 investment equate to a 50% *loss* and suddenly you're glad you're not in Tahiti after all. Since you couldn't afford a return ticket to see how much was left of your property.

Again, that is just a very basic example to show how leverage works to boost (or destroy) your returns. For actual real estate investments, you'll want to know how to perform more detailed analyses, which you will learn after doing your own research.

So you DON'T want to be a Landlord (but still like Real Estate)?

This lesson primarily focused on real estate investing through renting out property because that's what the investor did in the parable. Although that is a very traditional form of real estate investing, I would be remiss if I didn't note that there are other ways people try to make money in real estate. I will just make a few general points about other types of real estate investing.

Being a landlord involves tenants, and one popular type of real estate investing involves cutting the tenants out altogether. Here, investors never become landlords, but instead try to buy properties and resell them quickly for a profit. They might buy a property in need of repairs that no one else wants, hoping to make repairs and resell the house to people wanting something that is move-in ready. This is called "flipping" properties.

Of course, if you cut out the tenants, you also cut out the rent tenants pay. That means time is of the essence, and investors try to flip the property as fast as possible.

The earlier example showed how important leverage is for real estate returns, and many alternative real estate investing types, including flipping, usually involve the investor putting in as little of her own money as possible. Again, when this works, it works very well (in theory, you can have an infinite return if you come up with a scheme to use $0 of your own money, but still turn a profit). But when it doesn't work, it can be catastrophic.

Flipping property, and other types of real estate investing that do not involve becoming a landlord, are perfectly legitimate. But, they can involve a lot of risk, personal involvement, hard work, and unexpected problems. Before you get involved with any type of real estate deal, research what you're getting into. Real estate deals often rely heavily on leverage, or debt. Debt is an incredibly powerful thing when it works in your favor because you use a little bit of money to control a lot.

A final note is that real estate investing tends to be infested with shady types who make their money by selling other people their "secrets" to real estate riches, rather than actually making money in real estate themselves. Any time the real estate market does well for a while, gurus with a "system" come out of the woodwork to tell you how to make easy money (after buying their program, naturally).

Just remember, if someone knows how to turn dirt into gold, they're going to get rich by turning dirt into gold, NOT by selling you the secret of how to do it. A good rule of thumb (not just for real estate, but any type of investing) is that you are unlikely to do well with any investment being advertised on a two AM infomercial, or sent to you unsolicited in the mail.

Finally, another way to invest in real estate without becoming a landlord *or* buying property to resell is to investing in a "Real Estate Investment Trust" (REIT). The Appendix covers this investment option in more detail.

Financial Lesson 2: Don't Throw Good Money after Bad

Another valuable lesson from the parable of the landlord applies to any type of investing, not just real estate. That lesson is to know when to cut your losses and move on, and to stop putting new money into an investment that isn't working out.

The landlord sent a contingent of employees to collect the rent, but those employees were beaten and/ or killed. Then the landlord sent yet another contingent, which met the same fate. Finally, the landlord, who had already invested significant resources with no return, sent a third contingent *that included his own son*. And then he seemed surprised when the exact same thing happened for a third time and his son was killed.

This could be called "The Parable of the Landlord who was Terrible at Seeing Patterns."

The lesson applies to many investment types. In fact, real estate is actually one type of investment where this *isn't* a good lesson because a landlord has a contractual relationship with tenants to get money. In the landlord context, the lesson would be to follow the eviction process and have the sheriff evict dangerous tenants instead of doing it yourself. Maybe there was no local constable to evict tenants at the time of the parable.

Think about this parable's lesson in terms of many other investments you will make, where you have no guarantee. A common mistake people make is to keep putting money into a losing investment, thinking it will "turn around at any moment." It is very common for those investing in their own business, so let's look at an example.

Suppose Justin has always loved plants and dreams of starting a greenhouse. He researches his options and opens Justin Thyme Nursery for business. He uses his savings to rent a building, install UV lights and a watering system, buy inventory, advertise, and renovate the storefront to look like a cute little cottage.

But Justin Thyme Nursery doesn't do very well for whatever reason (maybe the name makes people think it's a nursery for babies and not plants). Months go by, but very few customers come in (except maybe a few confused ones with strollers, expecting bottles, but seeing begonias). The business isn't working out.

So Justin doubles down. He uses the rest of his savings to invest in specialized equipment that will let him raise and display rare orchids that no one else is selling within a 200-mile radius. But, only a handful of customers want rare orchids because they're hard to grow. Despite investing additional money into the upgrades and new inventory, Justin's sales do not go up.

(Tip: if you like orchids, Phalaenopsis is one of the easiest to grow and is the one you see for sale in every store that has a plant section. Other types can be very difficult to grow, depending on what you get. For more information on growing orchids, you can peruse section 635 of your local library).

Justin is not deterred, even though he has only sold ten plants this month (and two of those were to his Aunt Harriet). Justin convinces his brother to lend him some money to tide him over "until the business turns a corner," which it "absolutely will." After all, "it's almost spring, and that's when everyone buys plants." Despite more advertising, a new plant lineup, and hiring a local teenager to dress up like an orchid and dance around outside the shop holding a sign, Justin Thyme Nursery is forced to go out of business. And his brother looks at him disapprovingly over Thanksgiving.

Like the landlord in the parable, Justin made a classic mistake of throwing good money after bad. Sometimes you have to recognize that your investment isn't panning out and just let it go.

It's easy to read the story of Justin, cluck our tongues, and say, "What a foolish way to throw away his money." It's easy to say the same thing about the landlord in Jesus' parable. But that's because we have the advantage of hindsight and are on the outside looking in. It's much easier to see something objectively when you're not involved yourself.

And that's the point: personal involvement is the key warning sign to look out for. Any time you notice yourself making emotional connections with an investment, careful. Maybe you see the investment as the fulfillment of a longtime dream (like it was for Justin). Maybe it's personal pride (you don't want to admit to yourself or others that you made a bad decision). Maybe it's greed ("if things just turn around, I'll be rich beyond my wildest dreams").

Whatever the reason, once you attach emotions to an investment, it can be difficult to make rational decisions, such as the decision to let go. Unfortunately, it's a vicious cycle; the more you invest, the more of an attachment develop to the investment, and the more likely you are to throw more money in.

A basic concept in Economics is the principle of "sunk costs." Sunk costs are simply costs that you have already paid and can't get back. For Justin, as soon as he pays a month's rent on his nursery, that money is a sunk cost: it's gone (to a landlord, appropriately enough).

"Behavioral Economics" studies how people actually behave, compared to how a "rational" person would behave in the same scenario. This is a fascinating field, and one lesson is that sunk costs can cause people to act in ways contrary to their own best interests. Once we have sunk (invested) money into something, it suddenly becomes harder for us to avoid putting more money into it, even when the facts tell us it's a bad idea. By investing, we forge an emotional attachment.

It's not a character flaw; it's just how we're wired. If you like dogs, and if it makes you feel any better, I read an article a long time ago that said retrievers feel the same. When you throw the ball the first couple of times, the retriever brings it back with no problem. But, the dog eventually develops an attachment to the ball and it's harder for him to give it back.

The key to breaking free from a cycle of perpetual investment into a losing enterprise, or to prevent such a cycle from developing in the first place, is to gain some objectivity. This can be hard to do.

One technique to gain objectivity is to ask yourself some key questions that essentially force you into the position of an outsider. When you find yourself thinking about making another investment into something, especially something that has not done as well as you hoped, imagine you're sitting across from yourself, and ask the following questions:

"If you had no money invested in this already, would you invest in it right now for the first time?"

"What are the best three arguments you can think of to *not* invest in this?"

"Assuming this investment were not available for some reason, what are three alternative things you would do with the money you're thinking about investing?"

"If you were only allowed to invest in one thing for the next ten years, would this be it?"

Questions like those achieve two main things. First, they force you to stop and think before you plunk down your hard-earned money. Just giving yourself some time to think might be all you need to prevent a reactionary move you'll later regret. Second, those questions force you to shift your perspective and think more like an outsider. You stop being Justin or the parable's landlord and start being the objective reader who is perplexed by those people's actions.

Another technique to help you break out of the cycle of throwing good money after bad is to get an opinion from someone you trust. This can be useful even if the person you talk to isn't an expert in the subject because, again, it forces you to slow down gives you time to think before acting. Also, the other person has the advantage of not being you, which makes the task of giving an outside opinion much easier. Assuming you're willing to listen, you might hear ideas you had never thought of. Even if you end up making the investment, you will be better off for having considered alternative perspectives.

The "assuming you're willing to listen" part of the penultimate sentence of the last paragraph is very important. Having an open mind and the ability to set aside arrogance in the name of constant learning is a tremendous asset. Have you ever noticed that the most incompetent people also happen to be the most arrogant, while intelligent people are willing to consider that their position might be wrong?

This is not a new observation; even Shakespeare talked about it (from *As you Like it*: "The fool doth think he is wise, but the wise man knows himself to be a fool"). That always perplexed me, and I was absolutely thrilled to read a psychology article about a phenomenon called the "Dunning-Kruger Effect." This effect, named after the two scholars who have studied it extensively, provides a very elegant explanation for why imbeciles think they're geniuses, and why intelligent people allow for the possibility that they're wrong. It's beyond the scope of this book, but well worth reading more about.

Try not to be an arrogant idiot; it's bad for your finances and your life in general (unfortunately, if you happen to be one, the research indicates that you're unlikely to even consider that you're wrong, much less have the skills needed to change).

The lesson to take from the parable of the landlord is to think through your investing decisions, and to avoid continually putting your money into a losing proposition for illogical, emotional reasons. Whether it's a small business you started, stock in a company you believe in, or something else, remember that you're not infallible and try to take steps to objectively look at your decisions.

Incidentally, this same lesson applies to relationships. It's not unusual to see someone with a low-quality romantic partner continuing to invest time, money, and energy trying to make things better. The same sunk cost principle is at play. "Well, I've already bailed him out of jail twice and spent four years of my life trying to make this work. If I walked away now, it would be like all of that was for nothing." For anyone who has had a friend or relative in that situation, you know with crystal clarity how much easier it can be for someone on the outside to see problems than it is for the person involved.

Chapter 8: The Prodigal Son

Parable Summary

A father had two sons. The youngest son – we'll call him Mo (short for "Moron") – asked his father – we'll call him Carson (short for "Clueless About Reckless Son's Obvious Nonsense") – to give him his portion of the inheritance early. Instead of smacking Mo in the head for such an impertinent question, Carson divided up the estate and gave Mo his portion.

Mo promptly took all his money and headed to a far-off place to party (maybe to the ancient world's version of modern day Ibiza). He lived it up and spent his money on things like wine and prostitutes. He had a great time, right up until his money ran out.

Penniless, friendless, and hopeless, the best Mo could do was getting a job as a pig feeder on a local farm. He was so poor and hungry that he envied the pigs for getting all that delicious slop to eat every day.

(The parable actually says the pigs ate "pods" or "husks," depending on which translation read, but seriously, pigs will eat just about anything. We'll say "slop.")

Eventually Mo realized that his father Carson's employees back on the family farm were doing a lot better than he was, so he went home to beg his father for a job. He even worked up a little speech in his mind to deliver when he got home.

But, Carson spotted Mo as he was coming up the road. Carson ran to Mo, and, missing another prime opportunity to smack Mo in the head, gave him a big hug and a kiss. Mo delivered his little speech about how terrible he was, but his father was feeling very generous. Instead, Carson told his servants to bring Mo a fine robe, a ring, and some shoes. Then he told them to slaughter the juicy calf they had been saving for a special occasion and to prepare a feast to celebrate Mo's return.

Mo's brother – we'll call him Manny (short for "Man, does this story sound unfair to Manny") – was out industriously working in the field (as he had been doing every day while Mo was partying in Ibiza) and heard a party going on. Manny came in and asked a servant what was going on, no doubt wondering why he hadn't been invited to a party at his own house that even the servants were invited to. The servant filled him in.

Manny was furious at this turn of events and refused to join the party. His father tried to persuade him to come inside, but Manny was having none of that.

"What in the world is going on here?" Manny asked. "I've been out working in the fields and doing what you asked for years, and you never even gave me a scrawny, tough goat to roast up for a party with my friends. Yet, my worthless brother comes back from wasting money on prostitutes and nonsense and you treat him like royalty."

"Now, now, son" Carson replied, "Everything I have is yours. But we have to celebrate because your brother has returned. He was dead, but now he's alive; he was lost, but now he's found."

Where you can find it
Luke 15:11-32

The Religious Lesson
God has endless mercy and grace and forgiveness and will welcome back sinners who repent.

The Financial Lessons
This parable is full of financial lessons. We will leave aside some questions that the parable doesn't answer for us (like, how did Carson still have an estate for Mo to return to if he had already divided it up between his sons? Wouldn't what remained of the estate be Manny's if the father had divided it up between his two sons? And if it was Manny's estate, why was Carson still barking out orders and having calves butchered for his derelict son's benefit?).

Having sidestepped those unanswered logistical questions, let's hop on into the financial lessons.

Financial Lesson 1: Don't Squander your Money
One of the most obvious lessons of this parable is to avoid wasting your money on nonsense.

This story is often referred to as the parable of the "prodigal son." Don't confuse the word "prodigal" with the word "prodigy." "Prodigal" an adjective and a noun meaning "super-wasteful" and "someone who spends his money in a super-wasteful way." "Prodigy" is an unrelated noun meaning "someone who is extremely good at something." "Prodigy" is usually preceded by the activity that the person is good at (a "piano prodigy").

A lot of fairy tales begin with a young man going off to seek his fortune. By the end of the fairy tale, the young man has usually found a great fortune, wooed a princess, and is living happily ever after.

Mo's story is just the opposite: he gets his fortune first and then goes off to try to live happily ever after. His wastefulness is astounding (which is what makes it a good parable). He spends the time drinking, carousing with prostitutes, doing whatever the ancient world had to offer in terms of drugs (licking a psychedelic lizard, perhaps), and generally living it up.

I shouldn't have to say too much about the main idea that it's a bad idea to live a life of endless carousing to the point where you literally spend all of your money. Instead, let's look at several practical applications of this lesson.

How Prodigal are You?

Mo represents a cartoonish extreme. In reality, very few people are actually on track to spend *all* of their money on partying and useless nonsense (though I have known some people who seemed close).

To draw a meaningful lesson for your own life, think about the *types and characteristics* of things Mo bought, and then consider how much you spend on similar things. Mo spent his money on things that provided brief happiness. Wine, prostitutes, and partying were fun in the moment he was enjoying them. But the only way to recapture the fleeting pleasures those activities provided was to buy them again the next night. And the next. It was like pouring water into a sieve, hoping it would eventually be full.

Mo's purchases had no intrinsic or lasting value. You can probably think about your own spending and identify things you buy because of the fleeting pleasure they provide. The idea of "retail therapy" is a term that refers to the practice of buying things because of the temporary emotional high from making the purchase, not because the buyer needs the item.

Maybe you buy an expensive vehicle because you feel prestigious when people see you driving it. Maybe you opt for high-end vacations or clothes because you feel good posting pictures on social media. Or maybe you just make a lot of inexpensive impulse purchases to relieve stress or boredom.

Even though you aren't spending every penny you have on these things like Mo did, it is worth identifying similar purchases and considering the impact they have on your overall financial picture. If you identify things you buy purely because of the fleeting happiness they provide, you can figure just how much you spend on them overall. With knowledge comes power, and if you know how much you spend on this category, you can determine if it's unreasonable, and how to cut back.

The point here isn't to pass judgment on what you buy. There's nothing inherently wrong with buying things because they provide fleeting happiness. You might think those purchases are well worth their cost. The point is simply to make sure that you are thoughtfully allocating your money and know how much you spend on this category.

If you add up how much you spend each month on this category of purchases, you might discover that you have more in common with Mo than you are comfortable with.

Before we move on, let me provide a short defense of Mo. Earlier we noted that Mo's purchases had no "intrinsic value" and provided "fleeting happiness." At the most basic level, Mo was buying experiences. There is an emerging idea that experiences may be one of the better things to spend your money on because they provide ongoing, and even increasing, happiness as you reminisce about them over time. In that sense, experiences may provide more than "fleeting happiness."

So, maybe Mo was onto something with spending money on experiences. Given that he ended up penniless and envious of pigs and their slop-dinners, though, it is pretty clear that he went too far. Perhaps a wiser course of action would have been to enjoy a few parties and then spend the rest of his money setting up a stable life for himself. Then he could have looked back fondly on his party days from the comfort of the front porch of the farm he bought (maybe a pig farm, where he would always have a cheap source of labor in the form of newly-destitute idiots who had flocked to the city to squander their inheritances).

Don't be fooled by Large Numbers

Another nuanced lesson we can learn from Mo is to not overestimate how large a sum of money actually is. Humans are generally pretty bad at wrapping their minds around large numbers because numbers are an abstraction. Another characteristic of human behavior is that it changes dramatically from times of perceived abundance and times of perceived scarcity. When we think we have a lot of something, we tend to go through it quickly. When we believe something is running out, we suddenly have a tendency to conserve.

Combining an inability to grasp the meaning of large numbers with the tendency to behave differently in times of abundance can be a recipe for disaster.

In Economics, the tendency people have to spend more freely when they feel rich is called the "wealth effect." Imagine it's Halloween and you have a huge bowl of candy to hand out. You've never seen so much candy in one place, and you're ready for trick or treaters.

A cute little princess prances to your door with her big round eyes and little wand and holds out her basket. You give the sweet little thing two big handfuls of candy, can't even see where you've made a dent in your bowl, and give her another handful. Off she prances. Next, a super-scary goblin comes clomping up to your door, with a basket that looks like a severed head. You're very impressed and, again, you turn over a generous portion of handy.

This goes on throughout the night until you suddenly realize that it's still early and your bowl doesn't seem quite so full anymore. You go from handing out two handfuls of candy to one handful, and then to a half handful. By the time the last ghost comes floating to your door, you're rationing candy the way someone lost at sea rations the last cup of drinking water, and the last ghost that floats by is lucky to get a piece of black licorice and a smile.

You spend the rest of the night looking out the window, worried that egg- and toilet paper-throwers are lurking behind every shrub.

In our parable, Mo took his inheritance and immediately headed for a far-off land to have a good time. He had never seen that much money before, much less had it to spend as he pleased. As someone not accustomed to large amounts of money, he misjudged just how much he had and how long it would last.

In the beginning, it was probably hard for him to conceive that he could spend that much money in one lifetime. He probably hired someone to drive him to the far-off land in a fine horse-drawn cart. When he got there, he went to the nicest spots, bought the fanciest food and wine, and cavorted with the finest prostitutes.

But we know how it ended. By the end of the parable, Mo is walking back home. Like the bowl of candy, Mo's sack of inheritance money seemed like more than enough – until it suddenly didn't. And by then it was too late.

Lottery winners and professional athletes who suddenly receive big contracts are notorious for running out of money. The story is always the same. A person who never had much money is suddenly worth more than he ever imagined. Within a few years he is completely broke – usually in debt – after a spending spree on cars, houses, jewelry, lavish vacations, gifts to family members, and so on. This tendency comes from a fundamental misunderstanding of the amount in question.

On the other end of the spectrum, some people end up with the opposite problem. People who have saved a large amount of money over a long time, such as through retirement accounts, can be so used to saving that they *under*estimate how much they can safely spend.

Those who overestimate how much they can spend and those who underestimate it suffer from the same fundamental problem: they lack a clear concept of just how much money they have and what they can do with it. To be clear, in neither case is it a matter of not knowing how much money they have. It's a matter of not understanding what that number means.

How can you avoid this problem? For one, if you come into a large sum of money, plan ahead before you do anything. Do some research and talk to some vetted professionals like accountants, attorneys, insurance agents, and financial advisors *before* you make any major decisions. Put a plan into place before you even take possession of the money in the first place if possible.

Occasionally you hear about that rare lottery winner who waits months and months, right up to the last possible time, to claim the winnings. Whenever news outlets report on these stories, the reaction is usually, "How could she stand to wait that long." The answer is that she is probably smarter than the average winner and spent the last few months figuring out how to not be broke within a few months. I haven't seen any statistics, but I suspect there is a relationship between how long people wait to claim their winnings and how likely they are to end up broke.

Making a plan forces you to think through your options. If you are forced to put your desires into concrete terms, you are less likely to toss your money around like a drunken sailor on shore leave.

For example, if you sit down and write out that you want to buy a horse farm, give each of your five children a large inheritance, have a building named after you on your college campus, own a chalet in Switzerland, and live part-time in a penthouse apartment in Hong Kong apartment, you might find that your retirement fund or lottery winnings have a bottom after all. Better to find out in the planning stage with hypothetical dollars than with real money you can't get back. Maybe just have a bench named after you on the college campus.

Another way to decrease your odds of spending a seemingly-large sum of money too quickly is to make an effort to get your head around just what that number means. This relates to the human difficulty in understanding large numbers. As you mentally interact with the amount of money in question, you will begin to see it as a concrete thing, rather than a fuzzy abstraction.

Here is a little example exercise to explain what I mean by "mentally interact with the amount of money in question." Suppose you are 65, have $1,000,000, and are thinking about retiring. That seems like a lot of money. It has two commas, after all. But how much is it, really?

To start the mental exercise, imagine you will live for 30 more years. If you just had that money sitting in a basket in cash, how much could you take out each year until it was gone? The answer is that you could take out $33,333.33 each year ($1,000,000 divided by 30 years). That's a super-simple division problem to take a large number and put it in terms of smaller numbers that are more familiar.

In reality, that calculation isn't extremely useful. For one thing, you won't have your $1,000,000 sitting in cash in a basket (I hope). It will likely be in some sort of investment, even if it's in something very safe that doesn't yield much. For another thing, based on what we know about inflation from Lesson Two of Chapter Three, the $33,333.33 would buy you less and less each year, and would only be worth a fraction of that in real terms by year 30. And our calculation doesn't into account taxes, which is a big deal.

But that's not the point. Instead, the point of the calculation is to start with a large number and get your mind around it. While it might be hard to imagine how much $1,000,000 of something is, it's probably easier to think about how much $33,333.33 is. You can compare it to numbers you're familiar with: prices of things like a new car, a used car, or a refrigerator. You can compare it to your current salary, your rent or mortgage payment, and so on. This mental exercise helps you avoid seeing a large, multi-comma number and thinking of it as a limitless pool from which you can drink endlessly.

Another mental exercise that is more practical is to use the "4% Safe Withdrawal Rate," sometimes just called the "4% Rule." I won't go into the history of this rate, but it is a common rule of thumb that retirement-related books and articles might refer to, and is worth mentioning in this book.

Essentially, the 4% Rule says that if the potential retiree in our previous example has half her portfolio in bonds and half in stocks, she can withdraw 4% each year (adjusted annually for inflation) for 30 years and have little risk of running out of money. The 4% number was based simulations using historical data and there is a lot of debate about details such as whether the percentage should be slightly higher or slightly lower number, what the investment mix should be, how long it will last and so on.

Feel free to research the quibbling over the details, or even contribute to the quibbling yourself (look up "Trinity Study" to get started). For now, let's just repeat the same $1,000,000 exercise, only this time using the 4% Rule.

A retiree following the 4% Rule could withdraw $40,000 per year (4% of $1,000,000). Like our previous exercise, the point is simply to take a large number and reduce it to a more mentally-manageable number. It is easy to make $40,000 a practical – just compare it to how much you earn now. It's hard to really understand $1,000,000, but it's easier to understand the concept of $40,000 per year (adjusted upward for inflation each year) for 30 years.

By simply doing various calculations on a large number, it starts to become familiar and more concrete, and thus easier to worth with.

In our parable, it's easy to understand Mo's cluelessness about how large his inheritance was. He had been working on his father's farm his whole life, and probably didn't have much money of his own. When he suddenly came into his inheritance, he didn't understand what kind of money he was dealing with. He would have been much better off if he had done a few calculations like the ones above.

Had he performed a few mental exercises with the number, he might have realized that his inheritance wasn't an unlimited amount. As it was, he didn't learn that lesson until he reached into his wallet and found it empty.

The Principle of not spending the Principal

We can draw another good lesson from Mo's story by examining what type of money he was spending. Namely, it appears that Mo was spending his principal. The *"principal"* is the amount of money you put in – your own money. You can think of the principal as being sort of like your core amount. As we discussed in previous chapters, that principal – invested wisely – can itself generate new money in the form of interest or returns.

There is nothing in the parable to indicate that Mo invested his money in anything at all (land that he could rent out, a wine-making business, etc.). Nor is there anything to suggest that he bothered getting any kind of job until after he had already run out of money. So, with no money coming in, Mo was simply spending down the principal itself.

When you spend your principal, two things happen. First, and most obviously, you have less money available to you for spending later. Second, your now-lower principal has the potential to generate less future income in the form of investment returns. The opportunity cost (as we discussed in a previous chapter) of spending a portion of the principal is the money that portion could be generating for you, had you left it invested.

Imagine you have $100,000 in an investment that achieves a 5% return over the course of a year. At the end of the year, you have $105,000. Your $100,000 principal earned $5,000. But, now imagine that you started with $100,000, but withdrew $10,000 at the beginning of the year. You still get the 5% return during the year, only now you get 5% on $90,000 because of your withdrawal. Instead of earning $5,000, your lower principal of $90,000 only earns you $4,500. The $500 difference is the amount you gave up by withdrawing from the principal (the "cost").

Spending the principal isn't necessarily a bad thing. Most people will spend part of their principal each year in retirement. But, there are two key differences between these people and Mo. First, they generally spend a part of the principal *along with* earnings from the overall investment portfolio. Because they spend earnings generated by the principal, they can withdraw less principal, which means the money will last longer. Mo had no investment earnings that we know of.

Second, people who retire after a career of building up a large investment portfolio are in a very different position than Mo. A retiree with a well-thought-out plan spends money accumulated over a long time – usually decades. But Mo is young and is in the part of his life when he should be *building up* investments, not spending them. The younger you are, the more principal you need in order to generate sufficient income to support your lifestyle. Assuming you bother to invest it. Which Mo didn't. And his lifestyle during his spending period wasn't cheap.

Of course, those with very large principal amounts, combined with moderately good returns, sufficiently low lifestyle costs, and perhaps some additional income (from Social Security, a pension, or a side job) might not dip into their principal at all.

Had Mo bothered working even a little bit to generate some income, or had he invested even a part of his principal in something (say, a tavern, which seemed to be a pretty good business in that town), he would have been better positioned. He might still have run out of money, of course. Without knowing more details, there's no way to know for sure. But he might have been able to party a while longer, at least.

The most relevant lesson from this for modern readers, then, is to avoid tapping your principal too soon. Quite a few people (tens of millions) with retirement accounts take early withdrawals from those accounts every year. Some of these people simply take withdraws from their account. Other people take money out of their retirement accounts when they change jobs, rather than rolling the balance over into their new employer's retirement plan or into another account. These withdrawals might be for legitimate reasons, but many people see a retirement account as an untapped source of money that can be used for a purchase like a new car or nice vacation.

Taking money out of your retirement account early is the modern-day version of what Mo did, only worse. When Mo took his inheritance out of his bag of gold coins and spent it, at least he got to spend everything he took out. As I am writing this, early withdrawals from retirement accounts incur an immediate 10% penalty (not a *tax* – a *penalty*) as punishment for taking it out early. That is in addition to paying any taxes you might owe. The Appendix of this book discusses retirement accounts and some of the basic rules governing them in more detail.

Even assuming you didn't have any gains to be taxed on, 10% is a big deal. It would as if someone sat beside Mo, taking away one out of every 10 gold pieces he pulled from his bag. In this way, withdrawing retirement money early is even more foolish now than it was for Mo in the parable.

Regardless of what type of account you have your principal in, be very leery of withdrawing it, certainly while you are in the stage of life when you should be accumulating assets instead of spending them.

Financial Lesson 2: Trust in a Trust

Additional financial lesson hidden in this parable becomes obvious by simply shifting our focus from Mo to his father, Carson. Thinking of Carson in a modern context quickly leads us to the lesson that you should sometimes consider taking steps to protect those you care about from themselves.

As you read about Mo, you might think of the saying, "Easy come; easy go" because Mo got his share of his father Carson's estate relatively easily – just by asking for it – and he lost it just as easily. In that Mo-centric context, it is easy to reduce the parable down to "Yep, Mo's pretty stupid" and move on.

But it's hard to read this parable without thinking about Carson's actions. We are left to wonder why Carson agreed to Mo's request for an early inheritance. Maybe he was just overly-indulgent. Maybe he gave Mo too much credit for his level of responsibility. Maybe he was afraid Mo would kill him in his sleep if he said "No."

The parable doesn't give Mo's age, but it is clear that he is young. More importantly, he is foolish. The two are likely connected: because of his youth, Mo did not have the benefit of experiences that would lead to wisdom. Two things might have helped Mo: getting his money later in life, or getting it in installments instead of as a lump sum.

Had Mo come into his fortune later in life, he might have developed enough experience to manage his money better. For instance, he might have seen his father and older brother Manny keeping business records, or making deals to sell livestock, or saving some of the money they made, or doing any number of things that didn't include spending money on parties and prostitutes.

Similarly, Mo might have been better off if he had received his money in installments – on a monthly basis, for instance. Some people simply don't seem to learn from their mistakes and need to be protected from themselves (you have probably met a few). This fascinating specimen floats through the vastness of life's experiences as if coated with a substance that simultaneously prevents lessons from sticking and wisdom from penetrating. They would be no wiser at 60 than at 16.

Regardless of whether Mo's problem was that he simply needed more time to gain wisdom or whether he simply lacked the ability to run his own life, Carson could have better-positioned him for success.

As it happens, Mo's problem seems to be lack of experience. He doesn't seem like the kind of person who simply can't – or won't – learn. After all, once he lost all the money, he seemed to understand what he had done wrong.

The terrible Catch-22, of course, is that the experience of losing all his money is *exactly* the sort of experience that would have helped Mo not lose the money in the first place. Imagine he had received his money in monthly installments. He might have become a pretty good money manager after a couple months of running out of money the third day after receiving it.

The option of receiving his money later in life and the option of receiving the money in installments are not mutually exclusive. There are any number of combinations of the two that might have helped. Mo could have received his money in installments for a while and then gotten the remainder as a lump sum. Or, he could have gotten smaller and smaller amounts each year, as he learned how to make up the difference with his own sources of income (such as investment returns or employment).

This is a very real issue for anyone who wants to take care of someone who won't (or can't) think for himself. Parents, grandparents, and guardians who want to secure someone's future would do well to sit up, take notice, and ask what measures they can take to prevent Mo's fate from befalling their precious little bundles of potential disaster.

If you're in a position like Carson's, your children probably won't come up and ask for their portion of the inheritance early (if they do, you have problems well beyond the scope of this book – maybe try section 649 of your local library ("Child Rearing") (though it might be too late)). Instead, the more common concern is that you might die prematurely, causing them to inherit your estate at a relatively young age. Even if a law in your state would prevent them from inheriting anything until they were adults, remember that people are generally considered adults at 18, and most 18-year-olds aren't paradigms of responsibility.

You might not like the thought of your children or grandchildren flying off to Las Vegas and spending in a weekend what you took a lifetime to build. You won't be around to see it, of course, but still. What to do?

"If only Mo had gotten his money later in life," we said. "If only Mo could have received his money in monthly installments," we said. "If only Mo benefited from some combination of monthly payments and an eventual lump sum," we lamented.

Good news! You can do all of this, and more. I refer you back to the section about Trusts in Chapter One. Trusts can be specifically designed to avoid *exactly* the situation described in this parable.

If you want your children to get monthly installments instead of a lump sum upon your premature death, you can arrange that. Remember the "4% Rule" we talked about earlier? If you want money distributed to your children following something like that formula, you can arrange it through a Trust. Do you have some other, more simple (or complicated) system in mind? It can be arranged.

You don't even have to be dead. A Trust can go into effect while you're still alive. If you find yourself in the happy situation of having more money than you know what to do with, and want to give some money to your children and grandchildren while you're still alive, you can arrange it so the money is doled out however you want.

This is especially clever, because you can set up a Trust such that you can take it back if you want. That not only lets you see the beneficiaries enjoy the money while you're alive, but, perhaps more importantly, improves your odds that the beneficiaries in question will be nice to you (to your face, at least) as long as they are on the receiving end of your generosity.

The bottom line here is that a Trust, designed by a good attorney, perhaps in concert with an equally good financial advisor and accountant, can go a long way to prevent Mo's sad fate from befalling people you care about.

That's why we started this lesson noting that the focus is on Carson, not Mo. Who was in a better position than Carson to see that Mo wasn't ready to manage a large sum of money? There were certainly clues that Mo was irresponsible – the fact that he asked for all his money up front, while his father was still alive, for instance. If that didn't tip Carson off that Mo wasn't mature enough to manage a small fortune, I don't know what would.

We'll give Carson a partial pass. He probably couldn't walk down to an attorney specializing in Trusts and set up a legal instrument such as the ones described here. But, he could have required Mo to come back every year to get a portion of the inheritance. It was Carson's money, after all – he didn't have to give it away. He could have gone off partying himself, in fact.

That's the key to remember: if you have the money, you have the power. If you're the Carson figure in your situation, it's *your* money. And with ownership comes power. You can do whatever you want with your money. Assuming you are a not a contractual guardian (like a Trustee) with an obligation to do certain things with the money, you have no obligation whatsoever to give it away all at once. You don't have an obligation to give it away at all. It's yours to do with as you please, and if you decide that one way of giving it to someone is better than another, it's certainly up to you.

Just do it before you die without a Will or Trust, because then it's out of your hands.

Corollary Lesson: The Importance of Safety Nets

In the final section of this chapter, we will look at some powerful factors that worked in Mo's favor. This section does not contain lessons about what to do or avoid doing. Instead, the lesson is to be thankful if you have certain advantages in your own life, and to temper judgment of others who do not have them. Let's look at some of these things.

Youth

Mo's finances fall apart when he is still young. His youth is a huge advantage. The older someone is, the harder it can be to recover from a financial setback or from financial mistakes. It is much easier for someone who takes a big financial hit at 30 to recover than it is for that same person to recover at 60.

Mo frittered his money away through his own poor choices. But it would be a mistake to think that people are safe if they just make wise decisions. Financial disaster can come in unexpected forms: a costly divorce, large uninsured medical expenses, an extended stretch of unemployment, an expensive lawsuit, and so on. While there is no good time for such a devastating event, the timing can be the difference between how well someone recovers, or whether they can recover at all.

In Chapter Two we discussed how time is the investor's best friend because of the power of compounding returns. Time is also the saver's friend for obvious reasons – the more time you have to save, the more you can put away. A young person who has experienced a large financial setback has more time to get back on track – to find another job or to start saving and investing again.

The deck is often stacked against those who try to rebuild their finances late in life. Even when economic times are good, it might not be easy to just "go out and get another job." Age-related employment discrimination is a very real concern; some employers would simply rather not hire older people. There are laws that prohibit certain age-based discrimination, but these are notoriously hard to enforce, particularly when alleged discrimination occurred during the hiring process.

This lesson struck home in the aftermath of the "Great Recession," as the time between late 2007 and mid-2009 is known. Multiple financial markets experienced simultaneous collapses ranging from "bad" to "catastrophic" following a combination of factors, including a run-up in asset prices across multiple markets, risky actions by large financial institutions, and poor-to-nonexistent oversight. Even though the Great Recession technically ended in 2009, many people felt its effects for years afterward.

Retirement account values plummeted, and those who sold their assets in a panic locked in those low prices. Real estate prices dropped severely, taking with them the hopes of people who planned to use their homes' value for retirement. People who once thought they had secure jobs suddenly found themselves unemployed.

The most painful and notable aspect of the Great Recession was how long it lasted and its long-term effects. The word "recession" is an economic term that has a technical definition (two or more quarters where a country's Gross Domestic Product (the value of what it produces) declines). But the impact it had on people lasted well beyond the technical date the recession ended. Even though a period of economic prosperity followed, many people still had not recovered a decade later.

People of all ages felt the impact. In fact, the negative effects on young people were in many ways similar to those felt by older people (such as high unemployment rates). But, the Great Recession was especially devastating for many older people because they did not have time to recover. There are countless stories of people who lost their jobs and simply ended up being retired without ever intending to retire; they just never found a job to go back to.

Many of these people either lost large portions of their savings by selling out of investments that had fallen in value, or had to withdraw money early to pay for living expenses. Many never regained meaningful employment, and without time to rebuild, ended up in a retirement reality far different from the one they envisioned.

The point of this section is twofold. First, do what you can to put yourself in the best position possible to withstand financial hardships. But second, and most importantly, if you are young and experience a financial setback, at least look at the silver lining and be thankful that you have time on your side.

A lot of people say that "time is the most precious commodity." That's not true. A commodity, by definition, is something that can be bought and sold. You can't buy or sell time. Instead, time has an essentially infinite value by virtue of the fact that you *can't* buy or sell it. There's no market. It's something you have. Until you don't. Be thankful for it.

Health

Mo had another huge advantage – his health. After squandering his money, Mo went to work feeding pigs. Feeding pigs is physically demanding work. You have to carry the food back and forth and pour it into the trough. Pigs eat like, well, pigs, so you're making a lot of trips back and forth carrying buckets. It was terrible work, but he didn't starve. Had Mo been in poorer health, he might not have even been able to feed pigs.

"Health" is in a separate section from "Age" because the two do not necessarily go hand-in-hand. I once knew a man in his mid-80s who tried to show some high-schoolers a hidden overlook at the end of a mountain trail that they had heard about. Unfortunately, he failed to show it to them because the high-schoolers couldn't finish the hike.

Poor health at any age can prevent those who suffer a financial setback from returning to work, or from working as long as they would like. It has negative effects on the young and old alike. Older people who suffer from health issues may not have the option of returning to work after a financial setback, thus preventing them from rebuilding their lives. Young people in poor health can be in even worse shape – facing a longer life with few financial resources.

Some professions (carpet-installation and roofing come to mind) are notoriously hard on the body. A carpet installer who is forced to start over may simply find that his knees will not allow him to do so, even if every carpet-installation company in the tri-county area is knocking on his door.

White collar jobs are not immune, as chronic pain can make it virtually impossible to focus. And certain mental health problems can also make it extremely difficult for sufferers to maintain employment

After you suffered a misfortune, has anyone ever said, "Well, at least you have your health?" Usually meant as helpful optimism, it sometimes comes out sounding like, "Yep, things are pretty bad, but let me say anything I can think of to make you feel better." But, there's something to that saying; if you have suffered a big loss, but are still healthy, you have a lot to be thankful for.

In the parable, Mo was able to eke out a living for a while and then walk back home because he was still in good health. We can draw two lessons from that. First, we should remember how important it is to do what we can to take care of our health (per the related section in Chapter One).

Second, and more important, if you are in good health, be thankful for it and don't take it for granted.

In the previous section, I said that time is essentially priceless because you can't buy or sell it. Health is almost as valuable. Like time, good health can't be bought or sold. You *can*, however, sometimes buy things like medicine or medical services to improve your health. Note the difference – you're not buying health itself; you're buying a product or a service that can result in better health.

But there are situations where there is simply no amount of money that will improve your health. For that reason, good health is second in value only to time itself, and we should remember how fortunate we are if we enjoy good health.

If you ever find yourself taking your health or age for granted, by the way, volunteer at a nursing home for a few weeks.

Family that can (and will) Help

Mo had another key advantage in the parable: he had somewhere to go when things fell apart. More precisely, he had somewhere to go where he had family. Even more precisely: Mo had somewhere to go where he had family that was willing to help him.

I talked about the Great Recession earlier, and the concomitant rise in unemployment. During that time, the news media produced numerous articles about unemployed adults who had to live with their parents or other relatives. Some were in their late 50s and unable to find new jobs (like we discussed in the previous section). Others were younger and had only been on their own for a short time. Others were recent graduates who had never moved out in the first place. Some were single, some were married, and some had children.

Some of the news articles adopted a sympathetic tone ("what an unfortunate situation for this poor soul"). Others were critical ("tsk, tsk, what an absolute loser and failure"). All cited statistics about the rising number of multi-generation households.

Simultaneously, the news media reported on the rising level of homelessness throughout the country, particularly in metropolitan areas.

There is an important connection between these two storylines that I never saw explicitly made. Namely, a huge portion of those who moved in with (or received help from) family would have ended up homeless themselves, were it not for that family help.

It is hard to overestimate the important role that family (or friends, in some instances) played for many people during that time. Having someone who was willing and able to help financially was quite literally the difference between having a place to stay and living in a homeless shelter or on the street. And that was a huge advantage.

For all his troubles, Mo also enjoyed this advantage. When he reached rock bottom, he had somewhere to go, and someone willing and able to take him in. Recall that this was an era without robust government assistance programs. Without the safety net provided by his family, Mo would have died. Even if he hadn't starved to death, the combination of malnutrition and backbreaking work would have led to sickness or injury, in a spiral leading inevitably to the grave.

Having a family backstop has a second, and more nuanced, advantage as well. It allows those who have it to take on more risk. Knowing that you have someone willing and able to help you in the event of disaster lets you seize opportunities that you otherwise wouldn't.

When I graduated from college, I had two job offers. One appeared much better than the other, but required moving to a city where I didn't know anyone (like Mo, only without taking any inheritance). I ended up taking the better offer, which worked out. Even though I never needed any subsequent help from family, I knew that, like Mo, I would probably not end up on the streets if things went poorly. The mere fact that I *had* a safety gave me the ability to take a risk, which ended up leading to more opportunities.

Essentially, family can act like an insurance policy that lets you take on more risk and benefit from greater rewards. Cars have brakes so that drivers can go *faster*. If cars didn't have brakes, you'd be terrified of going 60 miles-per-hour. What if a deer bounced out in front of you? What if the car ahead crashes and you need to stop suddenly? Just as brakes give drivers the ability to go faster, knowing that a family backstop exists is enough to let many people take advantage of more opportunities.

There are two lessons. As with the other sections, one is to be thankful if you are fortunate enough to have a safety net that you could fall back on if disaster struck. The second is to be nice to your family.

Chapter 9: Good Times, Bad Times (You Know You'll have your Share)

Story Summary

This is a story that actually took place long before Jesus' time. But its financial lesson is simply too good and important to leave out. This story, about a biblical character named Joseph, is long and interesting, though I will summarize it as succinctly as I can, while providing the important parts for the financial lessons.

Joseph had the ability to interpret dreams. He interpreted a couple of his own dreams to mean that his parents and his brothers would bow down to him. He then told his parents and brothers about the dreams. That was ill-advised, because Joseph's brothers, who already didn't like him because he was their father's favorite, plotted to kill him. They didn't kill him, but sold him to some slave traders instead.

Joseph ended up in Egypt, working for a man named Potiphar. Potiphar was a super-important man who was close to the Pharaoh (king) of Egypt. Joseph was very industrious and smart, and became Potiphar's right hand man. Unfortunately, Potiphar's wife wanted Joseph to be *her* right hand man, if you're picking up what I'm putting down. Joseph was having none of Potiphar's wife's advances, which made her furious. So, she accused Joseph of trying to rape her and Joseph was tossed in the dungeon to rot away.

Joseph was industrious even in prison, and he quickly became the jailor's right hand man, helping out with dungeon chores. It so happened that Pharaoh had his royal wine taster and royal baker thrown into the dungeon. Each one had a dream and Joseph interpreted these dreams.

Joseph's interpretations came true. This was good for the wine-taster, since Joseph interpreted his dream to mean that he'd get his old job back in three days. It wasn't so great for the baker, as Joseph interpreted his dream to mean that the baker would be executed, stuck onto a pike, and that birds would pick the skin off his corpse. The wine-taster skipped happily out of prison three days later, promising that he'd never forget Joseph. The baker … well, you know what happened to him.

The wine-taster immediately forgot about Joseph – until two years later, when the Pharaoh was being bothered by some dreams that no one could interpret. Suddenly, the wine-taster remembered his old prison buddy Joseph, who was immediately brought out of the dungeon, cleaned up, and sent before the Pharaoh.

The Pharaoh told Joseph about two dreams. First, he said, he had dreamed that seven fat, juicy, delicious-looking cows came up out of the Nile River to graze. If that wasn't strange enough, seven skinny, pitiful-looking cows also came out of the river and grazed beside the fat ones. Suddenly, the seven skinny cows ate the seven fat cows.

The Pharaoh's second dream was very similar to the first, only instead of skinny cows eating fat cows, seven skinny heads of grain swallowed up seven fat heads of grain on a stalk.

Joseph said that he knew exactly what the dream meant. He said that Egypt was going to have seven years of great weather, good times, and bumper crops. Then, there would be a terrible drought and a resulting famine for seven years.

After interpreting the dream, Joseph said to the Pharaoh, "You know, you ought to find someone super-smart and wise, such as someone who can interpret dreams, and put that good-looking young man in charge of getting ready for the drought. That person, whoever he happens to be, should have a good plan. And, by the way, in case you're interested, *my* plan would be to create a government agency to oversee putting aside 20% of the grain harvest during the seven good years, such that Egypt would have it stored up for the seven years of drought."

Pharaoh said, "That's a fine idea, Joseph. In fact, it occurs to me that I should appoint *you* to do just that."

So, Joseph essentially became Egypt's Chief Operating Officer. Sure enough, there were seven good years, followed by seven bad years. Egypt was in good shape, though, because it not only had enough grain stored up to feed itself, but it had plenty left over to sell to people from other countries who came to buy it (people such as Joseph's brothers, who had sold him into slavery – but you can read that part of the story for yourself if you want).

Where you can find it
Genesis chapters 37-47.

Note: the financial lesson comes primarily from Genesis 41:1-57, but the entire story takes the ten chapters above.

The Religious Significance
Joseph and his family were ancestors of the Jewish people, and God worked through Joseph to save them from starvation and bring them to Egypt.

Financial Lesson 1: Get while the Getting's Good
The story of Joseph's life in Egypt is an excellent lesson about the importance of saving when times are good so you can survive, or even thrive, when times are bad.

Note the boom/ bust cycle in the story of Joseph. There are seven years when everything is going great. There's plenty of rain, crops are growing, harvests are gigantic, and everyone is happy. There's more than enough to go around. Then, suddenly, there are seven years when nothing goes right – it doesn't rain, nothing grows, and things look very bleak.

This boom/ bust cycle applies to things besides crops. The economy itself, along with investment performance and employment rates, are cyclical. You can pick any reasonably long period of time in U.S. economic history, for instance, and find the same boom and bust cycles as recounted in the story of Joseph. Interestingly enough, seven years is roughly the length of boom cycles (busts, or recessions, tend to be shorter).

Just looking at the time between the 1990s and the time of this writing in 2018, there was a short recession in the early 90s, followed by the boom associated with the dot com era. A bust followed, marked by both the September 11, 2001 terrorist attacks and a collapse of the dot com boom. That bust hit people pretty hard, but was followed by a boom period related to housing and related businesses like banking and construction that lasted until the late 2000s. The Great Recession, which we talked about in the previous chapter, followed, again bringing devastation. But, that was followed by a huge boom, which continues up to the time of this writing.

So, what do you think will be next?

I just talked about the last 30 years, but you can go back as long as you want. The boom/ bust cycle that Joseph experienced in Egypt is not an unusual thing; it is the very nature of economics. Good times are always followed by bad times. What goes up must come down.

Egypt had a distinct advantage: Joseph knew the exact timing and length of the next boom/ bust cycle. You won't have that advantage. Although many media pundits claim to be modern-day Josephs who can predict these sorts of things, they are almost always wrong.

Just remember this: even though you don't know *when* the next phase of the cycle is coming, you definitely know *that* it is coming.

The inherent problem is that people tend to think that the current environment they happen to be living in will continue on indefinitely into the future. When things are good, people think and behave as if things will always be good. When things are bad, people think and behave as if things will continue to be bad forever. Interestingly, those who think things will always be bad will shift over to thinking that things will always be good, once they have enjoyed a subsequent, sufficiently long, period of prosperity.

Why is that problematic? Because it leads people to do things that are the exact opposite of their long-term interests. When you have a good job with a good paycheck and get a raise, what better time is there to put money aside? But, what do people actually do when they get a raise? They spend it – sometimes *more* than the amount of the raise – on a more expensive lifestyle. A new car, a bigger house, an extra annual vacation.

That sounds great, except that good times are always followed by bad times. What happens when that great salary and raise disappear because of recession-related layoffs? Those who didn't put aside their money suddenly find themselves in doubly bad shape. First, they have no savings and are unprepared for extended unemployment. Second, they need *more* money than they did before the boom because they have to continue payments on the more expensive car or house that they bought with their extra money during the good times.

In the late 1990s, gas prices dropped down to around $1.00 per gallon. Suddenly, everyone was rushing out to buy larger and larger vehicles. The poor gas mileage wasn't an issue because gas was cheap. Suddenly, gas prices started going up, and people were rushing to sell those cars. Fascinatingly, gas prices later decreased again and people started buying those cars as if nothing had happened.

The lesson of saving when times are good is especially important for those with incomes that vary with the economic cycle. I can't think of a better example than real estate agents during the mid-2000s. The period from around 2003 through 2007 saw some of the greatest increases in real estate prices in U.S. (and global) history. Residential real estate agents are largely paid through commissions, earning 3% or 6% of the sale price (the buyer's agent and the seller's agent each get 3%, but if an agent represents both, he can get the full 6%).

In a commission-based business, the more you sell, the more you make. So, if you're selling $1,000,000 in real estate each year at an average commission of 4.5% (the average of 3% and 6%), you're earning $45,000 per year. If the real estate market suddenly heats up like it did in the mid-2000s and you sell $2,000,000 worth, your annual earnings double to $90,000. That doubling is not at all far-fetched. Note that in boom times, you are likely to not only sell more, but to sell at a higher price.

Real estate agents wise enough to set aside a portion of their windfalls ended up well-prepared for the bust that followed (I knew a few – they tended to be veteran agents who had lived through previous boom/bust cycles). Those who lived as though the boom would go on forever found themselves in much worse shape. Many had overextended themselves by inflating their lifestyles to a level that assumed a continuation of their boom-related higher income.

In fact, many had made large investments in real estate themselves (violating the advice in an earlier chapter about diversifying your income streams). This group suffered doubly during the inevitable bust – experiencing a large loss of income combined with a huge drop in their investment portfolio.

The main lesson, then, is to remember that neither good nor bad times last forever, and to take advantage of that knowledge by saving when things are good.

Financial Lesson 2: Don't Forget to Enjoy Yourself

Nothing in the previous lesson is to say that you can't enjoy yourself during a boom. In fact, a second lesson from the story of Joseph is to remember to enjoy an economic boom or financial windfall.

Recall that Joseph's plan was not to store up *all* the grain during the seven good years. Rather, his plan was to store up 20% of the crop, or one out of every five bushels. He had that 20% set aside, but for the rest it was business as usual.

It is interesting how the numbers in this parable track modern finance. Just as I noted earlier that seven years is about the length of a typical economic boom (a little on the long side), 20% isn't a bad number to shoot for as a savings rate, in terms of your income.

Egypt enjoyed the good times. It still had 80% of its grain to use and sell. And remember that this was 80% of a *bumper* crop – not a regular crop. It didn't miss that 20% savings off the top.

Think of it this way: imagine you earned $50,000 per year. Then, you experienced a huge boom and somehow tripled your salary for seven years. Now you're earning $150,000. If you follow Joseph's plan, you save 20% *of your new, higher salary*, and put aside $30,000, which is over half of your old salary. After seven years, you'd have $210,000 saved. That's almost four-and-a-half times your initial salary. More importantly, in our scenario, you would still have $120,000 available during the boom times (the new $150,000 salary, minus the $30,000 savings).

Of course, I just made up the numbers in the above scenario to illustrate the point. You are unlikely to suddenly triple your salary overnight. But, it shows the wisdom in taking advantage of good times. If you suddenly experienced an unexpected unemployment, and hadn't inflated your lifestyle too much during the good times, that $210,000 would come in very, very handy. Plus, you'd have enjoyed a higher income for those seven years, even after the higher savings.

The picture we're painting, then, isn't that Egypt lived a miserly existence for seven years and then had just enough to scrape by for the next seven. Instead, it lived well for those seven years – probably much better than in the preceding years. It just didn't spend all the excess. And it certainly didn't spend *more* than the new amount. Which is probably exactly what it would have done were it not for Joseph.

If you experience a financial windfall, such as more income due to a boom in a commission-based business, a period of generous overtime pay, an unexpected bonus, an increased paycheck due to a temporary tax break, being hired to do a project for someone on the side, and so on, remember to put some aside. Assume the windfall is temporary, even if you have reason to believe it isn't.

The lesson is not to live a bare-bones, unhappy existence during that time, only to use the extra money when times are bad to continue just barely scraping by. Rather, it's fine to enjoy some of the excess. Just remember that it's exactly that – excess – and save some of it.

That's not to say it's a *bad* idea to save all of the excess. If you are happy with your lifestyle and suddenly find yourself with an unexpected windfall, you might very well decide to save all of the excess, maintain the lifestyle you're already happy with, and be extra-prepared for the next downturn.

Financial Lesson 3: Keep some Powder Dry

A third important lesson from the story of Joseph is that wise actions in boom times can put you in a position of power during subsequent busts. Under Joseph's leadership, Egypt not only had plenty of grain to eat; it had plenty to sell to other places that lacked the foresight (and inside information) to save up.

This is the difference between a *defensive* and an *offensive* posture. Doing a good job of saving when things are going well puts you in a position to not only *survive* the inevitable bad times, but to actually take advantage of them and *thrive*. After all, the bust will inevitably be followed by a boom.

After the Great Recession, you could buy all sorts of investments at rock-bottom prices. Stocks and real estate were available at prices not seen in years. Many people were able to use money they had saved during the good times leading up to the recession to buy these inexpensive assets. Those who did that (i.e. the wise real estate agents I mentioned earlier) made large profits in the subsequent boom times in the years that followed.

In finance, this strategy is also known as keeping "dry powder." The "powder" in this metaphor refers to gunpowder, which doesn't explode when it's wet. The phrase comes from the time of muskets, when you had to stuff in gunpowder in order to shoot. If you were out hunting, you didn't want to be shooting at everything that moved or carrying all of your gunpowder with you in case it rained or you fell into a creek. Instead, you wanted to keep some of your powder dry – back at camp or at your house or wherever.

Then, if you suddenly heard about a particularly good hunting spot a few mountains over, you would have dry powder to give you the opportunity to shoot. It would be very frustrating to see a fat, delicious deer grazing in a meadow, but have to eat dandelion salad because you didn't have any dry powder left.

Or you could use a bow and arrow, I suppose.

In the financial context, if you have all your money invested when asset prices fall, you don't have any money sitting around to take advantage of those lower asset prices. Imagine you are a stock market investor with $100,000 in your portfolio. Then the market collapses and your portfolio is suddenly only worth $50,000. You are a long-term investor, so the drop isn't a problem. That $50,000 decrease is only on paper; you don't lose money unless you sell it.

Your real problem is that, as an investor, you see that you can buy the same stocks for half price. But, if you don't have any dry powder, you have no choice but to sit on the sidelines, not buying inexpensive assets, watching helplessly as prices recover a few years later in the next boom cycle.

Aesop: Of Grasshoppers and Ants (and Diapause)

I can't help but close this chapter by observing the similarity between the story of Joseph and one of Aesop's fables. I don't know if Aesop was thinking about the story of Joseph when he wrote (well, told – his stories were oral, and written down later) his fable about the grasshopper and the ant, but they both have the same financial lesson.

You are probably familiar with this fable, if only because it became very popular in cartoon form.

In his fable, Aesop describes a lazy grasshopper that idly wastes time through the spring and summer, singing songs and dancing, while ants industriously store up food for the winter. Winter came, as winters tend to do, and the grasshopper suddenly realized that he didn't have any food. He begged the ants for some food, but they snidely told him to dance and sing his hunger away, presumably before giving each other high-fives with three of their six hands, and disappearing into their food-filled anthill. The grasshopper is left to starve.

Again we see the cyclical nature of boom and bust cycles – spring and summer are boom times and winter is the bust. The financial lesson is again to store up in the good times so you can survive the inevitable bad times. The financial lesson in Aesop is easier to see than it is in Jesus' parable because Aesop's lessons were not limited to the spiritual sphere.

Just like people enjoying an economic boom have trouble thinking another recession will come, the grasshopper can't imagine a winter without food during the warm, bountiful spring and summer months.

Interestingly, the joke would have actually been on the ants, a fact that must have escaped Aesop. Grasshoppers have a significant benefit over ants, in the form of "diapause." Diapause is a biological mechanism that allows some creatures to enter a dormant phase and go for a while without eating. Diapause is specifically used by these creatures to survive cyclical periods when there is no food. Winter, for instance.

Some ants also enjoy diapause, by the way, though obviously not the ones in Aesop's fable, since they were so diligently putting food aside for the coming winter. It would have been funny to see the look on the ants' faces when they came out of their hole the following spring, only to see the grasshopper sitting in the same place, singing the same songs. The ants would have been pretty demoralized as they realized their lives were reduced to carrying food back and forth when it was warm, for the sole purpose of surviving through the winter, just so they could get back to work shuttling food.

Fascinating stuff. You can read more about insects and their various habits and abilities by visiting section 595 of your local library ("Arthropoda").

In a postscript to Aesop's fable, there was actually quite a bit of controversy around its message. It sounds pretty simple: save up when times are good so you don't starve when times are bad. But a lot of people, even in ancient times, took exception to the ants' behavior, and felt the ants were the bad guys for letting the poor grasshopper starve. Thus, there are some alternate-reality versions of this fable, where the ant is represented as stingy and the moral is to be generous to those who don't have anything.

Ants have a long history of representing hard work and industriousness. In fact, the Bible even has a verse in the book of Proverbs telling people to be hardworking like the ant. It says, to paraphrase, "Let the ant be an example to you, you lazy good-for-nothing; think about her industrious habits and be wise." Ants are nature's natural savers.

If you like getting advice (financial and otherwise), the book of Proverbs is worth reading.

Chapter 10: The Rich Fool, or How much is enough?

Parable Summary

A crowd of thousands of people had gathered around Jesus to hear him teach. Suddenly, someone in the crowd said, "Hey, Jesus, tell my brother how to divide the inheritance with me."

Jesus said to the man, "Who made me a judge over your squabbles?"

Then Jesus turned to the crowd and said, "Beware of all kinds of greed. Life isn't about possessions."

Having said that, Jesus told the following parable:

One year, a rich man ended up with a great harvest. He thought to himself, "What am I going to do? I don't have room in my barns to store all of this grain."

Then he had an idea. He said, "I know what I'll do. I'll tear down my current barns and build bigger ones to hold all my grain. Then I'll be set for years! I can sit back, relax, and take it easy – eating, drinking, and partying."

But God himself suddenly said to the man, "You fool! You're going to die tonight. Now who will get everything you have?"

After finishing the parable, Jesus said to the crowd, "This is what it will be like for people who store things up for themselves, but not with God."

Where you can find it
Luke 12:13-21

The Religious Lesson
Spiritual matters are much more important than material things.

Financial Lesson: Money isn't Everything
This parable stands for the financial lesson that there is more to life than money.

On the surface, the parable seems to go against all of the previous financial lessons we have learned. We have a man who gets a great harvest and doesn't know what to do with it. He thinks about it and decides to build new barns to store it. Then, he will be able to quit working and retire to a life of leisure.

It seems like this guy has it together. He seems like an example of *exactly* what we should all do. It sounds like this guy read all of the lessons in this book and is doing everything right.

He must have read Chapter One because he is sitting on a financial foundation strong enough to let him contemplate a good retirement.

He read Chapter Two's lesson on compounding, because the grain harvest that resulted in his bountiful harvest had to come from somewhere. He had likely been planting increasingly-large amounts of seeds as his yearly harvests compounded on each other.

He read Chapter Three because his grain-based portfolio has outstripped the scourge of inflation.

Regarding Chapter Four's admonition to diversify, he doesn't seem that diversified since most of his assets appear to be in grain. But, he might own the land on which he grew the grain, indicating a real estate portion of his portfolio, or he could have other investments we don't know about. It is also possible that he read the discussion in Chapter Four about concentration of assets and decided to go all in on grain and was fortunate enough to have it work out.

He read Chapter Five because someone with his amount of wealth certainly hired advisors (about the weather, fertilizer types, which land was best, new grain storage methods, pest control, etc.) and other professionals (barn-builders, silo engineers, etc.) for help along the way. By all indications, he properly vetted these professionals and received good advice, service, and products.

He read Chapter Six because he is not in the dungeon (or a tomb) due to failure to pay taxes, yet he also managed not to lose his fortune to tax overpayments.

If he earned any of his fortune by renting out property to tenant farmers, he seems to have read Chapter Seven and avoided the pitfalls associated with being a landlord or other real estate investment types.

He certainly read Chapter Eight and avoided foolishly squandering his money.

And he definitely read the previous chapter about Joseph in Egypt, because he is in a very similar position and is following Joseph's example. He has extra crops and is planning to put them aside.

And yet, in the parable God himself comes down and rebukes our hero, telling him that he is going to die that very night, and asking him what will become of his possessions. What's going on?

The financial lesson is that money isn't everything. This book is dedicated to sound principles of personal finance to help build a strong financial foundation, avoid some common pitfalls that can derail your financial life, understand some key concepts and terms, and prepare you to generally make good decisions. The Appendix of this book provides an overview of some specific investment types and investment account types, along with pros and cons of each.

But those things are all mechanics. As you find yourself on surer and surer financial footing, you are more likely to find that you have more than you really need for a happy, fulfilling life.

The journey to a place of financial fulfillment can be difficult. On a day-to-day basis, it might seem like a fierce battle in the trenches. You're working to advance your career or educate yourself for a new career. You're figuring out ways to put money aside and where to put it, on the lookout for pitfalls, educating yourself on financial matters, and so on.

During that journey, it is easy to lose sight of the bigger picture that we are actors in a larger society and world, and that, in the end, a meaningful life is not about how much money you had or how well your investments performed.

In the parable, God did not say to the rich man, "I am going to strike you dead tonight because you're a bad person." Instead, he simply stated, "You're going to die tonight." That statement is a reminder that, in the end, we all die. There is a finality. Money, investments, and possessions are fleeting in that context.

Think of God's comment as a reality check for the man in the parable and for you. That check essentially says, "Whatever you're doing, make it count."

God's question to the man – "Now who will get everything you have?" – is rhetorical. This is not a lesson about posthumous transfers of possession in the context of Wills, Trusts, and Estates (as discussed in Chapter One).

Instead, in the financial context, interpret this rhetorical question as "It ultimately doesn't matter what happens to your things or who gets them; it's what you do, and the difference you make with the one life you have that counts."

The rich man in the parable wanted to retire and eat, drink, and party. That sounds pretty sweet. In the financial context, don't take God's admonition and tough words as a warning not to enjoy yourself. Rather, just remember that, although eating and drinking and partying are fine things, there are other things to focus on that bring deeper fulfillment and more lasting happiness.

What really matters to you? What do you care about, and what impact would you like to make on the world? Do you want to bring clean water to villagers Africa? Defend an endangered species from those same villagers? Help support a gifted athlete's Olympic alpine skiing aspirations? Paint?

The man in the parable is already rich when he gets his bumper harvest; his barns are already full. He represents someone who has already made it financially, but who fails to look outward to matters bigger than himself. His only thought is of building bigger barns and then retiring to a life of leisure.

How much is enough? After your barns are full, you have access to a unique luxury. Once you have a solid financial foundation, are properly insured, have adequate cash for emergencies, and have sufficient assets to secure a satisfying retirement, you can turn your attention to things that actually matter to you as a person. Things that don't involve numbers in an investment account.

This is the last lesson in the book for a reason.

Appendix: Investments and Where to Put Them

Introduction: Investment and Accounts – Liquids and Containers

This book and Appendix do not attempt to give advice about particular investments or investment strategies. Instead, the goal is to provide an overview of some basic financial concepts and principles. The main book itself focuses on financial principles through the lens of parables and stories in the Bible. This Appendix focuses on some particular investments and accounts, explaining a few common types and some advantages and disadvantages of each.

Information about investments and account types is very practical for helping navigate the financial world. We discussed throughout the book how you should do your own research before making any decisions or consulting a professional, so you are armed with information. That remains true, but think of this Appendix as a place you can start your research.

To start the conversation, let's first discuss the difference between *investments* and *accounts*. The two are totally different, a fact that seems to confuse many people. In Chapter One, we discussed the connection between investments and financial assets, noting that a financial asset is something valuable you own in order to generate money in the future, through income and/ or a higher future price. You can think of investments and assets as being the same, since you invest your money by buying assets, or things of value.

Accounts, on the other hand, are not investments, but are instead places where you put investments.

Common questions people ask, such as, "Should I invest in an IRA?" underscore a fundamental confusion between an investment and an investment account (as you'll read below, an IRA is an account type into which you put investments; you can holds investments in an IRA, but you can't "invest in an IRA").

Think of investments as liquids and accounts like containers. You put liquids into containers. There are various types of liquids and there are various types of containers. You can put water into a bucket. But you can also put oil into a bucket. Or, you can put water or oil into a salad bowl. Some containers are better at holding certain liquids than others. Liquids and containers; Investments and Accounts.

Part One of this Appendix discusses various common investment types. Part Two discusses various common account types that can hold the investments from Part One. Some accounts are better than others and some accounts can't hold certain investments at all.

Let's start with Investment types.

Part One: The Liquid you pour in – Investments

This section will describe common investments, including some pros and cons associated with each one.

Remember that this is a starting point, and you should conduct additional research on your own before deciding which mix of investments is best for you. There are many more investments available to you than this book can cover. Even if you had a comprehensive source of investment types, new options emerge frequently and that source would quickly be outdated. In addition, the rules surrounding these investments can change.

This part of the Appendix will at least give you a place to start your research and better position you to ask smart questions when you talk to an investment advisor or accountant.

The investments discussed below are generally in order of increasing risk. The saying "with more risk comes more reward" is not exactly right in investing. A better phrase would be "with more risk comes more *potential* reward." The word "potential" is crucial. There are very few guarantees in investing. Generally, investing in riskier assets increases your chances of earning higher returns. But, those assets come with increased chances of losing money.

Certificates of Deposit: The CD you can't listen to

What is it?

A "Certificate of Deposit," or CD, is an investment product issued by a bank or credit union. Unlike a checking account or savings account (discussed in the next section), a CD is more like an investment than an account.

You agree to invest money into a CD for a certain amount of time. The bank or credit union (I'll just say "bank" from here on) agrees to pay you more interest than it would on money you have in a checking or savings account.

The time period can be anything the bank offers, but common time periods include six months, one year, two years, three years, or five years. Three months, nine months, 18 months, and other terms aren't difficult to find if that's what you're looking for. The longer the term, the higher the interest rate you get (check, though; sometimes there is very little difference between interest rates for short and long-term CDs).

Like children (hopefully) do, CDs "mature" at the end of the period, which means you get your money back, plus the interest that has accrued. You can also choose to have your interest paid to you periodically instead of credited back to the account, but that will lower the amount of interest you get at the end (since that money was not added to the principal to compound, as we discussed in Chapter Two).

Pros
Assuming the institution issuing the CD is insured by the FDIC or NCUA (and don't even think about doing business with one that isn't), there is very little risk of losing your money. You won't lose sleep at night with your money in a CD.

We will discuss FDIC and NCUA insurance in more detail in the "Deposit Accounts" portion of the "Accounts" section below.

Closely related to the low risk advantage is the certainty that comes with a CD. Given the interest rate and the time period in question, you know exactly how much you will have when the CD matures.

Another advantage is that you get to choose how much money you invest in a CD. Sometimes there is a minimum amount, but it is not difficult to find CDs with no minimum investment required. You can put $100, $1,000, or $70,319.71.

You can also choose how long you want your money locked into the CD. You can't choose any time period you want – you have to pick from the options offered by the institution. But, as noted above, there are plenty of short-term and long-term options available. This time period option is important. Since you won't have access to your money until the CD matures, you can decide whether you think you'll need the money sooner or later.

Cons

Despite the pros above, CDs are not without their drawbacks.

The most obvious drawback to CDs is that the returns (in the form of interest rates) are often low compared to other investments. We discussed the risk/ reward connection earlier. Since insured CDs carry low risk, they also carry lower reward. This is the flip side of the benefit of certainty. If you know for certain that you will get 5% for three years, then you also know that you will *not get* more than 5% on that money over the three years.

This disadvantage will be very apparent if your friends are all bragging about their high returns in riskier assets and you have your money in CDs. Of course, during periods when those riskier investments are in freefall and your friends are in a deep depression, you'll feel smarter.

Another big drawback of CDs is that your money is "locked in." That's the deal you make in exchange for higher interest rates – you agree not to withdraw your money until the CD matures at the end of the term. Because of that, you should only put money into CDs that you won't need for the time period in question.

That sounds easy, but what if something comes up and you *do* need the money? Maybe an unexpected expense comes up. Or maybe you find a much better investment opportunity and need to raise some cash to take advantage of it.

If you do need your money, you are in luck. The "lock" on your money isn't actually very strong, and you can get to it if you want. For a price, of course. Although you can withdraw money early from a CD, you will have to pay an "early withdrawal penalty." How much you have to pay varies, but it is often something like one quarter of a year's worth of interest. So, it is possible to actually lose money on a CD if you withdraw your money early enough that you forfeit more in interest than your CD has accrued.

Another disadvantage, closely related to the low returns, is the effects of inflation. As we discussed in Financial Lesson Two of Chapter Three, inflation chips away at your investment returns. This effect becomes more noticeable for investments with lower returns.

For example, if you have a CD earning 3% for a year, but inflation is 4% during that same year, you effectively have 1% *less* money at the end of the year than you had before you invested. Of course, that's better than having the 4% less you'd have if you left the money in cash under your pillow, but it's still not good. Inflation eats away at *any* investment; it is just more noticeable with lower-return investments like CDs.

CDs often have minimum deposit requirements. These can vary quite a bit, and might be more than you are willing or able to lock up for the length of the CD.

Similar to minimum deposits, you might see "tiered rate" CDs. Here, you get a higher rate if your investment amount hits a certain level ("tier"). So, you might get an extra .5% in interest if you are willing to put aside $5,000, and an extra 1% if you're willing to put aside $10,000.

Another drawback of CDs is that they are institution-specific. Mega Bank will have a 12-month CD at 3% interest, with a minimum deposit of $500 and an early-withdrawal penalty of one quarter's worth of interest, while Cute Credit Union will have a 12-month CD at 3.25% interest, no minimum deposit, and two quarters' of interest as an early withdrawal penalty.

If you want the better rate, you have to open an account at that bank if you don't have one already. And, which banks are offering which rates and terms can be hard to keep track of, especially if you regularly try to find better terms (fortunately, there are several good websites and apps that will help you sort through available options).

Banks and credit unions regularly have "CD specials" with great one-time rates as a way to get new customers to join. Those rates are often very good, but you have to open an account there to take advantage of the rate.

Final Word

Certificates of Deposit are safe investments that you can invest in by simply going to the bank you already do business with (in person at the branch, via phone, or (almost always) online). You won't get rich from CDs, but you'll sleep well at night. There are a lot of websites that help you compare CDs across financial institutions.

Both rates and terms vary significantly across institutions and change regularly, so it pays to do some research before deciding which CD is right for you. Although CDs are probably not the ideal investment upon which to build a financial empire, they can play a valuable role in your financial plan.

For instance, if you are saving money for something like a down payment on a house and you know will need the money in a certain number of months or years, and you absolutely do *not* want to see that amount of money lose value, a CD can be a great investment.

Bonds, Government Bonds

I have tried to distill this section down to its most important elements and walk the line between basic information and endless tedium. I must warn you up front, though, that even a basic bond discussion is not as interesting as, say, a novel about a unicorn-riding leprechaun who fights off dragon-riding trolls to defend his gold (note to self for next book).

What are they?

A government bond is an investment where a government (federal, state, local, or foreign) borrows money to pay for its activities. It's a loan, only by buying the bond, you're the lender instead of the borrower.

You know the federal government's gigantic budget deficit you always hear about in the news? That's essentially just a bunch of loans it took out (to the tune of trillions of dollars) by issuing bonds. Bonds issued by states, counties, and cities are called "Municipal Bonds" or "Munis."

A government wants to do something like build a park or put in a new light rail system. If it doesn't have the money to just buy the thing outright (which governments never do), or if it thinks it's smarter to borrow the money for some reason, it issues a bond. Those who buy the bonds (including other governments, companies, and the general public like you and me) then become lenders to the government.

The government agrees to pay you back your money, plus interest. This works much like the CDs from the previous section.

Pros

Bonds have several advantages. One is that they are guaranteed not to default by the government that issues them. What backs that guarantee? Governments either pay you back from money generated by taxes, or from revenue generated by whatever project they're building.

For terminology's sake, a bond backed by the government's taxing power is called a "General Obligation Bond" and a bond backed by revenue from a project like a toll road is called a "Revenue Bond."

You know how Cousin Jim comes to you every so often and asks to borrow $250 so he can buy "milk, potatoes, and a new Bible" and says that he "will absolutely pay you back as soon as next Monday's paycheck is in the bank" and that, he's "definitely not using heroin again?" There's a very good reason to be skeptical and not lend him the money. Even if you didn't see fresh needle marks on his arms and his sleazy new girlfriend lurking around outside in the yard, you have no reason to believe he even has a job, or any way of coming up with the money to pay you back.

With the government, at least you know it can generate money through taxes, or that it plans to make money from the project it is building with your money (like the toll road). That increases (but doesn't guarantee) the odds that it can come up with money to pay you back.

Generally, the bigger the government, the safer the bond. So, a U.S. (federal) government bond, issued by the Department of the Treasury, is generally safer than a bond issued by Slippery State, which is in turn safer than a bond issued by Catfish County or Sinister City.

Another advantage of bonds is that, like with CDs, you can find them for different time periods that suit your needs.

I should clarify something at this point. For simplicity, this section discusses "Government Bonds" as an all-encompassing term for debt taken on by governments. The United States Government, through the U.S. Treasury, actually uses three different words to describe the money it borrows over different time periods. A Treasury "Bond" technically only refers to debt for one duration – 30 years.

When the U.S. Treasury borrows money for mid-range terms (2, 3, 5, 7, and 10 years, to be specific), it just calls them "Treasury *Notes*." What's the difference? For all practical purposes, the only difference is the name. You still get your initial investment back, plus interest.

Any time the Treasury borrows money for one year or less, it calls them "Treasury *Bills*" (the actual available terms are 4, 13, 26, and 52 weeks). We can't have anything simple, now, can we?

They are all essentially the same – with Treasury Bonds, Notes, and Bills, the federal government is borrowing money. And you can buy those Bonds, Notes, or Bills as an investment. You can hold all three for the entire term (whether it's less than a year or 30 years), or you can sell them early.

There is one slight difference with Bills. With Bonds and Notes, you invest your money and you get your principal (initial investment) back plus interest (which is paid every six months). With Treasury *Bills*, though, you buy them at a discount to their face value and then redeem them at face value.

For example, you would buy, say, a $1,000 Treasury Bill for $950, and then after it matured, you'd get $1,000. The $50 difference, called the "discount," would be your return. The $1,000 you get is called the *face value*.

At the end of the day, Bonds, Notes, and Bills all essentially work the same. You're investing your money by lending it to the federal government for a certain amount of time in exchange for a promise that you'll be paid back more than you invested.

Another advantage of bonds is that the market is absolutely *enormous*. It makes the "stock market" seem tiny. There are a *lot* of bonds for sale any given moment. A big market is an advantage because it means you're less likely to have a problem buying or selling bonds.

By the way, an investment that is easy to buy or sell is said to be "liquid."

Some bonds have additional tax advantages. For instance, you don't have to pay state or local income taxes on U.S. government bond interest. And, you don't have to pay federal income taxes on the interest of most Municipal Bonds (issued by states, counties, and cities). Depending on which state you live in, you might not have to pay state or local taxes on the interest of those bonds, either.

That can be a huge advantage; an otherwise-bland interest rate can suddenly seem generous when you factor in tax savings. This is especially true if you are in a higher tax bracket, since that tax break is worth more (see the discussion of progressive marginal tax rates work in the first Bonus Financial Lesson of Chapter Six). Because of the tax implications, you should do your research when investing in bonds, especially municipal bonds, to make sure you know what your real after-tax return will be.

Governments all around the world issue bonds. Many foreign government bonds will have attractive interest rates, relative to U.S. bond issues. You might very well find that you can both diversify your investment portfolio from a global perspective and earn somewhat-higher rates of return in the process by adding foreign government bonds to your portfolio.

But, just remember that higher returns often reflect higher risk. If you find a country with a bond that is 10% higher than average, there's probably a good reason for it. If you invest in a bond issued by a country that gets overthrown by a revolutionary group, you can imagine what your odds are of ever seeing your principal or interest again.

Another advantage worth mentioning is that bonds have ratings. There are a few major companies that rate bonds. These ratings are designed to reflect how risky the bond is, based on the issuer's likelihood of defaulting. Each rating company has a similar, but slightly different-looking system. It is easy to look the ratings up. Ratings generally look like report cards (only they can be multiple-letters long, like "AAA"). Like report cards, an A is better than an F.

It is nice knowing a bond's rating – you know that someone has reviewed it, written up a report, and graded it. But, see the "Cons" section below for a counterpoint.

A final advantage worth discussing applies to U.S. government Bonds (and Notes and Bills). In the "Cons" section below, I will discuss that one disadvantage of bonds is that they can be difficult to buy. U.S. government Bonds (and Notes, and Bills), though, are actually easy to buy. The U.S. Treasury has a program called "Treasury Direct" that makes it easy to invest in U.S. government debt. There is an official government website (TreasuryDirect.gov) that is not only user-friendly, but lets you set up an account and invest (in $100 increments).

Cons

Government bonds are not without their drawbacks. First, just because the government guarantees your bond doesn't mean that it's absolutely safe. We noted previously that there are two kinds of bonds: General Obligation Bonds, which are backed by the taxing authority of the government, and Revenue Bonds, which are backed by the revenue from a particular project.

With Revenue Bonds, there is a risk that the project won't generate enough revenue to pay you back. Maybe the money raised from your revenue bond is used to build a toll bridge from Nowhereville to Losertown. And, as it so happens, no one wants to go back and forth because there's a perfectly fine alternative bridge a few miles away.

General Obligation Bonds are safer because governments can always raise taxes, right? Maybe, but note that governments can go bankrupt just like people and companies. Detroit, Michigan, for instance, declared bankruptcy in July of 2013. Although Detroit is a headline-worthy example, it is not alone; various other municipalities have declared bankruptcy as well.

At the time of this writing, no state government has ever declared bankruptcy. Technically, it might be illegal for states to file for bankruptcy, so state bonds are less likely than county and city bonds to default on (fail to pay) their bonds.

I say it "might be" illegal for states to declare bankruptcy. The legal aspects of this issue are far beyond the scope of this book. Suffice it to say that, while conventional wisdom is that states cannot declare bankruptcy, there are some theories as to how a state government might be able to legally do so. No more about that – just remember that almost nothing is truly risk-free.

The bottom line is that, while government bonds are much safer than many other investments, government bond repayments are not an immutable law of physics.

As a matter of historical fact, U.S. municipalities have rarely gone bankrupt as of this writing, and rarely default on their bonds. That sounds good, but it leads to another disadvantage of government bonds. Namely, rates tend to be low because the risk is very low.

Remember, with low risk comes low rates; highly-rated bonds almost always have lower interest rates than CDs for the same time period. This isn't always the case, though. Some high-quality municipal bonds will have higher rates than CDs, especially if they come with tax advantages (if you pay less taxes, your net (after-tax) interest rate will be higher).

We talked about the ratings agencies (companies that rate bonds) above and how the fact that they rate bonds is an advantage. Take that rating with a grain of salt. You'd assume that bond ratings would go down well before an actual default, right? A lot of evidence suggests that you'd be wrong. In fact, there are plenty of instances where bond ratings stayed high right up until the bond issuer was in default.

The lesson is to not expect bond ratings to be super-helpful for seeing the future. The differences in bond ratings at any given time are more useful; a higher-rated bond will be more likely to pay out than a lower-rated bond, and to have a lower rate of interest. Just don't expect a rating to change in time for you to sell and avoid a loss.

One of the most practical disadvantages of bonds is that they are not as transparent as other investments. They are generally more difficult to research than other investment types, and are also harder for the regular investor (i.e. anyone reading this book) to buy. Buyers and sellers in the bond market are mainly companies that specialize in bond trading, not individuals. There are various historical and practical reasons for this, but a major reason is that regular investors simply aren't as interested in bonds as they are in other investments. So, there is no incentive for a user-friendly marketplace to spring up (like there is for stocks, which we will discuss later).

You certainly can buy bonds through a broker (in person or online), but you will quickly find that bond information is still harder to come by, they are often more expensive to buy, and how much they are worth at any given time (before maturity) can be more complicated to determine than you might expect.

If you like the idea of owning bonds, though, do not despair – we will talk about another way to invest in bonds in another section. And, keep in mind that U.S. government debt is pretty easy to buy via Treasury Direct, as discussed in the "Pros" section above.

If you buy a bond and hold it for the entire period (two years, 10 years, 30 years, whatever), you will get what you expect – you know at the outset much you will get back at the end. But, you can sell the bond earlier if you like. If so, you might encounter another potential disadvantage of bond investing – interest rate sensitivity.

While there is no contractual penalty to selling a bond early like there is with a CD, you might find that there is a very real and costly "penalty" in terms of how much you can sell it for. And this "penalty" is out of your control and unknowable in advance. Remember, you buy a bond for a price and then you get interest for the life of the bond. In between the time you buy it and sell it, the price of that bond – what you can actually sell it for – is based on market forces (what other people are willing to pay for it).

What are people willing to pay for it? Well, that depends in part on what interest rates on other bonds are doing. Suppose you invest $10,000 in a 30-year bond with a 5% interest rate. Then, in year five, you decide you want to go on a cruise, so you want to cash in on that bond. How much can you sell it for?

It depends. Imagine that prevailing interest rates are now 10%. Why would anyone buy your 5% bond when they can just go out and buy a new bond yielding 10%? The only way they would buy your bond is if they could buy it at a significant discount. That means you will be going on a shorter cruise than you had hoped.

That example underscores a fundamental principle of bond investing – the price of a bond goes in the opposite direction of interest rates after you buy it. If interest rates go up, your bond is suddenly worth less. If interest rates go down, your bond is suddenly worth more. Of course, if you hold the bond to the end of the period – the full 30 years in our example – you get your $10,000 back, plus the interest you were guaranteed. But if you sell early, you sell at whatever the prevailing market price is.

Finally, note that there is a potential advantage hidden in the relationship between interest rates and price. Since you can sell the bond before it matures, and the amount you can sell it for varies with interest rates, doesn't that mean you can buy bonds and then sell them when interest rates move in your favor?

The answer is a resounding "yes, but..." *Yes*, it is very possible to make money buying and selling bonds. It is done every day, and a lot of money is made from it. *But*, you probably can't do it. For one thing, it is very hard to know which direction interest rates will go. Even if you know the direction, you won't know exactly when the rates will move. In order to have a good chance of knowing those things, you would probably have to devote your life to it. Even then, you probably can't do it.

Another problem is that interest rates usually don't move by very much. So, in order to make any money through buying and selling bonds, you would need a very large investment. Like, very, very large. Those who make money buying and selling bonds usually work for large institutions and do it professionally. These people – called Bond Traders – use the company's money to buy and get paid a salary and bonus. They often make leveraged bets, using borrowed money to magnify the amount of bonds they buy and sell. They would also be your competition if you tried to do it yourself.

So, it's a nice thought, but not feasible – don't bother. That's why the possibility of trading bonds isn't in the "Pros" section.

Here's a TIP(S)

There is a final type of government "bond" I will discuss, and I give it its own section for clarity because it is different from the others.

Namely, there is a U.S. government debt obligation you can invest in called a "Treasury Inflation Protected Security" ("TIPS"). The Treasury did a good job of choosing a descriptive name. TIPS do just what the name implies – they protect your investment from inflation (Chapter Three, Lesson Two discusses the problem of inflation in great detail).

TIPS are issued for 5, 10, and 30-year terms. They pay interest twice per year. TIPS factor adjust your principal amount to account for inflation, as measured by the Consumer Price Index (CPI).

Here's an example: if you invest in $100 in a 2% TIPS and inflation is 5%, your $100 is first adjusted upward by the 5% inflation rate. Then, the 2% interest rate is applied. So, instead of having $102 at the end of that period ($100 plus 2% is $102), you would end up with $107.10 (the original $100 plus the 5% inflation adjustment is $105, and then adding 2% to *that* gives you $107.10).

Because of the extra safety (inflation protection), the interest rate will be lower than the rate on a treasury note of the same term. That protection can pay off in periods of high inflation, though.

Also note that in periods of *deflation*, your initial investment is actually adjusted *downward* before the interest rate is applied. That can be a cold slap in the face. But, the Treasury does guarantee that you will at least get your principal (the amount you invested in the first place) back, regardless of what inflation does. So you won't lose money, at least.

TIPS are not a perfect instrument, and there can be some unusual tax consequences related to how interest is paid. We won't delve any more into TIPS here, but they are worth knowing about since this book discussed the negative effects of inflation in such detail.

Final Word

We used the word "bonds" in this section even though this category of investment is part of something called "Fixed Income" investing. That makes sense because your investment earns you "income" in the form of interest payments, and that interest income is "fixed" and won't increase. It's important to know the term, because if you are thinking of investing in a "fixed income" product, you'll know it probably involves bonds.

Government bonds are also useful as proof of a concept I mentioned earlier – that the financial landscape is always changing. If you talk to someone who bought bonds a long time ago, they might talk to you about "EE Bonds" or "I Bonds" or "HH Bonds." Those are all real things issued by the U.S. government (many people still have them at the time of this writing). But, the U.S. government stopped issuing them quite a few years ago. That is both the reason we won't spend time discussing them, and an example of the fact that things are always changing in the investing world – even in the staid old world of bond investing.

I will leave the discussion of government bonds here. They represent a huge market and are definitely worth knowing about. Like with CDs, you won't get rich investing in bonds, but they can play a role in your overall financial picture, particularly in circumstances where safety is more important to you than the prospect of high returns.

Bonds, Corporate Bonds
What are they?

Like governments, companies sometimes borrow money to fund their operations. There are various options for borrowing money. For instance, companies can borrow from a bank just like a person can. But, companies sometimes opt to issue bonds.

Bonds issued by companies are called "Corporate Bonds" and they work very much like government bonds. You invest some money by buying a bond issued by a company. Like with government bonds, you become a lender and the company now owes you your money back, plus interest.

All kinds of companies issue bonds, and if you perused a list of bond offerings you would recognize a lot of names.

Thinking back to Cousin Jim (the heroin-addicted relative in the previous section who asked to borrow money), you might be leery of companies borrowing money. "After all," you might reason, "isn't that a sign they're as financially irresponsible as Cousin Jim?"

Not necessarily. Some companies in dire financial straits do try to stay afloat a bit longer by borrowing money. But, very stable companies with plenty of money sloshing around sometimes determine that it is prudent to borrow money. Keep in mind that the company is presumably borrowing money to expand its business. So, the company might decide to borrow money at 6% and invest the borrowed money in a new line of business that it projects will return 16%.

Similarities between Corporate and Government Bonds

Given that Corporate Bonds are very similar to government bonds, many aspects have direct comparisons.

The same ratings agencies that rate government bonds also rate corporate bonds. The pros and cons with ratings and ratings agencies apply equally to corporate bonds as they did in the previous section to government bonds.

The fundamental relationship between interest rates and the price of bonds, discussed in the previous section, also applies equally to corporate and government bonds. This relationship – that interest rates and prices move in opposite directions – also implies that the same comments apply regarding whether you can make money by buying and selling corporate bonds when interest rates fluctuate favorably. It is certainly possible to do, but not for the individual investor like you and me – that sort of trading is squarely in the world of professionals working for large institutions that specialize in such investing.

Like government bonds, corporate bonds are part of the world of "Fixed Income" investing. Again, you are investing your money in exchange for your money back, plus a predetermined ("fixed") income stream in the form of interest payments.

Pros

Corporate bonds have a few advantages worth discussing.

The main advantage is that you can find higher interest rates within the corporate bond market than you can in the government bond market. For many people, the primary reason to invest in corporate bonds is that they want the safety of a guaranteed return combined with higher rates than they can find in the government bonds.

In addition, you can typically find a larger *range* of interest rates within the corporate bond market than you can within the government bond market. That is to say that you can find corporate bonds offering anywhere from fairly low rates to very high rates, while the spread between the highs and lows among government bonds will tend to be smaller. A larger range of available rates gives you more investment options.

You can invest in the bonds of international companies as well, which lets you diversify your corporate bond portfolio across countries. You will recall that we mentioned in the previous section that you can also diversify a government bond portfolio in the same way by buying bonds issued by different countries. Chapter Four of this book explains the importance of diversification.

Corporate bonds offer yet another layer of possible diversification that government bonds do not – industry diversification. Corporate bonds are guaranteed by the underlying companies that issue them. If an entire industry suffers a downturn, companies within it are likely to suffer financially, increasing the risk that they are unable to pay you back. The ability to buy bonds across many industries lets you diversify in a way government bonds do not.

Cons

Just as corporate bonds have some unique advantages over government bonds, they also have some notable disadvantages.

We said that one of the main advantages is the relatively higher interest rates within the corporate bond market, compared to the government bond market. But those rates are higher because companies are more likely to be unable to pay you back than governments. Corporations can't force customers to buy their products, but taxpayers can't easily avoid paying their taxes (they have to move to another place). So, corporations in general are more likely to be unable to repay bondholders during a downturn than are governments.

That is not to say that every government bond is safer than every corporate bond. A well-funded company with a long track record of making money in a stable country will almost certainly be safer than a war-torn country on the verge of its second revolution this year. In that instance, the company's bonds will have lower interest rates than the government's bonds.

That is a skewed comparison because it takes examples on either extreme. When comparing apples to apples (stable, high-rated companies and stable, high-rated governments), companies have higher interest rates because they come with higher risk of not being able to pay you back.

We said in the "Pros" section that corporate bonds give you a broader range of rates to choose from. That is true. Just remember *why* you have a broader range of available rates: because some companies have flimsier finances than Cousin Jim and the only way they can entice people to lend them money is to offer ridiculously high interest rates.

Corporate bonds with super-high interest rates are called "Junk Bonds," by the way (a more diplomatic name is "high yield corporate bonds"). Be wary if you are considering investing any of your money into this area, or if someone is trying to convince you to invest in such a thing. It is a perfectly legitimate type of investment, but don't see the word "bond" and automatically think "safe." If you see "high yield" anything, focus on that, and remember why it has a high yield.

Another disadvantage to corporate bonds is that high-quality (low risk) corporate bonds still won't have impressive rates compared with other investment options available to you. A bond is a bond, which is a guaranteed contract. Any investment with a guarantee will have a relatively low rate.

Similarly, remember that, as a bond holder, you are a lender, so your upside is limited. If the company borrows your money and then goes off and makes a fortune with it, you don't get any more than originally bargained for.

The above is a very important point, so let's look at an example. Imagine your brother borrows $1,000 from you to fund a software business he's starting. He promises to pay you back $1,500 at the end of the year. That promise is essentially a bond in our example. You recognize that he is offering you a fabulous interest rate, and you quickly take the deal, snickering at your good luck.

Your brother takes the $1,000 you lent him and buys some software and cables and such. At the end of the year, you open the mail to find a check from your brother for the $1,500 he owes you. At the same time, you are watching an interview with him on TV, where he talks to a business reporter about how he just sold his software business for $1,500,000. Now who's snickering?

The key is that, as a bond holder, you can only get what you bargained for – you don't get any extra, regardless of how successful the company you lent the money to is. The security of the guarantee comes with the understanding that you *only* get the guarantee – no more.

Corporate bonds also do not enjoy the same tax advantages that many government bonds do. That can be a big disadvantage. Of course, you (or your financial advisor) should consider the tax implications before investing, and it is not too complicated to determine whether a tax-advantaged government bond or a corporate bond with a higher interest rate is a better option for you.

Another disadvantage some corporate bonds have are "Call Options." Both government and corporate bonds can have Call Options, but I discuss them here because corporate bonds seem to have them more frequently. A Call Option gives the bond issuer the ability to redeem it early, but after a given amount of time has passed. Essentially, they can "call it in" or take it back from you by just paying a predetermined price. This can be a big disadvantage.

Imagine you predict that interest rates are going to drop over the next couple of decades, and that you further predict that no other investments will do very well. So, you run out and buy a bunch of 30-year bonds at the currently-high interest rates. Then, just as you predicted, interest rates fall and no other investments do well. You, however, are set, right? After all, you can sit back and enjoy the high rates you locked in for the next 30 years while less-prophetic suckers wallow in their own low-return-fueled misery.

Not so fast. If the bonds you bought had a Call Option that kicked in after five years, the issuer that borrowed the money from you can "call the bond." You get paid whatever the bond contract called for, and the company is free to issue new bonds at the now-lower rates. You don't look so smart, now, and are suffering in the same pool of misery as everyone else.

In reality, things aren't so bleak. For one thing, bonds with call options will pay higher interest rates than comparable bonds without call options in order to compensate you for taking the risk that the bond will be called. In addition, rates have to fall to the point that it makes sense for the company to call the bonds in the first place, based on the contractual price they have to pay you. Just understand what a Call Option is and what it means to you.

Final Word

The goal of this section is obviously not to turn you into a bond expert and get you ready to take over the trading desk at an investment bank. Rather, it is just to help you gain a working familiarity with corporate bonds, their positive and negative characteristics, and how they compare to government bonds.

Taking Stock: Investing in Company Stock

What is it?

We started out this section of the Appendix by talking about Certificates of Deposit (CDs), where a bank or credit union gives you interest if you agree not to withdraw your money for a certain amount of time. Then we talked about investing in government and corporate bonds, by lending money to governments and corporations.

Now we move into an entirely different type of investment: company stock.

With both CDs and bonds you have a *contractual* relationship with another party. CDs are contracts between you and the bank. With bonds, you enter a contract to lend money to a government or company in exchange for a certain guaranteed rate of interest. With company stock, on the other hand, you have an *ownership* relationship.

In keeping with the goal of this chapter, we will keep this discussion basic and not muddy the waters any more than we have to. The goal is to understand the principal concepts so you understand what you're doing and what this type of investment is.

As a typical investor, you can think about companies as being in two categories: private and public. Think of a private company as being owned by a small group of people – maybe a couple of friends or a family – and what goes on is none of your business. The company goes about its operations, but how much money it makes and what it does is secretive, and it would be very difficult for you to own a piece of it as an outsider.

I am simplifying matters with respect to private companies because we really want to focus on public companies. Think of public companies as the opposite of what we just described. Public companies are owned by lots of people and the company's business isn't secretive. In fact, anyone can find out how much the company earns and what it does because the company makes that information available to the public. More importantly, anyone can walk right up and buy a piece of the company if they want to (and if they have the money to do so, of course).

Public companies usually start off as private companies. At some point it becomes difficult for that private company to keep growing, so it looks for a way to bring in some money. One option is for the company to sell off all, or part, of itself. Essentially, the company breaks itself into lots of little pieces and then arranges for those pieces to be sold to investors from the general public. That should pique your interest because the "general public" is you and me.

Since the general public can buy these pieces, the company is said to be a "public" company.

Each "piece" of the company is called a "Share of Stock" or (a "Share" or "Stock" for short). A price is set for each share and people can buy them. The first time shares of a company are offered for sale is called an "Initial Public Offering," or "IPO." Shares are sold to the public and then people who bought them are free to sell them on the "stock market."

While you own, or "hold," shares of stock, you become a "shareholder" in the company.

As a shareholder, you own a piece of the company itself. That's pretty cool; you get to do cool things like vote on important issues. More importantly, if you own part of the company, you own part of the profits, or "Earnings." If the company has 1,000,000 shares outstanding and earns $1,000,000 for a given year, you own $1 of those earnings for each share you have ($1,000,000 in earnings divided by 1,000,000 shares equals $1 per share).

The company doesn't necessarily send you any of that $1 in earnings. The company's managers decide what to do with the earnings. The company might reinvest them into operations, with the hope of earning $1.50 per share next year. But, the company can also decide to pay out some of those earnings to the shareholders. Such payments, called "Dividends," are literal payments to you, in the form of an actual check or a direct deposit into an account.

When things are going well for a company, the price of its stock tends to go up because more people are interested in owning it (and higher earnings they expect it to make). When things aren't going well, the price usually goes down for the opposite reason. Over time, companies that earn more and more profits will tend to have stock prices that go up, while companies that lose money tend to have stock prices that go down, possibly to $0 when they go out of business.

Anyone can buy and sell shares of stock of public companies on various "exchanges" (like the New York Stock Exchange ("NYSE") or the NASDAQ that you might have heard of). An "exchange" is simply a place you buy and sell stock. It is really a bunch of computers talking to each and not an actual place. The NYSE *is* an actual place on Wall Street in New York, New York, but most of the actual trading takes place on its various computer servers all over the place, not on the "floor" of the exchange you have seen in movies where people run frantically around waving slips of paper in their hands.

The important thing about the fact that shares of stock trade on an exchange is that the price of each share of stock goes up and down all the time based on supply and demand.

Because people are buying and selling, there is a "market" for stocks, hence the phrase "investing in the stock market." Like an exchange, "the stock market" is not an actual place; it is a concept that refers to the buying and selling of all stocks on all exchanges. Because most buying and selling ("trading") takes place electronically on far-flung computer servers, there is no location of "the stock market" (the same true for "the bond market").

Pros

There are various advantage to investing in stock.

The primary advantage is that stock has the potential to earn much higher returns than other investments we have considered. Why would that be? It goes back to the relationship you have. With CDs and bonds, the amount of interest you make is limited because of the contract you have; you get your money back with interest, but no more.

With stocks, on the other hand, you own a piece of the company itself and your upside is essentially unlimited. Remember our hypothetical scenario in the bond section above about lending your brother $1,000? He paid you back $1,500, which was great, but he invested your $1,000 in a business that he sold for $1,500,000.

To understand the power of stock, imagine the same situation, only instead of *lending* your brother $1,000, you had *invested* the $1,000 in exchange for 10% of his company. Instead of getting back the $1,500 based on a *loan*, you would have gotten back $150,000 based on *ownership*.

The more your brother sold your company for, the more you would have earned because your upside is limited only by the sale price (it's 10% yours, remember). The key difference between being a lender and an owner is that your upside is not limited. The better the investment does, the higher your return. Historically, stock market returns (of well-diversified investment portfolios) have done well over long periods of time (meaning they have earned rates of return significantly higher than inflation).

If you liked the income potential of bonds (the fact that they paid you interest every so often), you can find that advantage with stock as well. As we discussed, dividends are cold, hard cash that the company can (not "must") pay you. You can find plenty of stocks paying dividends. But, unlike bonds, which pay a fixed interest, dividends can increase over time. So, if you buy stock in a company that does well, and regularly increases its dividends, you will not only end up with an income stream, but with an *increasing* income stream.

Even better, while bonds have a fixed term, companies generally have no set date when they cease operations. They can theoretically be in business until the end of time. So, dividends can potentially provide you with an increasing stream of income for life.

In addition to dividends, stock ownership comes with the potential for price appreciation. Price appreciation is simply when the price of the company stock goes up. Imagine buying a share of Supercorp for $10. At the end of the year, you find that you can sell it on the stock market (on a stock exchange) for $15. That $5 is the appreciation. If you happen to sell, you earn "capital gains," not "income." That's important because (as of this writing), the IRS taxes capital gains at different rates than income. For many, these rates are favorable.

Your "Total Return" is simply the price appreciation plus the dividends. Again, you invest in Supercorp at $10 per share and find you can sell it for $15 at the end of the year. In Supercorp paid you $1 during the year. Your total return is $6 – the $1 dividend plus the $5 in price appreciation. Of course, you have the sell the share of stock to get the $5 (it's called an "unrealized gain," not a "capital gain" since you don't have it in hand). The IRS taxes certain dividends at different rates than income, too. Like capital gains, these rates are favorable for many people.

Another key advantage of company stock is that it is relatively easy and inexpensive to buy. Each company will have a "ticker symbol," which is just some letters representing the company. If you want to buy shares of a particular company, you simply look up its ticker symbol and buy it through an account such as a brokerage account.

The price of most things goes up over time; the cost of buying and selling stock ("trading costs") has actually gone down. I bought my first shares of stock before Internet-enabled investing was common. It cost about $60 every time I made a purchase or a sale. Years later, I was able to make the exact same purchase and sale transactions for $10 apiece. Years after that, $5 trades were available. New companies are currently leveraging technology to make trades even cheaper.

In addition to being easy and inexpensive, stocks are a very liquid investment. You may recall a previous discussion on the importance of liquidity – how easy it is to buy or sell something. Large, powerful stock exchanges combined with a lot of people and companies buying and selling stock at all hours means that it generally only takes milliseconds to buy or sell as many shares of any given company as you'd like.

There is a lot more information available about stocks than bonds, which is an advantage for anyone who wants to research a company and its financial situation. We discussed how individual bonds are usually bought and sold by big companies instead of regular investors and how that fact leads to there not being as much information available about individual bonds for the regular investor. This is not true of stock.

Although big companies are still the major buyers and sellers of stock, buying and selling stock has long been a favorite pastime of the regular investor. Consequently, there is a lot of readily-available information about individual stocks. There are quite a few reliable resources where you can very quickly look up a tremendous amount of data about any given public company.

With bonds, you sort of have two types of research problems. First, how strong is the underlying government or company issuing the bond? Second, what are the term of the bond contract? That is quite a bit of research, especially in a less-than-transparent market. With stock, on the other hand, you really only have one research problem: how much do I think this company is actually worth, compared to what it sells for? That is still not an easy question to answer, but if you plan to buy individual stocks, it is one you should be prepared to look into. If you do, it is nice to know that at least there is plenty of information readily available about the company's financial history and plans.

You can find a lot of information for free, and there are also resources available for purchase that give you access to research that others have compiled for you.

I would be remiss if I failed to mention that mention that one advantage of investing in stock is that it can be a lot of fun. Many of the companies you know and love are publicly-traded and you can own a pat of them. Your favorite soft drink or car is likely made by a public company, and your favorite store might be public. It can be fun to do some research, find a company you think will do well, invest in it, and the watch how it does (it's always more fun if it does well, of course).

Cons

Stocks sound much better than CDs and bonds, but there are some key disadvantages to keep in mind.

Firsts, company stock come with absolutely no guarantees. Since that is the most important disadvantage of stock ownership, let me repeat that: stocks come with absolutely no guarantees.

With CDs, the bank or credit union contractually guarantees you it will pay the interest. That guarantee is usually backed by government insurance through the FDIC or NCUA (discussed in the "Deposit Accounts" section of Part Two of this Appendix). With government and corporate bonds, you have the guarantee of whoever issued the bond that they will pay you the interest. They might still default, but at least you have a guarantee.

But, remember that when you own stock, you are an *owner*, not a lender or a contract holder. That means that you can lose money, including the money you invest (your principal). Imagine buying a share of Supercorp for $10. At the time it is paying a $1 per share dividend.

But, after you buy your shares, Supercorp falls on hard times. It decides to discontinue its dividend to save money, and by the end of the year the price has fallen to $4. Your "Total Return" is *negative* $6. Your investment is actually worth *less* than you bought it for (this loss is called an "unrealized loss" since you haven't actually sold it). Supercorp's stock could always go back up to $10, or even continue on to $20 and beyond, but it could also go to $0.

That's a key difference. With bonds, the bond issuer pretty much has to declare bankruptcy before you lose anything. With stock, that is not the case. Always remember, the potential for higher reward comes with higher risk of loss.

Another disadvantage of stocks is that, even though it is easy and relatively inexpensive to buy them, it is not easy to know *what* to buy or *when* to buy it. Paradoxically, one reason for this is that there is so much information available. We mentioned the large amount of available information as a positive in the "Pros" section. But, you can suffer information overload when your research turns up a large amount of information, some of it contradictory. It can be hard to discern what would make for a good investment.

You may simply not be able to divine the right decision even if you know which pieces of information to look at. After all, you can't see the future. Maybe you think a restaurant is great, buy stock in it because there's no way it can lose money, and then the next day you read about several people getting food poisoning there, and the stock price suddenly drops to half of what you paid.

There's more to a good investment than simply finding a good company. There's a skill to determine how much you should pay for it and that skill can be exceedingly difficult to acquire. This is the "when" problem.

Maybe you find a company that you believe will make more money in the future. You buy into it, and sure enough, it makes money hand over fist. But, to your amazement, the price only goes down. How could that be? If the price you pay is too high relative to how much the company is actually worth and how much people are willing to pay for it in the future, it is entirely possible for a company to earn profits while the price of its stock goes down.

The bottom line is that knowing which stocks to buy, and when to buy them, can be very difficult.

Like bonds, another disadvantage of stocks is how expensive it can be to diversify. There is stock available from companies in all different industries, in all different countries. There are big companies, small companies, and mid-sized companies. In order to diversify, as advised in

Chapter Four, you might have to buy stock in hundreds of different companies. Even with relatively low trading fees, that can get expensive fast. And, you'll need to invest enough in each company to make it worth your while since any gains will need to offset those trading fees.

The time required to research all the possible investments you could make in company stock would also be enormous. Public companies are required to make lots of financial information available. Within minutes, you can have on your screen a copy of any public company's annual report, which contains its balance sheet, income statement, and cash flow statement. Or, if you like holding the documents, the company will be happy to send them to you in a few days if you simply call. Even if you have enough accounting knowledge to make sense of those documents, it would take a long time to research one company, much less hundreds.

We noted a disadvantage of bonds is that they are sometimes "callable," meaning that the issuer can pay you a set amount and cancel the bond in certain circumstances (all of which are circumstances where it would be better for you if they didn't call it). While stock is not technically "callable," there is a very close parallel. A company can sometimes "go private."

We discussed earlier how a private company "goes public" by selling shares of itself to the public. The reverse can happen. A private investor, or group of investors, can put some money together and offer to buy a company. If the company's Board of Directors agrees, the company sells itself to those investors and the company "goes private." If you were a shareholder, you get paid something, of course, but the terms are usually unfavorable from a long-term perspective.

Why are terms unfavorable? Because the private investors who buy the company aren't just random wealthy people who walked in off the street and said, "Hey, here's a company we can buy." Of course not. The private investors who buy an entire public company almost always have some inside track, special knowledge, or access to superior research to indicate that the company is a bargain at its current price.

In other words, the private investors have determined that the company is worth a lot more than it currently sells for. For instance, the company's shares are trading at $10 apiece on the stock market, but the private investors have determined that the shares are worth $100. They make an offer to the Board of Directors for $15, which gets negotiated up to $20. The shareholders get to vote on the deal, but the Board of Directors advises shareholders to vote for it. The motion ends up passing, and you get $20.

On its face, that sounds good – you got $20 for a stock that was trading at $10. But the problem is that it was actually worth $100. This is particularly bad if you had done your homework and bought in for $10 in the first place because you knew it was worth quite a bit more.

This happened to me once. During a particularly bad market for a particular industry, I found a company that I had calculated was worth far more than it traded for on the market. I bought it for, say, $7 per share. A year or so later, a group of private investors (led by the founder of the company – an insider who knew the business like the back of his hand, and who had made his first fortune when the company went public in the first place) took the company private for $14. I was the unhappiest person who ever doubled his money in one year. Because I knew very well that the private investors had walked away with a steal.

An even worse scenario is if you buy a company's stock, it goes down due to some temporary issue, and then a group of private investors buys the company for more than it currently trades for, but less than you paid. Maybe you buy it for $20 per share, it falls to $5, and then private investors take it private for $10. Here, you actually lose $10 even though you had no intention of selling and would have preferred to wait for it to recover.

The fact that you rely on a management team to run the day-to-day business activities can obviously be an advantage. You might not have the time, energy, expertise, or interest to run a multinational corporation. But, a disadvantage to having a management team running the business is that you don't know what they're up to. If they mismanage the money, make foolish decisions, and run the company into the ground, you're largely out of luck.

First, the law provides pretty strong protections for company managers making regular business decisions, even if those decisions are terrible. Second, even if the managers are flat-out corrupt and are sent off to federal prison, that doesn't help you much. It is probably too late for your investments and you are very unlikely to get your money back in any subsequent lawsuits.

Finally, just as I couldn't help but note the advantage of the fun to be had buying stocks (it's called "playing the stock market," after all), I must also mention that many people see the stock market as essentially a casino. Be careful not to conflate "investing" with "gambling." If you are putting down your hard-earned money into the stock of individual companies with absolutely no research or inkling of how much the company is actually worth, you are no longer investing. You are simply gambling.

Gambling is fine as long as you acknowledge that's what you're doing and recognize that it's as a poor strategy for securing your financial future. If you like gambling in the stock market and want to pick winners like you're at the racetrack, try this: set aside a small portion (10% at the most) of your portfolio for gambling on the stock market, and use the rest for smarter investment strategies. This will let you simultaneously indulge yourself, while minimizing the risk of losing all your money on ill-advised nonsense.

Leveraged Investing

Let's talk a bit about "leveraged" investing. This is as good a place as any to discuss the concept because we just talked about those who confuse investing with gambling. I will discuss leverage here in the section about company stock because a lot of people use leverage in the stock market.

We talked about leverage earlier. The concept is very simple. "Leverage" refers to the idea of using borrowing money. Just like you can pay a small down payment and buy a house that you otherwise couldn't afford, you can do the same thing in other markets, including the stock market.

Leveraged investing is also called buying "on the margin." When you buy on the margin, you have some of your own money invested, but your money serves as collateral for a loan that lets you buy even more investments.

People buy on the margin because it magnifies their gains. You're able to invest more money than you can actually afford. You pay interest on the money you are borrowing, but if the stock you invest in goes up, it can easily offset your interest payments. After all, you can earn profits on all of the stock you control through leverage – not just the shares that you could actually afford to purchase.

The key word in that last sentence is "can." Certainly not "will." You "can" earn profits. You also "can" lose money. Not only do you have to pay interest on your borrowed money when you invest on the margin, you also have huge downside risk if the price of what you're invested in falls. If the price goes down, it can wipe out not only the amount you put in (your principal), but the amount you borrowed as well.

If the price falls far enough, you get "margin call," where the company you're borrowing from actually requires you to put in more of your own money just to keep going. You read that right. With margin investing you can actually lose *more* than you started with. If you don't have the money to put up in the event of a margin call, the people who lent you the money can actually sell your investments to get their money back.

You can't stop them, either; you have to open a special type of account in order to trade on the margin, and one of the provisions of such an account gives the company on the other side the right to sell your investments in order to cover your losses.

We said stocks were risky because they had no guarantee and that you could lose all the money you invest. But, with regular stock market investing, you can only lose so much. Specifically, you can only lose however much you invest in the first place.

Recall the parable of Mo, the Prodigal Son who wasted all his money in Chapter Eight. There, we discussed the "principle of not spending your principal." Even the wasteful Mo only lost his principal (i.e. everything he had). Normally, if you invest $1,000, the most you can lose is $1,000. With margin investing, you can invest $1,000 and lose *more than* $1,000. And you still owe interest on the loan, of course.

Needless to say, this is a very risky endeavor that is definitely not right for most people. Because of the magnified downside risk, this is ill-advised for even a small portion of your portfolio. Be very, very careful before you buy anything on the margin. If you want to gamble, go to Las Vegas. At least you get free drinks while you're at the table.

Money for Life: Pensions

This section about company stock is relatively long because many investments that people end up relying on for retirement are heavily dependent on stock.

In the past, people were not so dependent on investments in company stock for retirement. It was common to work for one or two companies over a career then retire with a generous pension.

A "pension" is simply an employment benefit that guarantees to pay a defined amount of money (usually every month) to someone who retires from a company. Workers usually have to work for a certain number of years to be eligible, the benefit is based on how much they earned while working, and the pension's terms become more generous with each year after that minimum retirement age. Some people have retired with extremely generous pensions that paid something like 75% or more of their pre-retirement salary for the rest of their lives, adjusted for inflation.

Obviously, someone who automatically earns 75% of her pre-retirement income after she retires is much less dependent on other investments. That is particularly true if she is also eligible for Social Security income (discussed a bit later on).

A generous pension reduces your need to make savvy investment decisions. It's like riding a bike with someone around to catch you. Which is great. Unfortunately, employers offering pension plans are becoming rarer and rarer. Thus, the need to secure your financial future with other investments is increasingly important. The "other investments" in question are likely to include stock-based investments.

We will return to the discussion about pensions again in Part Two of this Appendix, when we discuss Employer-Sponsored Defined Benefits plans. I also include a pension discussion here to underscore why stock-based investments have become so important to modern-day retirement planning.

Final Word

Although this section about company stock is very basic, I went into more detail than in other sections. That's because there is a lot of misinformation floating around about what a share of stock actually is, and yet, practically speaking, stocks will end up being an important part of almost every investor's portfolio. It is simply very difficult for most people to even have a chance of building an adequate financial foundation without the help of stock.

Most people will not end up with a portfolio of individual stocks that they have chosen themselves as their principal retirement strategy (see the following sections). But, most people will rely on retirement investments that depend heavily on stocks. Thus, it is important to understand what a share of stock represents and what you actually own when you become a shareholder.

If you had enough money, you could get by with bonds alone. But the word "enough" in the previous sentence is important. I happen to be writing this during a period of historically low bond yields. The 30-year U.S. Treasury Bond yield is around 3%.

Think about what that means. If you were 65 and wanted to retire with as little risk of running out of money as possible, you might want to put your money into a Treasury bond and just live off the interest. Suppose you had $1,000,000. That sounds like a lot of money, right? But 3% of $1,000,000 is only $30,000. That might not seem like very much money for a million-dollar portfolio to generate.

Stocks represent a higher risk of losing money, but also come with the prospect of higher returns, and will inevitably play a key role in the investment strategy of almost everyone who is reading this book. It pays (literally and figuratively) to know about the things in which you are going to be investing in, even if you rely on an investment advisor for help.

Joining Together: Mutual Funds
What are they?

The previous sections discussed government and corporate bonds and stocks. We noted how investing in bonds is tantamount to lending money to a government or company in exchange for a return of your initial investment (principal), plus interest. We also looked into how investing in stock is taking an ownership interest in a company's earnings, with your return coming in the form of dividend payments and/ or an increase in the stock price.

You might be very leery of investing in stocks or bonds after reading over the rather extensive list of "Cons" associated with each. Your hesitation is well-founded. Even if you or your financial advisor determine that stocks or bonds are a good investment for you, the mere complication and expense of buying a diversified mix of them is daunting.

Achieving a meaningful diversification of your portfolio might require investing in government and corporate bonds, in companies of various sizes, across countries, and across industries. That would require a very large investment of both time and money.

You would have to buy hundreds, if not thousands, of individual stocks and bonds. It would take a tremendous amount of time and expertise to find, buy, and monitor these investments. Just the fees required for a broker to actually buy them for you would be very expensive, not to mention the money you are actually investing in the bond or company itself.

That might be enough to make you quit before you start. Fortunately for us, there is a much simpler option: Mutual Funds.

A "Mutual Fund" is simply a way for a bunch of investors to pool their money together and hire a professional, or team of professionals, to buy a collection of investments for them. It's a "mutual" investment of a "fund" of money into stocks or bonds.

For example, imagine that you would need $1,000,000 in order to achieve meaningful diversification. But, you don't have $1,000,000 laying around to invest. In fact, you only have only saved $1,000. That means you need a thousand times again your current savings.

So, your only option is to just pick the one stock or bond you think will do well and invest everything it, right? Or, since you have so many options and don't know which one is best, you might as well spend your $1,000 on malt liquor and horse-racing bets. Right?

Well, you could do either of those things, but there is a third option. Imagine you had 999 friends who also had $1,000 to invest. If all 1,000 of you got together, you'd have the $1,000,000 you'd need to invest in a diversified portfolio. Those numbers are simplifications, of course. Each person might bring a different amounts of money to the table, and the overall amount might be much more than $1,000,000.

A mutual fund is simply when a bunch of people get together, pool their money, and invest as a group. Each person owns a percentage of the total investment based on how much they invest. If you put $1,000 into a $1,000,000 fund, you own 1/1000th of the investments in it. And, of course, you also own 1/1000th of any interest, dividends, or price appreciation the investments earn.

In practice, a mutual fund obviously isn't formed by a bunch of people randomly finding each by happenstance. Instead, a company that specializes in putting these sorts of things together sets up mutual funds, and then people who want to invest can join in.

The company takes investors' money, pools it together, and hires a management team that invests the money and handles administrative tasks. The investments aren't made willy-nilly; each mutual fund has a particular strategy for what it will buy. This strategy is usually implied by the name itself, but is explained in detail in a document called the "Prospectus."

One mutual fund might specialize in low-risk Fixed Income investments, while another will focus on the higher-risk stock of small companies. The Fixed Income prospectus will probably describe how it will buy highly-rated bonds, while the fund focused on small companies will probably only invest in stock of companies that are worth a certain dollar amount, or below (for instance, it will only invest in companies valued at one billion dollars or less).

When this book refers to the idea of "buying investment *products*," mutual funds are an example of a product. Just like carpet for your house is a product you can buy, a mutual fund is a product. Both are created by a company and sold to people for a fee. The difference is that the carpet is not an investment because you didn't buy it with the expectation of it becoming more valuable or earning you money.

Pros

There are substantial advantages to investing in mutual funds rather than buying individual stocks and bonds.

One of the biggest advantages of mutual funds is that you get built-in diversification. Rather than having to buy a bunch of individual investments one at a time, a mutual fund gives you access to a portfolio that already consists of many investments.

You still have to decide what *type* of investments are right for you. Like we discussed in the previous two sections, there are government and corporate bonds, and various types within each category. There are lots of companies of all different sizes across numerous industries. Investments range from almost risk-free bonds to very risky companies whose future hinges on the success of a single product. You could find a mutual fund diversified across either of those extremes. So, you need to figure out what kind of mutual fund or funds you want.

We discussed above how mutual funds have guidelines that determine what they will and will not buy. One bond fund might only buy the very safest bonds issued by municipalities within the United States, while another bond fund might only invest in the riskiest of corporate bonds (junk bonds). One stock fund will buy only very large companies, while another stock fund will buy teeny-tiny companies that will either strike it rich or go out of business. And everything in between.

Once you determine which kind of investments you want, based on how much risk you're willing to take, you can find a fund that will allow you to diversify within that area. Although you still have to decide what kind of investments you want, and how much of your money to put into each, it is much easier than buying stocks and bonds one at a time.

Another big advantage of bond funds is that you have access to a professional manager and a management team. We talked earlier about the enormity of the bond market. There are a lot of potential bonds to invest in, and information about them is fairly difficult to come by, even if you have the expertise (or desire) to find and analyze that information.

There is a lot more information available about stocks, but it is still very difficult to sift through it all and decide what to buy.

With a mutual fund, the manager and his or her team do the work for you. They do the sifting and analyzing and researching of the available investments and decide which ones to buy and which ones to sell.

The management team does more than just decide what to invest in. It also advertises and brings in more investors. Why should you care about their advertising? Recall from our example that you needed 999 friends to raise enough money to properly diversify your investments. You probably don't have 999 friends willing to invest with you, much less to invest in the particular types of things you want to invest in. By advertising, the mutual fund brings in the other investors required to get enough money together to invest in the first place.

The mutual fund management team also handles the administrative tasks associated with investing so you don't have to. If you invested in 1,000 different bonds on your own, you'd have a *lot* of work ahead of you. First you'd have to figure out which 1,000 bonds to buy, out of the huge universe of possibilities. Then, you'd have to actually make 1,000 separate purchases. You'd need to keep track of the maturity dates and interest payments for all 1,000. You'd also need to keep up with your bonds' prices throughout, in case interest rates have moved in such a way that makes it attractive to sell some. And, of course, you'd want to keep an eye on the rating of each one, in case it slipped. At the end of the year you'd need to know how much income you made for tax purposes, keeping in mind that the type of proceeds received from bonds can vary (capital gains versus interest), so you'd have to split that out.

Like I said, it is a big advantage having a mutual fund management team doing that work for you.

If you want income and are buying stocks or bonds for their dividends or interest, a mutual fund can still provide that. Income funds (mutual funds designed to generate income) will send you a check – usually monthly – of your dividends and/ or interest payments.

If you don't need the income right now, almost all income funds also give you the option to reinvest your dividends or interest payments back into the fund to buy more stocks or bonds. Reinvesting the income will help you achieve compounding returns, as discussed in Chapter Two, since your principal continues to grow, and future income is generated by the increasingly-larger principal.

You have likely already deduced another advantage of mutual funds: they are very easy to buy and sell. Each mutual fund will have an associated symbol (a series of identifying letters that always ends with an "X"). Once you have decided which ones are best for you, that symbol is how you make sure you're investing in the right thing when you actually buy it.

An advantage equally important to *ease* of buying is the *inexpensiveness* of buying mutual funds instead of individual stocks or bonds — at least if you want a diversified portfolio. Just any person off the street can't legally sell you stocks or bonds; you have to buy these investments through a registered broker. How you pay depends on what kind of account you have.

A broker will charge a fee each time you buy or sell. If you buy 1,000 different stocks, you'll pay 1,000 different fees (though you only pay the fee on the *trade*, not on a per-share basis; it costs the same to buy 100 shares of stocks it does to buy 1,000 shares). Remember that you'll pay another 1,000 feels when you sell.

In contrast, buying a mutual fund containing 1,000 different companies only incurs one fee. If you own your shares directly through the fund company, you can invest money directly into your account and not pay a "fee" to invest. But, you'll still pay an annual fee that takes into account all the buying and selling the mutual fund company had to do. We'll talk more about fees in the "Cons" section, and discuss accounts in the next part of this Appendix.

The mutual fund company will be able to buy and sell cheaper than you can, too. Think of them as a "bulk" purchaser that gets special trade pricing that you can't get (unless you have many billions to invest like they do, of course).

Buying mutual funds is the equivalent of buying lots and lots of individual stocks or bonds at once. You kill a lot of birds with one stone and end up paying far less than you would if you diversified yourself, one investment at a time.

Cons

Mutual funds sound great, but they are not without disadvantages.

First, mutual funds are only as safe as the investments within them. Just as there are no guarantees with any individual stock, there is no guarantee with a stock mutual fund. This is offset by the diversification, of course: you no longer have to worry about losing all of your money if one company goes under. But, you might be taking on more risk than you think if you own a mutual fund that is heavily invested in one "sector."

A "sector" is a particular "area," such as one industry. If you invest in a mutual fund that focuses on the mining industry, and the mining industry itself suffers for some reason, you can expect to take heavy losses. You still get diversification – even if a few companies in the mining industry go out of business, you won't lose everything. But, you are diversified *within that sector* so your fund's performance will be sort of like the average of what the mining industry itself is doing.

Remember: mutual funds are only as safe as what they're invested in, so you should know what your funds hold.

If having a professional management team doing the work for you is a big advantage, the flip side of that coin is that you are now disconnected from your actual investments. By hiring someone to do the investing for you, you no longer get to choose which particular investments within the mutual fund to buy and sell. You pick what *kind* of mutual fund you want, but you don't control the actual investments within it.

If you clean your own house every week, you are in control of the process: how long you spend on each room, whether one area needs more attention than another, whether you use that little angled vacuum cleaner attachment to get into the corners between the carpet and the molding. If you hire someone to clean your house for you, you suddenly lose control of the process. Maybe they'll do a better job than you; maybe they'll do worse. It's the same way with mutual funds. Do you often use the phrase "If you want something done right, do it yourself?" If so, you might be the sort of person who has trouble with the hands-off nature of mutual funds.

This is a very important thing to think about. Consider what having an investment manager between you and your investments means. It does *not* mean that you no longer have to do any research. It means you have to *change* what you are researching. You are now investing in a fund, so you need to research the fund itself, rather than the individual companies within it. There is a lot of research available on individual funds, but it is still a very inexact science.

How are you supposed research the fund itself — more specifically, the people managing your money and what types of things you're invested in? You could always look at how well the fund has done in the past, but that is a notoriously unreliable predictor of future success. Indeed, every single piece of mutual fund literature will say something to the effect of "past performance is no indication of future returns." Take that warning to heart; studies continuously show that the funds most likely to do poorly in the future are ones that have done well in the past.

You can read reviews of the fund, the company issuing the fund, and the management team. Such reviews are available — some free and some for a price. But, now you have simply compounded your problem because you now have to trust in the *reviewer* of your fund, just as your original problem was whether you should trust in the management. The reviewer might simply be wrong. If you tried to review the reviewer, you'd be heading down a rabbit hole leading to madness.

You could read the prospectus, but it will only provide general guidelines of what the fund will invest in. You could research the backgrounds of the management team itself. But they will all have impressive Ivy League educations and boast of a successful track record.

There is an alternative way, and it is important enough that I have given it a separate section below, titled "Index Funds."

High fees can be another disadvantage of mutual funds. We discussed above that a mutual fund is a cheaper way to diversify than buying a bunch of individual stocks or bonds. That is generally true, but it is important to note that mutual funds aren't free.

Mutual funds charge a fee for their services. That fee, called an "Expense Ratio," is expressed as the percentage of your balance that you pay each year. If the expense ratio is 2%, for example, and you have $10,000 invested, you will pay a $200 fee for the fund's services (2% of $10,000 = $200). Note that the fee is something you pay every fiscal year, not a one-time fee.

The Expense Ratio is definitely something you can, and absolutely should, research for every mutual fund you think about investing in. Expense ratios, even for the same type of fund, can vary wildly and you should know how much you'll be paying.

This fee is sort of tricky. A bond fund might even seem like it's free because you never get a "bill" from the mutual fund company. That's because the fees are taken right out of your account – it's seamless. There are rules saying the fees have to be disclosed, and they will be on your statement, but if you don't pay attention it can be easy to lose track of just how much you're paying each year.

This is not to say that fees themselves are bad. The mutual fund's management team can't be expected to work for free. They are buying and selling the investments so you don't have to, and those trades cost money. They also pay for the advertising we talked about and need a staff of people to answer phone calls and mail and so forth. Running a mutual fund isn't cheap. Those costs will all be rolled up into the annual expense ratio and passed on to you.

Not all funds are created equally. Some are much more expensive than others, even though they invest in the same type of things. These fees are incredibly important. If you recall our discussion on compounding returns, returns added to the principal year after year lead to an ever-larger principal, which in turn generates larger returns. Expenses come right out of your investment portfolio, and every dollar you pay in fees is a dollar that you will not have to compound out into the future.

Taxes are another important potential disadvantage of mutual funds. Just because you are investing through a mutual fund doesn't mean you escape taxes. This book is certainly not designed to provide tax advice, and an involved discussion of mutual fund taxes is further into the weeds than I want to go. Every situation is different for taxes, and a strategy that works for one person would be foolish for someone else.

But, I will make a few general statements to give you something to think (and ask your financial advisor or accountant) about with respect to taxes. Tax complications can stem from the fact that different types of investment returns are taxed at different rates. Income is taxed at one rate, while profits from selling an investment (capital gains) are taxed at a different rate. Those rates can vary, depending on things like how long you owned the investment in question and your income. What kind of account you have your money in can dramatically affect the amount of tax you owe (see Part Two of this Appendix for a discussion of accounts). And the rules are always changing; the rules might have changed three times between when I write this book and when you read it.

Given the above, gains from your mutual fund investment might be a mix of different types of returns, and taxed at different rates. Knowing how much of each kind is not the problem; the fund will send you the relevant tax documents each year, breaking it down for you. Rather, the problem is that you won't know at the outset exactly what kind of gains you're going to make in any given year, or in what proportion.

At the beginning of this section, we said that you are disconnected from your specific investments in a mutual fund because someone does the buying and selling for you. Taxes are where this disconnect is most noticeable. When you are directly in charge of your specific investments, you decide when to buy and sell them. You can prepare for exactly how much of each kind of gain (or loss) you will incur each year for tax purposes. You can hold off on selling something for another month if your accountant advises you that it will save you money on your taxes.

With a mutual fund, you can't call the manager up and say, "Hey, man, I see that our fund owns Supercorp. Because of my tax situation, if you sell that this year, I'm going to have a bigger tax bill – can you hold off on selling that until next year?" Well, you *can* call the manager, but it won't do any good. The fund manages money for the collective group of owners (the "mutual" part of "mutual fund"), not for *you* as an individual.

So, ownership of mutual funds can lead to some unexpected tax consequences. Some of these can be mitigated; others cannot. I won't delve into this area any more, but it is important to understand this disadvantage of mutual funds, why it exists, and be able to research (or ask your advisor about) how it affects you.

Of course, keep in mind that all of these tax "disadvantages" we discussed assume you make money. Worrying about tax complications on your profits is a good problem to have. It's certainly better than the alternative, and completely possible, problem of worrying about losses.

Having said that, there are even tax consequences to losses, as losses can offset gains in some instances. Even with investment losses, mutual funds have the same disadvantage of you not being able to choose when you sell something for a loss. Like I said, tax consequences are too complicated and person-specific to be within the scope of this book, but are something to keep in mind, research, and speak to your accountant and financial advisor about.

Index Funds: Where Lazy and Smart Coexist

There are two basic types of mutual funds. One type called "Actively Managed" and the other is called "Index." As the name suggests, "actively managed" funds are actively managed by the fund management team. This is what we talked about up until now: the team buys and sells whenever they see fit. Their goal is to get as high a return as possible, within the limits of what the fund is allowed to buy.

"Well, obviously," you say, "of course that's what they do – that's what I'm paying them for, right?"

Think about what all that buying and selling means. Mutual funds incur costs when they buy and sell just like you do. The more active the managers, the higher the costs tend to be. If the higher costs resulted in substantially higher returns, that would be fine.

Unfortunately for mutual fund managers, they are competing with each other. There are only so many stocks and bonds to buy, and managers can only buy within the limits of what their type of fund allows. The abundance of funds relative to available investments often results in hyperactivity and hyper-costs, but without the hoped-for hyper-gains.

In fact, over time, most actively managed mutual funds do worse than the average returns that they could have gotten if they just invested in a general mix of stocks or bonds and did nothing. In other words, if they had just settled for an average return. These types of "average" returns are called "indexes" and you can buy mutual funds that just track certain indexes instead of actively trying to get better returns.

This type of fund is called an "Index Fund." You buy and sell them just like any other mutual fund. Index funds identify a particular index (collection of stocks or bonds meeting a given criteria) and then buy everything in it. Index funds have managers, but they only buy or sell to maintain their fund's adherence to the index (if a company drops out of index, or appears in it, the manager will sell or buy). Otherwise, the manager's job is to sit still.

Index Funds have big advantages. First, they tend to have lower Expense Ratios (fees) than actively managed funds. Some are *much* lower. They don't incur the high trading fees and they don't have to pay exorbitant salaries to the hotshot fund manager *du jour* who can supposedly beat the market averages.

Second, it is much easier to analyze whether an index fund is performing. It should just track the index it is benchmarked against. If the index itself is up 5%, the index fund should go up by 5%; if the index is down 5%, the index fund should be down 5%.

Third, it is much easier to research the fund and its management team itself. Namely, you can just focus on whether it has indeed tracked the average and what its fees are. You're not that interested in the team's pedigree, since its job is to fade into the background and simply track the index. Most index funds do a good job of tracking a given index. So, your analysis can generally come down to which ones have the lowest fees. This is far easier than trying to determine which mutual fund manager is going to be able to get you a good rate of return.

Study after study has shown that most actively managed funds do worse than index funds over time. The longer the time period in question, the fewer actively managed funds beat index funds. Numbers vary with each study, but the percentage of index funds outperforming actively managed mutual funds over 10 or 15-year periods is something like 85% – 90%.

The main drawback to an index fund is that you give up the possibility that you'll do much better than average. If you are invested in an index fund that tracks the S&P 500 Index (a very large group of companies), then your performance is going match the S&P 500 index. You're not going to find that you have earned 20% in a year when the S&P 500 Index was up 4%. With an actively-managed fund, you always have that possibility. Given the percentages in the above paragraph, though, you shouldn't lose too much sleep over that disadvantage.

Keep in mind that you still have to decide what kind of index fund you want. There isn't "an index" that index funds track. There are all kinds of indexes – large companies, small companies, highly-rated bonds, junk bonds, various sectors (such as particular industries, countries, geographic regions, etc.). And so on.

Exchange-Traded Funds

I will cover Exchange Traded Funds (ETFs) here, rather than in a separate section from funds. ETFs are not exactly mutual funds or index funds in the sense we have been talking about, despite the "F" in the name.

ETFs are similar to index funds in that their prices go up and down based on a particular index. The index can be a group of companies, commodities, or pretty much anything. ETFs are seem similar to stocks because they trade on a stock exchange just like company stock. They have a symbol just like a stock, the price bounces up and down throughout the day, and when you buy and sell them, the process is identical to buying shares of stock from your point of view.

ETFs are a (relatively) new investment category, but are still very liquid and easy to buy and sell. They tend to be available in more specific target investments than many mutual or index funds, and let you invest in very narrow areas (though broad areas are widely available as well). Because of that, ETFs can help you invest some of your portfolio in a specific category, but in a diversified way. It would be hard to dream up an industry, country, commodity, or option that you couldn't invest in with an ETF. They also tend to have slightly (sometimes not-so-slightly) lower expense ratios than an equivalent mutual fund, or even index fund.

Fortunately for us, the specifics of how ETFs are established and what makes them different from index funds and stocks is rather esoteric and would add no value to this book. For practical purposes, they work like index funds, and represent a large, well-established, widely-used investment option.

"Socially Responsible" Investing

Before concluding the section on mutual funds, let me make a remark about "socially responsible" investing. Socially responsible investing comes in two forms. One is to actively invest in industries you find socially beneficial. Another is when you try to avoid investing in things you find unethical or socially irresponsible. For instance, you might like solar and wind energy, and invest your money into that industry. Or, if you think smoking tobacco and drinking alcohol are social ills, you might avoid investing your money in companies that make those products.

I thought it useful to include a brief discussion of socially responsible investing for two reasons. First, this type of investing has become increasingly popular with mutual fund companies, so quite a few readers might have heard about it and appreciate a discussion. Second, this area of provides an opportunity to discuss the "secondary market" – an aspect of the stock market that was a bit too detailed for the stock market overview section earlier.

Many mutual fund companies have responded to increasing interest in socially responsible investing by rolling out actively-managed funds in this category. Like any fund, the prospectus will outline the parameters of what the fund will, and will, not invest in. Because people differ in what they find socially irresponsible, fund guidelines will vary.

Assuming you find a fund that supports (or avoids) investing in thinks you like (or dislike), how effective is it?

One problem with socially responsible investing deals with the difference between the "primary" market and the "secondary" market. Recall from our earlier discussion about company stock that most companies start out as private companies and then raise money by "going public" and selling pieces of themselves (shares) to the public. We noted that the first sale of those shares to the public is called an "initial public offering" or "IPO."

Those who invest in the IPO are quite literally funding the company. They are buying shares from the company and the money goes directly to the company to fund operations. This sale from the company to the public takes place in the "primary market" – it's the first time the shares were offered.

After the IPO, those who bought shares can sell them to others. Those people sell them to still others and so on. All of this buying and selling after the IPO takes place in the "secondary market." The company itself has already raised its money and the buyers and sellers are essentially selling "used" shares to each other.

It's like if you buy a chair from a carpenter, your money goes to the carpenter. After that, you can sell the chair to me, I can sell it to Aunt Eunice, Aunt Eunice can give it to Cousin Jim, Cousin Jim can pawn it to raise cash to pay for heroin, the pawn shop can sell it back to me, and so on. But the carpenter doesn't benefit from the sale after my initial purchase.

Why does that matter? Because the mutual fund you own will largely buy and sell shares of stock in the secondary market (unless it happens to focus on IPOs). The money you invest is not actually going to the company you either like or find objectionable. The idea of socially responsible investing largely rests on the mistaken belief that money invested in a share of stock is a direct investment in the company itself. That is simply untrue for any shares of stock bought after the IPO.

However, note that corporate *bond* investments *do* directly benefit the company (although socially responsible funds focusing on stock seem to be more common).

Another problem with socially responsible investing is that these funds are actively managed and have the associated higher fees. It's hard to have a socially responsible index fund because the manager has to keep up with what companies are doing to know whether they qualify for investment or not.

If the fund doesn't invest in companies that sell alcohol, for instance, and it owns stock in a chain of grocery stores, it will have to monitor whether that chain decides to sell alcohol at some point. Many people are fine with paying higher fees for perceived benefits associated with socially responsible investing. Just keep the fees in mind.

Another problem with socially responsible investing is that it gets philosophically difficult very quickly. It becomes hard to determine what is, or is not socially responsible. For instance, suppose you find tobacco objectionable, and invest in a fund that doesn't own stock in cigarette companies. Simple, right?

But how do you feel about stores that sell tobacco? What about e-cigarettes that contain nicotine, which is a drug found *in* tobacco, but which is itself not tobacco? What about a bank that lends money to thousands of companies, some of which happen to be tobacco companies? Or what about a credit card company whose customers use their credit cards to buy cigarettes? What about a company totally unrelated to tobacco, but whose president sits on the Board of Directors of a cigarette company and helps it make good business decisions and sell its products to more people? You see how this can go on and on and become increasingly nuanced.

The "answer" to that philosophical spiral is simple from the mutual fund's point of view. Its prospectus will define what it will and will not invest in and the management team will make its investment decisions based on its interpretation of that. But, again hearkening back to our discussion that the mutual fund company removes you from direct control over your investing, you might not agree with those interpretations. Or you might not even know that a mutual fund management team has excluded an investment that you would have been fine with (or invested in something that you would have found objectionable if you knew more).

The point is simply that, even if socially responsible investing actually had a direct impact on a company's funding, it can be difficult to ascertain exactly which companies are and are not objectionable. Even if you can get through the philosophy and find a fund you like, you still ultimately rely on a management team to make the day-to-day decisions for you.

There is a related philosophical drawback to socially responsible investing. Namely, if you affirmatively decide to only invest in companies you find unobjectionable, are you implicitly accepting moral responsibility if your fund invests in something you find unethical? The philosophical idea here is that you are not obligated to try to make an ethical judgment about what you invest in. But, if you affirmatively choose to take on that obligation, you should ask yourself if you are now responsible for investing decisions in something you find horrible made on your behalf. Maybe you are; maybe you aren't. It is worth thinking about.

Another, less philosophical, drawback to socially responsible investing is probably the most obvious. By limiting yourself to socially responsible investments, you might not be able to take advantage of opportunities for large gains.

A good example is marijuana companies. As of this writing, companies that produce and sell marijuana are beginning to appear on stock exchanges. If you find marijuana company stocks to be morally problematic, and invest accordingly, that is an entirely new industry that is off limits to you. Even if you happen to think it will be wildly profitable, your idea of socially responsible investing might prohibit you from taking advantage.

Similarly, you might take the opposite stance and purposefully invest in the stock of marijuana-related businesses. This is problematic in a different way. Here, you are taking on a risk of losing money in an unproven new enterprise purely because you want to express your support for the industry, and not because you think it's a good investment.

Finally, recall that ownership has its privileges. In addition to enjoying price appreciation and dividends from your investments in company stock, as a shareholder you also get to vote on some important things. You don't get to decide on day-to-day corporate activities, but you can vote on big things, such as who sits on the Board of Directors, and large matters of corporate policy. You can also raise an issue for the company's consideration as a shareholder.

Because of shareholder voting rights, there is a good argument to be made that socially responsible mutual funds have their strategy *exactly wrong*. After all, what better way is there to effect change than to vote on corporate policy and who sits on the Board of Directors? If you opt not to invest in a company, you ensure that you get no vote on what it does. Perhaps a better strategy for socially responsible investing would be to *only* buy shares of companies that investors find objectionable, and then raise issues and vote according to stated values.

I apologize if this section read more like a Philosophy text than a personal finance book, but socially responsible investing is at heart a philosophical issue. Hopefully this section will give you a framework for thinking about the ethics of your investing, if you're interested in that sort of thing.

The bottom line is that, if you decide to invest responsibly, you should take the time to think through the implications of what that means. If it makes you feel better or helps you sleep at night, socially responsible investing might be for you. Just don't expect to make your mark on the world by owning a socially responsible mutual fund.

Final Word

There are significant advantages to investing in mutual funds that own stocks and bonds, rather than making individual investments yourself. Mutual funds provide a cost effective way to hire a professional management team to diversify your portfolio for you, regardless of what type of investments you are interested in, and they are easy to buy and sell.

Mutual funds are not without their drawbacks, one of which is the cost of active managment, but index funds and ETFs are a good way to minimize expenses and invest in broad stock market averages.

Given the fading importance of company pension plans, people are forced into a more do-it-yourself investing world. Regardless of which types of investments you determine are best for you, you will likely end up owning, or at least considering, some type of mutual fund.

'Til Death (maybe) do we Part: Annuities

What are they?

Annuities are based on a very simple idea. But, like almost everything in the financial world, they have become more and more complicated over time.

This area has become so complicated that we will have to walk a very fine line in the amount of detail with which we discuss it. We will consider three different types of annuities. This section will cover "Fixed Annuities." The second section will talk about "Variable Annuities" and the third section will discuss "Indexed Annuities."

As with everything else in this book and appendix, the goal is to develop a basic understanding of the underlying concepts, answering in broad terms the questions, "What is this thing and what are its benefits and drawbacks?" This book omits some details about annuities in favor of explaining the major points. In practice, annuities are the most complicated investment covered in this appendix and if you take nothing else from the discussion of them, please research them before investing.

Fixed Annuities

Let's start with Fixed Annuities. The basic idea of a fixed annuity is straightforward. You pay an amount of money up front and in exchange you get some money every month or year for a certain amount of time. The amount of money you pay up front can be a lump sum (one big amount all at once) or periodic payments (i.e. a monthly amount for a certain number of years). The amount of time you get paid can be anywhere from a few years to life.

Here's a simple fixed annuity concept: you pay a lump sum up front and then get a *fixed* (hence the name) amount of money for life.

Social Security is, in fact, an annuity program administered by the federal government. You pay a portion of your paycheck each month while you work and then, when you retire, you get a fixed amount for life (adjusted for inflation, but let's not quibble here).

Financial institutions can also offer annuity products. The financial institution in question might be a bank or an insurance company. Note the word "product" again. Like a mutual fund, an annuity is a product offered by a company that you can buy as an investment. An annuity is a contract between you and the institution.

In a very simple example of an annuity, you go to a financial institution, write them a check for whatever amount you have to invest, and they give you a written contract saying they will pay you a certain amount every month for the rest of your life. Or, you don't have a lump sum, but go to the financial institution and agree to pay them money over time until some point when you "annuitize" the amount you have built up and they start sending you a fixed amount every month.

The amount they will pay you depends on various factors, such as how old you are, your gender, when you want the payment to start, and how much money you give them.

If you're 25, only have $10,000 to invest, and want the payment to start immediately, you won't be getting much at all. If you're 90 years old, have $1,000,000 to invest, and tell them they can start paying you in ten years, you can expect the company will promise you a very large monthly payment.

Why is that? Here's how annuities work behind the scenes. The company issuing the annuity isn't doing so out of the goodness of its heart; it plans to make money. So, it takes your money and invests it. The company consults various tables to estimate how long it thinks you will live and what sort of return it thinks it can get on your money. Based on that, the company will offer you an amount that it believes will give it a profit and you a monthly payment you'll accept.

That explains why the 90-year-old who won't start collecting for 10 more years and who has $1,000,000 to invest will be promised a much more generous monthly payout than the 25-year-old who only has $10,000 and wants his money right away. The odds that the 90-year-old will be alive to collect anything in 10 years is very small. And even if he is alive at 100, he probably won't be collecting the monthly payout for very long.

If this sounds like betting on when people will die, it's because that's exactly what it is. Only the company isn't betting on any particular person. Instead, it bases its calculations on large numbers of people and makes its decisions based on people's average life expectancies. The company estimates how long a person your age and gender is expected to live, takes into account how much you're investing and how much it thinks it can earn on your money, and then makes you an offer. It makes the same deal with thousands of other people in addition to you. So, the person who lives to be 120 is offset by the person who dies at 45 in a car accident.

If you find those calculations interesting, by the way, people who run these numbers for companies are called "Actuaries." If you're good at math and you're deciding what to do with your life, Actuaries are in high demand and earn relatively high salaries.

Pros

Let's consider some advantages of Fixed Annuities. This discussion will touch upon some of their additional features not discussed in the overview.

First, fixed annuities are easy to buy. As noted above, they are issued by financial institutions like banks and insurance companies.

Second, fixed annuities offer security in two ways. They are fixed in terms of both how much you get and the length of time you get it. The number of years can be for a specific number, like 30 years, or it can be for life. So, you can invest your money by buying an annuity that guarantees you a fixed dollar amount for life.

If you recall our previous discussion about pension plans work, we talked about how people contribute to their employer's pension plan (i.e. every paycheck), and then, upon retirement, the employer would start paying them a fixed amount for life. While pension plans are now a rarity, you can essentially create a do-it-yourself pension plan by investing in a fixed annuity. Indeed, company pension plans are a form of an annuity into which you make periodic payments.

Alternatively, if you end up with a large amount of money you don't know what to do with at some point (in retirement or otherwise), a fixed annuity offers you a way to turn that lump sum of money into a lifetime of income.

In Chapter Eight we talked about the parable of the Prodigal Son, who took his inheritance early and then went off and squandered it. I ended that chapter by admonishing the father for giving the obviously-foolhardy son all the money at once. I noted that, rather than give the son a lump sum of money to go spend on prostitutes and partying, the father could have set up a trust fund for the son that paid out a little bit of money every month. That trust fund would essentially function like an annuity (only created by a person instead of a company).

Fixed Annuities offer another form of security in addition to knowing how much you'll get and for how long. Like the Certificates of Deposit and Bonds we talked about earlier, annuities are a contractual agreement between you and the company that issues them. Thus, your income stream is backed by a written contract.

Another benefit to an annuity that we alluded to in the hypothetical situations of the 25-year-old and the 90-year-old is that you can generally decide *when* you want to start receiving your money. Why do you care? Wouldn't you always want your money as soon as possible? No. Remember, how much you get is a function of how long the company thinks you'll live. So, the longer you wait to get your fixed payments, the higher they'll be.

In other words, the ability to choose when you start receiving your fixed annuity payments gives you flexibility depending on your circumstances. If you're retiring and want to take part of your portfolio and turn it into an immediate stream of income, you can do that. Plunk the money down and immediately start receiving benefits. If you're younger and just came into a lump sum (like lottery winnings or an inheritance like the Prodigal Son) that you want to turn into a stream of guaranteed income, but want to keep working for a while longer because the lump sum isn't extremely large, you can arrange for the payments to begin in 5, 10, 20, etc. years. That will increase the amount you'll get and give you security of knowing that you have a guaranteed income when you reach a certain age.

You can also make payments into an annuity over time, in exchange for the security of a future income stream. This is helpful if you don't anticipate having a lump sum, but want to put money aside every paycheck when you have it.

Another advantage annuities have is a "survivorship" option. Annuity payments last for a set number of years, up to your lifetime. But, suppose you are married and want your spouse to receive money for the rest of his or her life if you die first. Most annuities come with a survivorship option, which guarantees exactly that. Of course, you will pay for the privilege, in the form of a lower payment or higher fees (or both). But it is available and can provide peace of mind. You have enough to worry about on your death bed without picturing your spouse living on the streets at 80 years old due to you not checking the "survivorship" box.

Fixed Annuities have the benefit of being simple – certainly relative to the other types of annuities that we'll profile in the next two sections. You basically pay in and then get paid. You have to choose a few things, like when to start taking it, how much of your portfolio to invest, whether the survivorship option is smart, and so on, but the basics are simple.

The final benefit I will mention is that annuities are transparent. Like mutual funds, all annuities come with a prospectus that you can read. The prospectus will outline exactly what you are getting into, including all terms and fees. That's a huge advantage. The companies issuing these things, by law, have to tell you the terms. Of course, you have to actually read those terms, but you will have them in black and white.

Don't complain that they are too complicated to read. If you are about to invest a large portion of your life savings into anything, you know very well how important it is. If you aren't equipped to read the prospectus yourself, hire a professional to do it for you and tell you what it means.

The very first chapter of this book covered the importance of paying for professional help. I never ceased to be amazed by the number of people who will think long and hard over whether to pay an extra $15 to insure the cost of a $50 blender, or who will agonize over which sport package to get on their new car, but who invest their life savings into a product they know nothing about *and have taken no steps to understand*. Don't be one of those people.

Cons

Fixed Annuities come with drawbacks.

First, don't forget about inflation, which can eat away at any investment especially fixed income products. The second financial lesson in Chapter Three discussed how inflation (rising costs) reduces your ability to buy things over time. Prices of most things go up, not down. That is an extremely important concept when you are thinking of investing in anything "fixed."

When inflation is low, as it has been for quite a while as of the time I am writing this book, it is easy to overlook. It's easy to assume that the price of a gallon of milk today will be about the same as the price of a gallon of milk a year from now.

But when inflation starts to rise, those with fixed incomes notice it first. Imagine you have a fixed annuity whose payments exactly covers your groceries and utilities. Then, the price of groceries and utilities start to rise. Every dollar by which those bills increase is a dollar you have to come up with from somewhere else (other investments if you are retired, your income if you are still working, or maybe even by going back to work if you were retired).

Another disadvantage of Fixed Annuities is that there is no upside. Like bonds and CDs, your income is fixed. You get what you get. That's good in the sense that you get what you bargain for, but bad in the sense that you are guaranteed to *only* get what you bargained for.

Some annuities come with an inflation adjustment, but, of course, that's something you have to pay for in the form of lower monthly payments, higher fees, or both. Nothing is free in the investing world.

Also keep in mind that the money you pay in is gone. Whether you invest a lump sum into a fixed annuity or pay into it over time, you are turning over a large sum of money that you got from somewhere (job, retirement savings, inheritance, lottery winnings, money you stole during an armed robbery) to a company in exchange for future payments.

Imagine you amassed $1,000,000 over your career and decide to invest in an annuity. An insurance company offers you a generous-sounding monthly income for life in exchange for it. You still have to actually turn that money over. And once you do, it's gone. You signed a contract to exchange the lump sum for income. That might be harder to do psychologically than you think, especially if you're writing a check that has two commas in it.

If you suddenly decide you want that money back, too bad. You signed the contract. Of course, there *is* a way to get money back out of an annuity. But, it involves entering into *another* contract with another company that will give you a lump sum in exchange for the payments you are scheduled to receive from the first company. Such a contract will be very expensive, in the form of you getting paid a steep discount to what your annuity payments are expected to be worth.

Unlike stocks and bonds, annuities are illiquid. You can't buy or sell them easily. You can buy and sell stocks and bonds all day. With stocks and bonds, if you push the "buy" or "sell" button while simultaneously dropping your coffee cup, your order will probably be executed before your cup hits the floor. Not so with annuities. They are generally non-transferrable contracts that you can't easily escape. There's no liquid market for them and no one to sell them to, other than to a financial institution. Even then, as discussed in the previous paragraph, the sale will be very costly.

There are various fees associated with Fixed Annuities as well. There are various types, and I won't go into them all. Their names seem to keep changing, and new ones crop up frequently. The important thing to remember with fees is that, like with mutual funds, they are all explained in the prospectus. That is your touchstone document that will tell you what you're getting into and what you have to pay.

We said that fixed annuities enjoy the security of a guarantee. That is true, but keep in mind that a guarantee is only as strong as the person or company that makes it. Good old Cousin Jim the heroin addict can guarantee you that he'll pay you back your $100, but you know very well you'll never see it again. Financial institutions tend to be a better bet than Cousin Jim, but their promises are not absolute guarantees.

When a company issuing a fixed annuity says it will guarantee you a fixed amount of money for life, it means that it will guarantee you a fixed amount of money for life, *assuming it doesn't go out of business*. If the company issuing your annuity goes bankrupt, all of its contracts, including the one guaranteeing your annuity, are suddenly on very shaky ground. You can't get blood out of a turnip, after all.

How do you know that the issuing company won't go out of business? You don't. But, you can at least research the financial health of the financial institution issuing your annuity. Suppose you are considering buying an annuity from an insurance company. That company will have a rating, just like a report card, on its financial health. An "A" rating for example, means that means that the rating agency believes the company to be in great financial health. Even that is no guarantee, which underscores the main point: even guaranteed annuities are *not* absolutely guaranteed.

Final Word
Fixed Annuities can be a good financial tool when used correctly. In their simplest form, fixed annuities offer you the ability to turn a lump sum of money or a set of payments into a guaranteed income stream. That fixed stream of income can offer you peace of mind. It comes at a cost, though, and is only as solid as the company making the promise.

Variable Annuities
What are they?
A Variable Annuity starts out looking like the fixed version we just discussed. You start by investing a lump sum of money, or a series of periodic investments.

That's about where the similarity ends. Unlike a Fixed Annuity, with a Variable Annuity you choose from a smorgasbord of investment options, into which your money is invested. You still receive income at some point, but it is not fixed. Instead, your eventual income *varies* based on how well your underlying investment options do.

The things you can invest in might look very much like the other investments we have discussed in this appendix – bonds, stocks, and mutual funds. In fact, that's why we are talking about annuities here instead of after CDs, which are actually conceptually more similar.

Pros
Variable annuities share certain advantages with fixed annuities. They are easy to buy. You can decide whether to start getting your income immediately or after some time has passed. You can add a survivorship option such that your spouse will get payouts for his or her life after you

die. Variable annuities all have a prospectus that lays out their terms and fees.

Variable annuities have some additional advantage over fixed annuities. The main advantage – indeed, the primary reason people buy variable annuities in the first place – is that they offer the prospect of a higher annual income than fixed annuities do. Remember, with variable annuities your money is invested in things like mutual funds that offer more risk, and more potential reward.

Another advantage is that you can customize a variable annuity to suit your needs. Since a variable annuity is just a contract, you and the financial institution that issues it can agree to add on various "riders" to address specific desires. A "rider" is just some language in a contract that specifies a particular agreement.

You might remember that we discussed "riders" in the insurance context in Chapter One. Indeed, there is a close relationship between annuities and insurance – they are often offered by the same companies, and one can start to look like the other as riders start to add up.

Suppose you like the idea of having a variable annuity with a larger potential upside. But, you read this book and know that those higher potential returns come with risk, so you want to ensure that you get at least a minimum payout from the annuity, regardless of whether your underlying investment makes money. You can add such a rider (guarantee) onto most variable annuities.

And that's just one example. A key features of variable annuities is that they come with lots of options and are very customizable.

Cons

Variable annuities have many disadvantages compared to fixed annuities that you should keep in mind. A key disadvantage of variable annuities is that they are almost always more expensive than fixed annuities. Much more expensive. It is not unusual for a variable annuity to have expenses that are four times as high as a fixed counterpart. Why would that be? The primary reason is all of those customizable "riders" we talked about in the "Pros" section above.

The financial institution selling you the annuity isn't dumb. If you have a rider that guarantees you a minimum payout regardless of your investment performance, the institution is suddenly exposed to more risk. It is going to compensate itself for that risk by charging extra fees. The more features and protections you add, the more you're going to pay.

Another disadvantage of variable annuities is that they are much more complicated than fixed annuities. The ability to customize them with riders and options is one source of complication. Not only do you have to understand what riders are available, you also have to understand what they mean and how much they cost.

In addition, remember that a variable annuity requires you to choose which investment options you want your money invested in until your payout. Understanding those choices are yet another complication, and also requires you to make investment decisions like you do with mutual funds.

It doesn't help that your main source of "information" will likely be a pushy insurance salesman whose company is paying him to sweet talk you into signing up for the annuity. Even if the salesman doesn't outright lie to you, he isn't going to go out of his way to explain the drawbacks to whatever you're signing up for. He wants you to sign as quickly as possible so he can go out and sign up someone else.

Variable annuities can be extremely lucrative for the companies and salespeople selling them. A complicated financial product coupled with a lucrative commission for the person selling it is a toxic combination for the average investor.

Another crucial disadvantage of variable annuities is that your returns (income) are variable. You do not get the same income guarantee that you have with fixed annuities. The only way to get a similar guarantee is to add on the expensive riders we talked about. At their worst, variable annuities can essentially just serve as a much more expensive and complicated way to invest in mutual funds that you could have just bought on your own without fooling with an annuity.

Even if you buy a variable annuity that works out all right, keep in mind that you might lose the peace of mind that attracts many people to annuities in the first place.

Like with a fixed annuity, a disadvantage is that once you put up your money, it's gone. The annuity itself is a contract, which guarantees you whatever you have signed up for, but the guarantee is only as strong as the company issuing it. Even if the company remains in business, but you want out, you have to go through a complicated process to get another company to buy it for a lump sum.

Taxes can be another disadvantage with annuities, particularly variable annuities. Because you have potentially-complicated underlying investments behind your annuity, your tax situation can grow more complicated. If your underlying investments generate multiple types of returns, you'll pay taxes on them as if you had purchased those investments yourself. Like in previous sections, I won't discuss taxes very much except to say that everyone's tax situation is different and you will do yourself a favor to run any major decisions by a tax professional before writing a check.

One thing to keep in mind is that a fixed annuity with lots of riders on it can start to look an awful lot like a variable annuity. If you happen to want the peace of mind of a fixed annuity and speak to a salesman (who will be called an "advisor" or something better-sounding), don't be surprised to find yourself pushed slowly into more and more complicated products. You start out wanting a fixed annuity. "I can certainly do that," the salesman says. "Of course, you won't get any upside to that, and inflation could rear its head at any moment. We also have this other option that gives you the potential to make a little more money..."

Final Word
Variable annuities are not evil incarnate, as the "Cons" section of this chapter might lead you to believe. You might find yourself in a position where you think one is right for you.

But keep in mind some history. Fixed annuities have been around in recognizable form for over 1,000 years. They have evolved over time, but the idea of trading a fixed amount of money for a stream of income is not new. That concept is attractive because people want certainty of knowing how much they will get, and for how long.

Then, less than 70 years ago (as of this book), financial institutions came out with the idea of variable annuities. Investors are still drawn to annuities for their stable payments, but the variable annuity plays to investors' desire for higher returns and more income.

In a world where many people don't understand even basic financial concepts, very few people will be equipped to understand exactly what they are signing up for with a variable annuity. I have seen people retire and invest all of the money they had accumulated over the course of multi-decade careers into complicated variable annuities. Many of these people lost sleep at night, lost money, and ended up finding expensive ways out of the situation they had gotten themselves into.

The bottom line is the same as it is with every other investment, only redoubled: educate yourself, or hire someone to educate you, before you make any major investments. Don't put your hard-earned money into something when you have absolutely no clue how it works or how much it costs.

The Hybrid: Indexed Annuities
What are they?
Always eager to come out with inventive new products, financial institutions rolled out a third type of annuity in response to the drawbacks of variable annuities. This third type is called an "Indexed Annuity."

An Indexed Annuity is a cross between a fixed annuity and a variable annuity and claims to incorporate the best aspects of each.

Here's the basic idea of how they work: like any annuity, you put in your money up front. Then, like a fixed annuity, the issuing financial institution guarantees you a minimum return on your money (a guaranteed minimum income when you take the annuity). But, the annuity is also tied to an index, such as a stock market index, and you get a portion of those gains as well.

For instance, suppose you put your money into a hybrid annuity. You might get, say, a 3% guaranteed return as your fixed portion. In addition to that, you might get some percentage of however well a stock market index does – such as 50% of the gains of the S&P 500 Index we discussed previously.

That's the hybrid nature. You get a fixed portion, plus a variable portion based on a given index's watered-down returns.

The details vary widely. Companies use various indexes. Some indexed annuities give you a higher percentage of the index than others do. Some give you one rate for the first few years and then a different rate for the remaining years.

Pros

Like fixed and variable annuities, indexed annuities have some basic advantages. They are easy to buy. You can decide whether to start getting your income immediately or after some time has passed. You can buy an annuity with a survivorship option such that your spouse will get payouts after you die. You can easily get a prospectus that lays out terms and fees.

The primary advantage of indexed annuities is that you do, indeed, get the secure nature of a fixed annuity, along with the potential upside associated with a variable annuity. They are still contracts, after all, and you get what the contract says.

Cons

Like all annuities, the "guarantee" backing hybrid annuities is only as strong as the company issuing it.

You will recognize some of indexed annuities' other disadvantages from the previous section on variable annuities. First, they are complicated. There are a lot of moving parts. What is your guaranteed return? What index is it tied to? How much of that index's upside do you get? Do these provisions change over time? If so, how? And when? Are there any other provisions that can limit how much you can earn? You should know the answer to those questions before investing.

Indexed annuities are usually expensive, certainly compared to fixed annuities. Again, the company has to compensate itself for the attractiveness of the terms if is offering.

Indexed annuities suffer from the disadvantage of limiting how much you get of a given index's gains. You might only get 50%, or even 25%, of the index's gains. Or, you might get 75% of the index's gains – but only for a few years, after which it drops to something much lower.

Another, related, disadvantage related to your upside potential is that most indexed annuities come with a "rate cap." This is a clause that essentially says, "Regardless of how well the index does, your upside is capped at X%." That is a very important clause to know about.

Suppose you have an indexed annuity that offers 50% of the S&P 500 Index's gains. You are pleased to see that the S&P 500 gained 20% for the year … until you find out that your annuity has a rate cap of 6%. In other words, the most you can make in any year from the variable (indexed) portion of your annuity is 6%. So, instead of getting 10% (half of the S&P 500 Index's 20% gains), you only get the 6% cap. A rate cap serves as a ceiling on the variable part of your annuity and is an often-overlooked provision of indexed annuities. Until it kicks in, of course.

Finally, just because your indexed annuity comes with a guaranteed rate of return and is guaranteed not to lose money, note that your guaranteed return could be 0%. Many indexed annuities guarantee you a small rate of return – 3% or less. But, watch out for ones with a 0% fixed rate of return.

If you buy an indexed annuity with a 0% fixed rate of return, note that what you have really bought is a variable annuity with a rider guaranteeing that you won't lose money. That's not necessarily a bad thing – if that's what you mean to do.

Final Word
Indexed annuities do what they claim – you get the benefits of both fixed and variable annuities. They have broad appeal and are fairly easy to sell because investors get downside protection combined with upside potential.

Indexed annuities can play a role in your investment portfolio, but the bottom line is the same as it was with variable, and, to some extent, fixed annuities. Annuities are a notoriously complicated product, often sold by fast-talking salesmen. Be sure you do your homework first: read the prospectus, do some research, hire a trustworthy financial advisor (not a salesman) or tax professional to help you determine whether the investment is right for you if you have questions (maybe even if you don't have any questions – you might just not know what to ask).

A "Real" Investment: Real Estate
What is it?

Recall that Chapter Seven of the book covers real estate in some detail. This section of the Appendix should be read in concert with Chapter Seven.

Real estate investing is simple on its surface. Rather than buy stocks, bonds, or mutual funds, you buy a piece of real estate. The term "real estate" is very large and includes land, houses, condominiums, townhouses, duplexes, apartment buildings, strip malls, huge office towers, and so forth.

You can buy real estate by paying the full price, or you can pay a "down payment" and borrow the rest. Most people borrow money to invest in real estate, but keep in mind that this is essentially buying "on the margin" like we discussed at the end of the section about stock market investing and opens the investor up to losing more than she puts down.

When I talk about real estate "investing," I am *not* talking about buying a house to live in. Rather, investment real estate refers to properties bought in order to make money from (i.e. by renting them out and/or selling them at a gain). Chapter Seven discusses this in more detail.

I am also going to focus on simple residential real estate investing in this book. If you are considering investing in something like apartment buildings, commercial real estate, or raw land for development, you are well beyond the scope of this book. Everything will be different in that context. You will often have to work with either partners or investors, loans will work differently, and legal issues go from nuisances to potential landmines. Before you invest in commercial real estate or complicated residential real estate, I suggest you read the "Real Estate Investment Trust" section below.

Pros

Real estate comes in all shapes and sizes in all different parts of the country and world. If you are a "hands on" person, you can certainly get the "hands on" experience with real estate. Unlike stocks or bonds that are (almost always) electronically traded and you will never see, a piece of real estate is something you can go to and physically stand in or on. Many people like the idea of being in control of all the decisions associated with the day-to-day operations of their investments.

Real estate can offer you profits in the form of cash flow (if you rent it out) or capital appreciation (if you sell it for more than you paid) or both. In that sense, it has some elements of both bonds (routine payments) and stocks (increasing price).

You can also increase your profits significantly if leverage (borrowed money) works in your favor. If your down payment is sufficiently small and the interest you pay on your loan is low enough, your rental income might give you a positive income each month. In addition, if the price of the property goes up and you sell, your gains will be magnified even more if you have put down a small amount.

There can be many tax advantages with real estate, but this is an area of tax law that changes, or threatens to change, frequently. Your tax situation, combined with whether you are renting out the property or selling it for capital gains, what state you're in, how long you rented it out, and so on can dramatically affect your tax bill. Unlike many other investments, expenses you incur on your property can sometimes lower your tax bill. There are many other tricks of the trade as well that can help you put off paying taxes for a long time, and even help your heirs avoid taxes altogether.

I won't say any more about the tax benefits of real estate investments, but you should definitely consult a tax professional or tax attorney before you consult a real estate agent if you are planning to invest in real estate.

Cons

A positive aspect of real estate is that it is a hands on investment. A negative aspect is that it is a hands on investment. Your hands might very well end up being on a clogged toilet at 2:00 AM if a tenant calls. You definitely have the ability to control the day-to-day operations of a real estate investment, but those operations may quickly prove overwhelming or unpleasant. There is more to real estate investing than cashing checks.

Speaking of tenants, one of the biggest drawbacks of real estate investing is dealing with tenants (assuming you are investing for rental income). Chapter Seven discusses this in much more detail; the parable in that chapter is a case study in tenant problems.

Real estate is relatively illiquid – you can't just snap your fingers and sell it like you can with stocks, bonds, and mutual funds. It might take months or years to sell a piece of real estate. You might have to take it off the market and put it back on several times, lowering the price each time, before you can sell it.

While the costs associated with buying and selling other investments has steadily decreased over the years, the cost of selling real estate through an agent has remained stubbornly at around 6% (the seller pays both the 3% commission to his own agent as well as a 3% commission to the buyer's agent). Recent technological advances have promised to reduce this commission, just as technology has reduced trading costs in other businesses, but as of this writing, the 6% commission holds steady. On a $200,000 house, a 6% commission means the seller pays $12,000 to sell it.

In addition to the expense of selling real estate, there is the expense of maintaining it. Chapter Seven discusses this idea in more detail, but expenses like property taxes, insurance, repairs, and maintenance can be very expensive. This is especially true for rental real estate, since tenants tend not to care for your property the way you would.

It is difficult to diversify real estate. Real estate markets are very local and property rents and prices go up and down based on what is happening locally. Maybe you had no trouble renting out a house you bought a few years ago, but then factory that employed half the town shut down. That local event will likely have a big impact on your rent and eventual sale price. It would be nice to diversify and have houses in various towns, but such an investment would be very expensive to buy and maintain.

Real estate is more complicated to own than many other investments. It is a one-on-one transaction and each transaction has its own details.

Because of that, it is very illiquid. You can't just go out and buy a piece of property like you can a bond. You have to go through a series of machinations each time. You find the property, inspect it, negotiate offers and counteroffers, walk through it again at the last minute to make sure everything looks okay, and sign a mountain of transaction-specific documents before actually taking possession of it. Selling a property is just like buying it, only from the other side. Renting it out involves tenant screening, and contracts. Tenant problems might involve going to court and other hassles.

The leverage that can make a real estate investment profitable can also work against you. If the price of your investment goes down, and you only put down a small down payment, you can end up "underwater" (owing more than your investment is worth).

On the subject of leverage, getting a loan can be difficult. Banks often require higher down payments for investment property (traditionally, 25% versus 20%). That means you might have to come up with more money to invest, but it also means your potential returns will be lower. You can always try to borrow money outside the traditional banking system (people who specialize in lending money to real estate investors are called "hard money lenders"), but you will pay for the privilege.

And, of course, there are no guarantees with real estate. There is nothing to say that you will be able to rent your investment out, or that the price will go up. If you can't rent out an investment property, or can't rent it out for as much as you had hoped, you can end up losing money each month.

Real Estate Investment Trusts

What if you are interested in investing in real estate, but don't know a hammer from a crowbar, don't like dealing with people, or are too lazy to put your hands on anything besides the TV remote and a bag of chips? There is a product you should know about called a "Real Estate Investment Trust" (REIT).

A REIT is a company (technically a "trust") that trades just like a stock. You can buy and sell REITs on the same exchanges where you buy and sell stock. You technically buy "units" and not "shares" of a REIT and are a "unitholder" and not a "shareholder."

There are two kinds: Mortgage REITs and Equity REITs. Mortgage REITs own mortgages on properties and Equity REITs own properties themselves. This section only focuses on Equity REITs, which are akin to owning actual real estate.

The Equity REIT (hereafter, I'll just say "REIT" to mean "Equity REIT") owns and manages a portfolio of properties. These can be residential properties like houses or apartment buildings, or commercial buildings like strip malls and office towers. REITs usually specialize in one category of property, and generally own a large number of properties within that category. In this way, it is sort of like a mutual fund.

REITs make money by renting out and selling the properties they own and then pass most of that money on to the investors in the form of dividends. As of this writing, if REITs pass at least 90% of their taxable income on to investors, the REIT itself doesn't pay federal income tax. That is a big advantage for the company, and its owners (the shareholders).

Because of that 90% distribution rule, most REITs pay fairly large dividends compared to non-REIT companies. Like any business, if the REIT does well, it can expand. A larger portfolio of companies can mean more rent coming in. Thus, your dividend payments can actually go up over time, unlike a bond, which has fixed interest payments.

Don't let bond-like returns fool you. Like stocks and mutual funds, REITs come with no guarantees. There is the potential to lose some, or all, of your money in REITs. But, keep in mind that you can always buy mutual funds that own REITs.

In the world of real estate investing, REITs are worth knowing about because they offer a way to invest in a diversified real estate portfolio without actually having to do the "hands on" work. Of course, there are tradeoffs. You have to trust a management team like you do with a mutual fund, for instance.

And, just because the REIT doesn't pay federal income taxes, don't assume *you* don't have to. In fact, taxes can be a major drawback of REITs, depending on your tax situation. REIT dividends are generally taxed differently from other dividends in your portfolio because the REIT itself enjoys favorable tax treatment. So, make sure you consider your tax situation before buying because you could owe much higher taxes on REIT dividends than on other dividends.

Final Word

Real estate is fairly common, and it gives you the ability to earn both rental income and price appreciation, while controlling the day-to-day operations of your investment. Investing in real estate can be expensive and complicated, however, and is not for the faint of heart. See Chapter Seven for a longer discussion of real estate investing based on a parable.

Real Estate Investment Trusts (REIT) offer a more efficient way to invest in real estate than owning actual properties. These investments, which have mutual fund aspects, generally pay high dividends, and those dividends can increase over time. REITs are not guaranteed and can lose money, and their dividends come with slightly less favorable tax considerations (for the individual) than regular company dividends, so you should look into the current tax rules before investing.

Things: Investing in Commodities

What are they?

If you have ever seen the 1983 movie "Trading Places," starring Dan Aykroyd and Eddie Murphy, it has an excellent scene where the owners of a commodities trading firm explain commodities to Eddie Murphy's character. It's a great movie, and you'll appreciate that scene even more after reading this section. It's a Christmas movie, so watch it on vacation if you haven't seen it.

A commodity is just a raw material that is bought and sold. That's it. Commodities include metals like gold, silver, and copper. They can be agricultural products like cattle, potatoes, or soybeans. The commodity you probably hear about most frequently in the news is crude oil.

It is easy to understand what commodities are. The market for commodities is also fairly easy to grasp. People buy and sell commodities all the time. A company that makes cereal, for instance, buys truckloads of corn.

As a regular investor, you can also buy physical commodities. Investors who buy commodities to actually hold onto for investment purposes usually buy things like gold and silver, not barrels of oil, for obvious practical purposes.

For investment purposes, most people invest in commodities through "futures contracts." Futures Contracts are simply agreements to buy a particular commodity at a fixed price on a future date. People entering into the contracts have no intention of actually buying the commodity. They are simply buying and selling the contracts. That might sound disingenuous, but it's not – that's just how you go about buying and selling commodities and it's perfectly legal.

Here's a very simplified example. If you agree to buy a barrel of crude oil for $60 on March 30, and on March 30 the price of crude oil is $70 per barrel, you essentially make $10. But in practice, you don't take possession of an actual barrel of oil and then haul it over to someone else to sell at the higher price.

Instead, to make your $10, you would simultaneously "buy" the barrel by using the contract you already have, while executing a second contract to "sell" the barrel at the current market price of $70. A delivery truck never shows up at your door with a barrel of oil; this all takes place electronically on the "commodities market."

The same thing happens in reverse. If you think the price of oil will go down by March 30, you can buy a contract to "sell" oil. It doesn't matter that you don't actually have a barrel of oil to sell; what you're really buying and selling is a *contract*, not oil.

There are two general types of commodities traders. One type is a business that buys the contracts as a strategic decision to hedge a risk of some sort. For instance, an airline knows that if oil prices rise it will have to pay more for fuel. So, it might buy some futures contracts that let it profit if the price of oil goes up. Then, if the price of oil does go up, the airline loses money when it pays more for fuel, but it offsets those losses by cashing in its futures contracts. This is called a "hedge."

The second type of commodities trader is a person or a company with no underlying business-related profit to protect with a hedge. This investor buys a contract hoping that the commodity in question goes the way he thinks it will.

If that sounds like gambling to you, congratulations; you have been paying attention. Commodities trading by the second type of investor (which would include you, I imagine) is exactly like gambling; it's pure speculation. When you enter into a futures contract, you are speculating on the direction of prices over a period time. It's often a short time period.

Of course, you have reasons to think you're right. Maybe you think the wheat harvest in the Midwest will be very good, which will make prices go down. So, you buy contracts to let you profit from falling prices.

Whether you buy actual commodities like gold coins, or futures contracts, you are betting that the price will go up. Or, you're betting that the social order will collapse and that the only items of real value will be tangible things.

At the end of the day, these are bets.

Pros and Cons

I won't say much about the pros and cons of commodities because this is not an area that many serious investors can do well in.

If you own physical commodities like gold, you have to store and insure it, which is costly. If you start talking to people who stockpile large amounts of gold, you quickly get into conversations about government collapses and eking out an off-the-grid existence. If the world gets to that point, your gold probably won't do you that much good in reality, and you have bigger things to worry about.

Having said that, commodities like gold often go up when the stock market goes down. Thus, some people own commodities to diversify their investment portfolios and hedge against recessions. If you choose to own gold, you might want to look into mutual funds that track gold prices instead of actual gold coins or bullion (gold and silver is called "bullion" until it is made into coins). That is a much easier way to own gold, and you won't have to worry about people breaking into your house to steal it. And you won't have to buy a safe to put it in.

Note that actual physical commodities don't pay any dividends. Their only returns come in the form of price appreciation (or maybe trading a bag of gold for your life if a post-apocalyptic horde of nomadic derelicts wanders through your encampment in a nightmarish future world). In fact, if you insure your gold or buy a safe to put it in, you actually have to pay to keep it. If you look at holding physical commodities through that lens, they start to look more like liabilities than investment assets.

As for futures contracts, "good luck" is about all I can say if you decide that commodities trading is right for you. Maybe you'll get lucky. If you devote all of your time and energy into following commodities markets, maybe you can even get an edge. I doubt it, but it's possible. Like I said, this is the world of betting that you are right about price moves. If you decide to become a one-person commodities trading shop, keep in mind that your competition is made up of extremely well-funded veterans backed by large institutions, most of whom trade via sophisticated algorithms programmed into massively powerful supercomputers. Like I said, good luck.

Final Word
I won't tell you not to invest in commodities. I will tell you to think through your plan first (which means you should have a plan). If you plan to hold physical commodities, ask yourself how much of your portfolio you want to invest, and what your underlying logic is. Make sure your "investment" doesn't become a liability.

Also keep in mind that you pay trading fees in order to buy and sell commodities contracts. And you have to pay taxes on any profits you make. Fees and taxes eat into any profits you happen to make.

If you plan to trade futures contracts, you are wading into a very high-risk world and your potential for loss is extremely high. Make sure your "investing" doesn't turn into pure gambling. Like I said before, if you want to gamble, go to Las Vegas; at least you get free drinks at the tables.

Collectibles
What are they?
Like commodities, this is another investment that is unlikely to occupy a very large portion of the average investor's portfolio. Collectibles can be

anything from the glass figurines your Aunt Marjorie keeps in the case in her bedroom, to the original Da Vinci that sold for over $450,000,000.

Because we're talking about investments, we'll exclude from our discussion any collectibles that someone buys for pure enjoyment (sorry, Aunt Marjorie). For a collectible to be an investment asset, it has to meet our definition. Namely, it has to be something of value that the buyer expects will return him a gain in the future, either through income or price appreciation.

Many things fit that definition: certain watches, antique cars, artwork, stamps, rare books, and coins all come immediately to mind.

Virtually none of these things generate an income stream for the owner, so investors generally buy them with the hope of future price appreciation.

Pros

The main advantage of collectibles is that they can hold their value, and even appreciate, over time. The art market, for instance, works like any other market. People buy and sell and the price of any particular piece of art, or of works by any individual artist, can go up or down, depending on what people are willing and able to pay.

If you happen to be holding a collectible and demand for it rises, you will enjoy price appreciation in the same way you would any other investment whose price went up. Of course, you'd have to sell it to realize those profits.

Many people buy collectibles as a "store of value" for their perceived price stability, especially things like expensive artwork. The theory goes that only very wealthy people can afford to buy such things, and that people wealthy enough to buy expensive artwork aren't affected by market fluctuations like the rest of us. Besides, the theory continues, art has built-in scarcity (Monet certainly isn't producing any more paintings, after all). Therefore, the idea is that wealthy people will always buy and sell in expensive markets for scarce items that serve as trophies. This idea can trickle down through the markets, such that people start to also apply this theory to less-trophy-like assets.

Before you buy into the above theory, just know that the market for collectibles, including expensive art, *does* fluctuate. And, while there will always be wealthy people, collectibles tend to appreciate when other, unrelated markets do well. For instance, when there is a boom in the oil market, you might see a rise in seemingly-unrelated collectibles markets like art and exotic cars. That is because the people buying collectibles often do so with money that they made through ownership in oil businesses.

Many people invest in collectibles for diversification. The idea is that prices of collectibles like art will move up and down on different cycles from other assets. Collectibles certainly have their own cycles; just remember our discussion above about how those markets often move in tandem with seemingly-unrelated markets (where the buyers of collectibles made their original money).

There are some potential tax advantages associated with collectibles. Some states allow a tax deduction for lending collectibles to a museum, or for donating them to certain institutions. If you are buying collectibles as a serious investment strategy, it goes without saying that you should be talking to a tax attorney and an accountant about tax benefits.

Finally, art is an investment you can enjoy. If you like ancient Chinese jade artifacts, and buy some for investment purposes, you can enjoy them while you wait for them to appreciate. Even if they never appreciate in value (or if they depreciate), you can still enjoy their look and historical significance. There is more than one type of "appreciation" in collectibles investing.

Cons

Be very careful about investing in collectibles as part of a serious investment strategy, though, as there are many disadvantages.

First, our note about doing your research applies here as well. Many "collectibles" are really just nonsense that someone slapped together and called a "collectible" in order to sell it. Weekend newspaper inserts and magazines are full of "collectible" coins, plates, dolls, and so forth that are available "in limited quantities for a limited time, if you act now." If you're going to buy collectibles because you like to look at them, buy whatever you want. If you are buying them as an investment, be more discerning.

Research whether there is an actual market for the thing you're buying and whether there is any reference for prices of the collectible in question. Many "collectibles" are in reality not worth anything more than the twenty-five cents you'll get at a yard sale when you move (maybe to a smaller house after you waste all your money on collectibles and are forced to downsize). Remember, the price of anything depends on what you can sell it for. If there's no market, you can't easily sell it.

In other words, collectibles are not very liquid compared to things like stocks and bonds. You can't just buy and sell them at the push of a button.

Even legitimate collectibles have the disadvantage of being expensive to buy and maintain. To buy collectible-caliber pieces, you might have to spend some serious money. And, this category of investments can contain exorbitantly expensive items. Even buying less-expensive, investment-quality collectibles can add up quickly.

There are high transaction fees, too. Collectibles are pretty illiquid, meaning there's often not a huge market of buyers and sellers. Because of that, many collectibles are sold by specialized dealers or auction houses that charge a high fee for their services. They are able to charge this fee because they advertise extensively and have a network of clients, including professional dealers. They essentially help create an active market and generate a higher selling price.

Even after you own them, collectibles come with additional costs of ownership. First, you'll want to insure them against loss and theft. Collectibles are an investment with the potential to literally go up in smoke if your house catches on fire.

Second, you probably can't just store valuable items in any old place. Lighting, humidity, contact with other surfaces, and even materials used for storage affects the quality (and value) of many collectibles. You might have to buy a humidifier or dehumidifier, special lighting, a safe, or any number of other specialty products to store and protect your investment.

Keep in mind, too, that collectibles have little-to-no intrinsic value. "Intrinsic value" is how much something is inherently worth based on what it actually is. For example, what is the actual value of a 1943-D Lincoln bronze penny worth? The answer is one cent. Any coin collectors (sorry, "numismatists") reading this just fell off their chairs. To them, the answer is closer to two million dollars. But that's the difference between something's intrinsic value and its market value.

The penny I mentioned above is incredibly rare (only one is known to exist) and it last sold for $1,700,000. But that's its *market value* – its value as a collectible. If you went to a convenience store and the cashier didn't know about its market value, you couldn't even buy a soda with the penny because its perceived value – *its intrinsic value* – is one cent.

Similarly, in 2014 a Ferrari 250 GTO sold at auction for almost $40,000,000. What is its intrinsic value? However much you could get for the scrap metal on the commodities market. A few hundred dollars, maybe (this time my friend Pete, an avid car collector, just fell off his chair).

The point is that the intrinsic value and the market value are wildly different, and the only thing propping up the price of the Ferrari and the penny as investment-grade collectibles is whether someone else will come along later and pay that amount for it. If, suddenly, no one cared about the price of the penny as a collectible, it would be worth exactly one penny.

I just mention intrinsic value to contrast collectibles with other investments. Stocks have an intrinsic value – each share has earnings (unless the company is losing money) and might pay you a dividend. The price itself can be much higher (or even lower) than the intrinsic value, but the asset itself has some value. Bonds are the same: bonds carry with them a promise to return your money to you, along with interest. So, it is possible to calculate an intrinsic value.

I will not go into various methods for determining a particular investment's intrinsic value, by the way. That is so far outside the scope of this book that it might as well be in another universe. There are plenty of resources available if you would like to learn more about asset valuation, though (a good starting place is section 332 of your library – "Financial Economics").

Finally, collectibles can have tax disadvantages as well. This applies not only to the sale, but sometimes just to the ownership of certain collectibles. Taxation is state-specific, so you definitely want to check on this aspect. There are people who specialize in this field. If you decide to put any serious money into collectibles, find such a person.

Final Word

Collectibles can be fun to own and look at, and can be a valid part of an investment portfolio. They are probably not going to be a large part of your investment strategy, and come with significant risks. Collectibles' costs and benefits of ownership are more nuanced than other investments, and are in many ways speculative, especially since they usually have very little intrinsic value.

Mind your own Business

What is it?

A lot of people think about owning their own business. The good news about investing in your own business is that you probably don't need a long tutorial on what that means. The idea is simple. You come up with a product and/ or service and start selling it.

Like buying stock, you are investing in a company. Only this time it's *your* company. You own the whole thing (or a large portion, if you have a partner). You become an "entrepreneur," or "person who starts a business."

Businesses are so varied that it would be impossible to go into great detail about all of the possible advantages and disadvantages. I also won't go into the various forms your business can take (many of which are state-specific). Instead, let's look at some of the very basic pros and cons associated with going into business for yourself.

As with all the other investment possibilities discussed in this section, you should do your research before jumping in. This advice is particularly important with a business, where the levels of complexity can become enormous. It is easy to make mistakes after you start and find yourself in over your head financially or legally.

In addition, you will be susceptible to mistakes of omission, where you could be doing things better, if only you knew enough to ask. Well before you begin selling anything, talk to attorneys and accountants specializing in small businesses. You should find out whether your financial advisor has experience working with business owners. If not, find one who does.

Pros
Let's look at some general advantages to owning your own business.

First, owning your own business is "hands on," like real estate investing we discussed earlier. Indeed, if you become a real estate investor, you might very well end up running a regular real estate investment business. The pros (and cons) associated with the hands on aspects of real estate ownership apply to other types of businesses. You also have control over daily operations and don't have to vote on anything if you own it.

You might be interested to learn that owning your own business is one of the most common ways of building great wealth – not just becoming wealthy, but becoming extremely wealthy. If you look at a list of the richest people in the world, most of them earned their money through business ownership (the ones who didn't generally inherited their money – from someone who started a business).

Your business offers the chance for both income and price appreciation. That should be obvious, since we discussed earlier that owning company stock offers the same things, and your business is just a company that you own. Not only can you generate income through your operations (selling your product or service), but you can potentially sell the business (or a piece of it) for a profit.

There are a lot of tax advantages to owning a business. These change frequently, and you should be careful to research the tax implications of business ownership so you don't make mistakes. For example, you can offset your business income with certain business expenses, but you will have to prove how much you spent. If you don't know that in advance and fail to record your qualified expenses, you might lose some of those advantages. An accountant specializing in small businesses can be worth many times her fee in tax savings alone.

Bankruptcy laws allow you to legally discharge your business' debts through an orderly process. The bankruptcy laws are another advantage you'll have as a small business owner. What's that? You think bankruptcy is a bad thing? Consider this: bankruptcy is essentially a built-in insurance policy that limits a business owner's downside.

Imagine yourself in this situation. You start a business with high hopes, but it doesn't go well. You don't get many customers, so you borrow money to invest in the business. Your business still doesn't do well, and now you owe a lot of money to various people – those who lent you money to build the business, people you bought supplies from, the landlord you rent a space from, and so on. These people all sue you.

Do you know what used to happen in some places to people in that situation? They went to debtor's prison where they rotted away until they could pay their debts. Which they couldn't do. Because they were in debtor's prison. Now, however, you (or your company) can declare bankruptcy and have your debts absolved. Your assets are divided up among the lenders, of course, and no one will be lending you money for a while, but it beats debtor's prison.

If people could still land in debtor's prison, how likely do you think they would be to go into business in the first place? Not very. So, bankruptcy laws encourage people to start businesses by limiting their downside. In essence, the legal system provides an insurance policy to backstop entrepreneurs and limit their downside. The social policy behind this is that it's a good thing for people to innovate, so the legal system encourages that through bankruptcy laws. You can still lose most everything you have, but if your business gets too far into the red, you have a way out. That is a big advantage.

Cons

Owning a business isn't all profits and parties. Let's consider the Cons for a moment. I will talk about them a bit more than I did the Pros because most people considering a business already have plenty of ideas about the upside, but need to understand the downside.

Starting and running a business is hard work. It can be all-consuming and drain your energy and interfere with your relationships. People usually start businesses to sell products and services they are passionate about. That is a good thing, but has the potential to become an obsession. If you read interviews with successful entrepreneurs, especially ones who have since retired or stepped away, you will notice a recurring theme of regret about missed time with friends and family while they were running the business. Once that time is gone, you don't get it back. Like we said in Chapter One; time has an essentially infinite value.

Small businesses have a tremendously high failure rate. I have seen various statistics over the years, but anywhere from 80% to 90% of businesses fail in the first couple of years. Keep in mind that, for the remaining 10% to 20%, "succeed" means "don't go out of business." A lot of people thinking about going into business for themselves develop a condition where their pupils are replaced by cartoon dollar signs. Be careful and take a big sip of reality juice. If nothing else, knowing the failure rate will help prevent you from becoming complacent.

If you thought understanding variable annuities was complicated, issues surrounding starting and running a business make them look simple. You will be faced with understanding federal, state, and local regulations governing various aspects (environmental, consumer protection, zoning, insurance, etc.) of whatever industry your business operates in. Federal, state, and local tax rules will vary. You will have to determine what type of "entity" is best for your business: you can establish your business as a sole proprietorship, an LLC, an "S-corporation," a "C-corporation," or other state-specific types, each of which comes with its own requirements, pros, and cons. Business insurance is very different from personal insurance, and has to cover a broader range of risks. You will have to take care of day-to-day operations such as billing, shipping, production, and customer complaints. If your business grows to the point where you need to hire some employees, your complications increase dramatically. There are myriad logistical matters that will come up.

Your business will require upfront costs, so you will either need to save or borrow the money. In addition to hiring professionals to help you establish your business, you might need to rent space, buy raw materials, advertise, pay licensing fees, and spend money on various other startup costs. Entrepreneurs have a tendency to underestimate these costs. You should think through your startup expenses carefully, and then add a cushion for safety. Assume the business won't make money for the first year.

In Chapter One we discussed the idea of Opportunity Costs. In the investing context, that means that money you put into one investment is money you don't have for another investment. Opportunity costs are a big concern. Money you pour into a business is money you don't have to invest in other things like index funds. If you spend money on your business, just be aware that you are choosing not to invest that money in something else.

We talked about the high failure rate of small businesses, but in some ways, a bigger risk is mediocre success. A somewhat successful business can be worse for your long-term financial future than a business failure. People who attain middling success are sometimes tempted to go "all in" and invest more heavily in the business, hoping it will turn a corner. Sometimes they quit their jobs to focus on the business full-time. This can lead to years of lost time and income in a traditional job, and foregone investments. Remember this book's discussion of sunk costs in Lesson Two of Chapter Seven.

It's something to think about if you are planning to go into business for yourself.

Final Word

It is important to understand that a business is an investment just like anything else, although there is no way to discuss small business ownership in any meaningful detail in a book of this scope.

With risk comes potential reward, as we have discussed before. Owning a business is a big risk, but can be extremely rewarding. In many ways, investing in your own business is investing in yourself. There are a lot of advantages, and bankruptcy laws can often prevent you from ending up in a hole from which you can never escape. But, owning a business is a big responsibility, with a lot of potential pitfalls and complications.

The decision to invest in your own business shouldn't be taken lightly. Like any investment, do your research, and consult with professionals, to minimize missteps up front. The best mistakes are the ones you avoid.

Cash is King
What is it?
It might seem odd to talk about cash in the context of investments, but as we will discuss, it has characteristics that fit the definition. I put the discussion of cash at the end of the "investment" section because it is a good segue into the next section about accounts. Namely, our first discussion in the next section will focus on Deposit Accounts, which only hold cash.

First, to be clear, when we talk about "cash," we're not *only* referring to the physical dollar bills in your wallet. Because Economists and finance types are the natural enemy of simplicity, there are various definitions of "cash." For investing purposes, "cash" refers to coins and paper currency, as well as money you have in deposit accounts like checking, saving, and money market accounts (discussed in the next section). Some definitions also include money in government bonds.

The underlying idea is that cash is currency and anything you can quickly turn into currency at rational prices. Government bonds often make the cut because of the "rational price" provision; because government bonds are guaranteed, you can sell them at any time for a stable amount. That is opposed to corporate stock, which can fluctuate wildly.

Just think of cash as money in the bank for purposes of this section.

Cash meets our definition of an investment because it is an asset that you hold that has value and generates income. It can also go up or down in value. Most people get the income-generation part; money in a savings account can generate income through interest. What about the value fluctuations? A dollar is always worth a dollar, right?

The reality is that currency prices go up and down in value all the time, *relative to other currencies*. This fluctuation takes place on the "currency market." Today your 1 United States Dollar (USD) might buy 100 Japanese Yen. Tomorrow that same 1 USD might be worth 105 Yen. The dollar is said to have "appreciated" in value relative to Yen because the dollar buys more Yen. The same thing happens in reverse if the dollar buys 95 Yen the next day; there, the dollar has "depreciated" relative to Yen.

There are actually people who buy and sell currencies to make profit off the difference. Someone buys 105 Yen for 1 USD today and then sells those 105 Yen for more than 1 USD later. This is called "currency arbitrage," it takes place on the "foreign exchange" or "forex" market, and is a form of investing.

I won't bother covering currency trading as a separate investment because it is very complicated and only for investors who like taking a lot of risk. Usually the people who make money trading currencies are professionals working for large companies that specialize in it.

The important thing to note is that cash is not just a boring thing that sits in your bank account; it earns interest and fluctuates in price. Thus, it counts as an investment.

Let's look at some of the pros and cons of cash. We are *not* talking about intentional currency trading here; we are simply talking about pros and cons of hold cash versus other potential investments.

Pros

First, when we discuss advantages of hold cash, we are talking about the advantage of holding cash *instead of* other potential investments. We're obviously not talking about the advantage of having more cash versus less cash; you don't need a book to tell you that.

One advantage cash has over other investments is its liquidity. With other investments like stocks, the liquidity advantage meant that they could quickly and easily be sold to generate currency. Cash is already currency; it's as liquid as you can possibly get.

The liquidity of cash leads to the primary advantage of cash: it represents options. You use cash to buy all of the other investments we talked about. So, in the investing world, cash represents all the investment opportunities you could take advantage of.

Hence the common saying among investors: "cash is king." At no time is that more apparent than in times of crisis. At the height of the Great Recession, investors with cash on hand were able to buy up investments at rock bottom prices. There were also stories of big, seemingly-bulletproof companies that ran low on cash and had to go, hat-in-hand, looking for lenders to tide them over. Those with cash to lend were able to negotiate very favorable terms (along those lines, the investing world also has a "Golden Rule" – "the one with the gold makes the rules").

Cash also lends a measure of security. In Chapter One we discussed the idea of having an emergency fund, or cash on hand, in case something bad happens (like a job loss). When an emergency strikes, it is reassuring to have some money readily-available to get you through. If you have all your money in various investments, you'll have to sell ("liquidate") some in order to raise cash. That might result in negative tax consequences, force you to sell when prices are low, or incur selling costs.

Cons
Cash is not without drawbacks.

Inflation, discussed in Lesson Two of Chapter Three, is cash's worst enemy. Cash in your wallet or in a safe is the worst cash of all because it generates no interest income whatsoever. The value of the money you have in actual, physical cash decreases each year as inflation eats away at it. Cash in deposit accounts (like savings accounts) is better because it earns interest, but that interest is often lower than inflation. It's like one step forward and 10 (or more) steps back.

Cash represents investment options and the cost of holding it is opportunity cost – the money you could be making by investing it. Over the long term, for instance, index funds covering a broad swath of the stock market have earned good, inflation-beating returns. The actual return depends on what time period you're looking at, of course.

Assuming you held cash earning 0% during a time when an index fund could have earned you 8%, your opportunity cost is the 8% difference between what you actually earned and what you could have earned.

Essentially, you can think of that 8% difference as the "fee" you paid for the safety of knowing you couldn't lose your money. But, to return to our earlier inflation discussion, if inflation was even 2%, remember that you actually *did* lose money. You lost 2%. It just doesn't seem like it since it's really your *purchasing power* that has diminished rather than the actual dollar figure in your account.

Finally, if you decide to keep a lot of money in physical cash – actual currency – remember that money can be lost, stolen, burned, chewed up by the dog, and so on.

Final Word

Cash might not seem like an "investment," but it meets the criteria. For investing purposes, cash as a percentage of your overall portfolio will vary over time. A reasonable amount serves as a comforting emergency fund, but cash is susceptible to inflation and the cost of holding it is the opportunity costs of investment returns you could be earning if you successfully deployed it.

Our discussion of cash is a good segue into Part Two of this Appendix.

Part Two: The Container – Accounts

Part One of this Appendix discussed investment *types* – assets you could invest in, like stocks, bonds, real estate, and so on. Part Two (remember when this was a book about biblical parables?) will discuss investment *accounts* – where you put your investments.

For example, if you own stock, you can have it in various different types of accounts. Not every account can hold every type of investment, but in many cases you can choose which type of investments to put in which type of account.

This Appendix will not cover every possible account type, just as it didn't discuss every possible investment type. The idea is just to discuss some of the more common account types and some pros and cons of each, so that you have a basic understanding to guide you and help you ask smart questions.

Deposit Accounts
What are they?

"Deposit Accounts" are the easiest to start with because you are probably already familiar with them. These are the accounts you open at a bank or credit union (we'll just say "bank" for short). Deposit accounts include checking accounts, savings accounts, and money market accounts.

Deposit accounts hold only one type of asset – cash. You can't put real estate, stocks, or bonds into a deposit account. But, as we noted in the previous section, cash is a type of investment, which is why we cover deposit accounts here.

There are three main types of deposit accounts. As the phrase "deposit accounts" implies, you deposit your money into them. The bank administers your account and pays you interest. The bank then loans your money to other customers to make a profit.

You can write checks from your checking account and (to a more limited extent) money market accounts. Money market accounts usually pay a higher rate of interest than savings accounts, which pay a higher rate than checking accounts. The difference between savings and money market accounts is too esoteric and historic to merit discussion here.

Pros

Bank accounts can be insured by the Federal Deposit Insurance Company (FDIC), while credit union accounts can be insured by the National Credit Union Association (NCUA). The FDIC and the NCUA are federal agencies that regulate banks and credit unions, respectively. The FDIC and NCUA also provide insurance on deposits up to a certain amount (currently $250,000 per person, per institution, per account type, but it can change). Most banks and credit unions carry this insurance. Never do business with one that doesn't.

FDIC and NCUA insurance is a huge advantage. If the bank goes out of business, the government will step in and give you your money back. It might take a while, but you'll get your money.

Bank accounts are easy to open and maintain and provide ready access to your money. Checks and check cards let you get to money in your checking account, while savings accounts are easily accessible via Electronic Funds Transfers. Paychecks, tax refunds, and other income streams can be deposited directly into your deposit accounts, and you can pay bills directly from them.

Cons

The main disadvantage of deposit accounts relates to fees. This drawback is not so much with deposit accounts as a category, but with deposit accounts at particular institutions (I'll say "bank" from here on out, but I mean "bank or credit union").

Almost all accounts will have fees, but the types and amounts vary wildly. Some banks charge fees just to *have* the account. Others will waive fees if you keep a minimum amount on deposit. If your deposit goes below a certain amount, the fee suddenly pops up. There is almost always a fee if you overdraw an account (i.e. try to withdraw more than you have on deposit), but the amount varies from bank to bank. Even one fee per year can easily outweigh any interest you earn.

The main takeaway is to research the bank you are doing business with and make sure you understand what fees you are being charged. Look at your statement each month and make sure you don't see anything weird.

It is not unusual for a bank to suddenly start charging a small "maintenance fee" each month. The fee would have been disclosed to you beforehand.

But by "disclosed," I mean it appeared in line 28 of paragraph 16 of the innocuous-looking account update you got in the mail or in an email. If you don't look at your statement, you might not notice the $5 per month that mysteriously starts disappearing from your account.

CDs: Accounts or Investments?
We covered CDs in the "investments" section, but you might be thinking that they sort of function as deposit accounts. After all, you go to a bank, deposit some money into the CD, and the bank holds it for you and pays interest. CDs can only hold cash and are eligible for FDIC or NCUA insurance, just like deposit accounts. Also, CDs will have an "account number" at your bank and the "D" stands for "deposit." So, which is it?

It really doesn't matter how you think of CDs, as long as you understand what they are. But, a CD is really an investment product — a contract between you and the bank. That's why we already talked about CDs in the "Investments" section. But, there's no real harm in thinking about a CD like an account.

Final Word
It is difficult to get by without deposit accounts. They facilitate most aspects of financial life and often serve as the "hub" by which money flows into your life from your income and out into investments and other things. Any deposit account worth having will be insured by either the FDIC or NCUA.

The main drawback lies in fees, and you would do well to research the fee structure carefully before opening an account with any bank. Even after you have an account, monitor it regularly for hidden fees.

Employer-Sponsored Plans: Defined-Benefits
What is it?
"Employer-sponsored" retirement plans come in two basic types: Defined-benefit Plans and Defined-contribution Plans. Let's look first at defined-benefit plans since they are more straightforward.

"Defined-benefit Plans," as the name implies, define at the outset what benefit you will ultimately get from them. The *benefit* (i.e. monthly or annual payment) you get in the future is *defined* up front. The benefit might be a set dollar amount, or (more likely) an amount that varies according to a formula. The "pension plans" we talked about in the previous section are a type of defined-benefit plan. If you have a pension plan, consider yourself fortunate since employers offering these plans are rarer and rarer.

For instance, your pension benefit upon retirement might depend on a formula that considers how long you worked for the company, how old you are when you retire, and the highest amount you earned while working. Pension payments are usually adjust for inflation every year or so.

Because you don't have much control over your pension benefit other than working longer (they're defined benefits, after all), the main advice here is to make sure you understand how the pension formula works. Your HR department can help with this by providing plan documentation. Your monthly amount in retirement might be substantially higher if you work an extra couple of years.

We won't discuss defined-benefit plans in much more detail because you don't pick and choose investments for them. The company itself puts money into investments behind the scenes (or, more likely, hires an investment firm to do it) so it can pay you when you retire. These plans are accounts (you have an account number), but they are unusual because you don't get to decide what your money is invested in and have limited control over how much you eventually get in retirement.

Pros
The primary advantage of defined-benefit plans is that you can estimate up front how much your stream of income will be in retirement. With a pension plan, you know what your annual income will be in retirement, based on how long you work for the company, how old you will be when you retire, and what your salary is when you retire. Someone else (your employer) is doing all of the investing work for you in the meantime.

In addition to knowing how much your annual income will *be*, you know how long it will *last*. Most pensions (like other employer-sponsored defined-benefit plans and Social Security) last for your lifetime. So, there's not much hand-wringing over whether you will live for five years after you retire, or 50.

Most defined-benefit plans let you make provisions for a surviving spouse, in the form of taking a lower payment during your life, such that your spouse gets payments for the remainder of his or her life.

Pension plans remove much uncertainty from retirement planning. It isn't a coincidence that the popularity of personal finance books like this one rose at the same time pension plans are in decline. If you have a generous pension, your retirement planning can be pretty simple – a matter of estimating how much you will get from it in retirement, adding in Social Security, and seeing if there is a shortfall you need to make up.

A huge benefit to pension plans is that they are somewhat insured by a government entity called the "Pension Benefit Guaranty Corporation" (PBGC). I say "somewhat insured" because there is a limit.

Companies can reach out to the PBGC to take over their pension plans. This often happens when companies face bankruptcy, but companies can actually reach out and ask the PBGC take over even if they *can* continue paying pensions. In any case, the PBGC can take over the company's plan and the plans assets and make sure that those collecting pensions get their money (up to a maximum legal amount that can change from year to year).

As of this writing, the PBGC isn't funded by our tax dollars. It gets money from insurance premiums that companies pay, assets collected from companies, its own investments, and other non-tax sources.

Employer-sponsored defined-benefit plans like pensions are a very luxurious retirement benefit to have. However, luxury comes at a price. And, since these plans are "employer" sponsored, the employer pays that price. That is the reason they have become so rare.

Cons and Final Word

There really aren't many disadvantages to employer-sponsored retirement plans like pensions.

One disadvantage is that you usually have to work for the employer in question for a certain number of years before you "vest" (become eligible to receive benefits).

Another disadvantage is in the word "defined." Your benefit is a set amount based on a formula. You don't have much control of your future income stream, unless you work longer or manage to earn a higher salary before retirement.

You also can't control how your pension fund is invested – a trustee or board will do all of the investing behind the scenes. You can get information about how it is invested and will get statements, but you don't have much control over it.

Note that those disadvantages are all in the context of a very employment good benefit that you really don't have to set up or manage. With defined-benefit plans, employers do all of the hard investing work and take much of retirement planning out of the hands of employees. As I said earlier, personal finance books like this one have become popular at the same time that pension plans are in the decline.

Pension plans have largely been replaced by things like the defined-*contribution* plans you will read about next, and *individual* retirement accounts that you will read about after that. That shift cannot be understated; it represented a shift of the burden of retirement planning from employers onto their employees. And employees are (for now) people, very few of whom ever receive even a basic financial education, such as this book's overview.

That is a very unfortunate shift, and many people near retirement are unprepared, and many people who should be planning for their own retirement are not equipped with the knowledge they need to prepare in the first place.

Social Security
I will only talk briefly about Social Security because it is a defined-benefit plan that operates like a pension. Rather than being an employer-sponsored pension, Social Security is a government-sponsored pension that employers are required to help administer on behalf of their employees.

If you have a job, you "contribute" to the Social Security "pension plan" by paying taxes from your paycheck, up to a maximum annual amount. You don't choose whether to pay Social Security taxes. They are deducted automatically from your paycheck. When you retire, you then get a fixed amount of income based on your earnings and age.

Because it is required for anyone with a job, you don't get to choose any investment options, and the benefit is based on a formula, Social Security doesn't merit too much discussion. There isn't much you can control, after all. It is important to mention it after the pension section, though, since it works like a pension and can factor heavily into your future retirement situation. For some, Social Security might be the only income they have in retirement.

There is a lot of concern that Social Security won't not exist in a given number of years. Perhaps. A likelier scenario might be that inflation will have caused the eventual payout to be worth less in real terms. Your guess is as good as mine. Social Security is inflation-adjusted, but that is a year-by-year decision. If you are concerned about your lack of control over Social Security's viability or long-term value, that is all the more reason to focus on investments and accounts that you *can* control.

Numbers and Letters: Employer-Sponsored Retirement Plans
What are they?
Having discussed employer-sponsored defined benefit plans, let's discuss the second type of employer-sponsored retirement plan – the "Defined-Contribution" plan – and the mechanics of some common types.

Defined-contribution plans you might hear about, or have access to, include 401(k), 403(b), 457(b), and TSP plans.

With "defined-contribution" plans, you and your employer are both allowed to contribute money to your account. If your employer contributes, the amount is usually based on how much you contribute, and is limited to a certain percentage. The amount you and your employer can contribute is "defined" in the sense that it is capped by a legal maximum.

Companies can offer 401(k) plans to their employees. Non-profit organizations (including some public schools, religious institutions, and other qualifying tax-exempt entities) can offer 403(b) plans. State and local governments can offer 457(b) plans, as well as non-government, tax-exempt entities. Federal government employees have access to the TSP, which stands for "Thrift Savings Plan."

The crucial thing these all have in common is that they are offered by an *employer* (they are a type of "employer-sponsored" plan, after all).

This isn't a legal textbook by any means, but in case you're interested, the numbers and letters for the first three plans refer to the particular section of the Internal Revenue Code (Title 26 of the U.S. Code) that establishes them. The TSP is created by a separate law (in Title 5). These plans all have to be created by law because, as you will see, many of their benefits would be straight-out tax evasion otherwise. Fortunately, the federal government allows employers to offer these plans to help people legally save more money for retirement than would otherwise be legal.

All of these plans have basic similarities. One primary difference, as discussed above, is that the type of retirement plan your employer is allowed to offer you depends on what kind of organization it is. I will use "401(k)" generally in this discussion, but keep in mind that many of the rules are very similar for all three.

The plan types are *not* equivalent. The 457(b) is the most different. I will provide a brief overview at the end of this "Employer-Sponsored Retirement Plans" section to discuss a few major differences with 403(b) and 457(b) plans. The key is that, if you have access to one of these plans, familiarize yourself with it when (or, better yet, before) you take the job and then keep up with any changes to it throughout your employment.

Now, let's look at one particular form the 401(k) can take: the *Traditional* 401(k).

Defined-Contribution Plans: The Traditional Way

There are two types of 401(k) plans, but let's look at the traditional form first (we'll look at the other type in the next section). For this section, "401(k)" means the "traditional" form, and remember that much of this discussion will help you understand a 403(b), 457(b), or TSP plan if you have access to one.

To take advantage of a traditional 401(k), you first set up an account within your company's plan. Remember, this is just an *account* – not an investment. It sits empty until you contribute money to it. If your company has a plan, it will usually help you set it up when you start working. Sometimes it will automatically open an account for you. If your company has a plan, but you're not enrolled, make haste to the HR department to open one.

After your account is set up, you contribute money from your paycheck into it. These contributions go into your account before you pay taxes on them. Just a note about terms: you "contribute" money to retirement plans, versus "depositing" money like you do with a savings or checking account. It's the same thing, just a different term.

Your employer is also allowed to contribute money to your account. This is optional on the employer's part, but many do. Employers' contributions often match a certain percentage of your own contribution. For example, they will agree to match your contribution to the account, up to 5% of your salary.

You can invest the contributions you make into your account by choosing from a pre-defined list of investment options. You don't have to do this each time you make a contribution; you usually specify what percentage of your contributions should go into which investments. You can change your investments, how your money is allocated among them, and how much you contribute at any time.

Investment options usually include mutual funds that cover a range of investment options like bonds, stock in small companies, stock in big companies, stock in international companies, and so forth. You might also have access to "Lifecycle" mutual funds, which are designed to automatically change their investment mix from stock-heavy to bond-heavy as you approach retirement age (to reduce your risk and potential for loss as you near retirement).

The 401(k) is the account (container) into which you put the investments.

The investments within your 401(k) operate in the same way we discussed in the first part of this Appendix. Remember: the *investments* are the things we talked about previously, like mutual funds. They just grow (or shrink) within your 401(k) account. If things go well, you enjoy compounding returns over the life of your plan. You do not pay taxes until you withdraw the money.

You can start withdrawing money from account after certain events occur. These withdrawals are called "distributions." The most common events allowing you to take distributions are when you reach 59.5 years old or stop working. There are some other conditions when you can make withdrawals, such as a disability, separation from the employer's service, if the plan ends, certain defined "hardships," etc. If you take money out before a qualifying event happens, you'll have to pay a penalty in addition to taxes.

The above paragraph covers when you *can* start withdrawing money. On the flip side, you *must* start withdrawing a certain amount of the money when you reach 70.5 years old (you'll need to consult a financial historian to figure out why the ages are in half-years; I have no idea).

At 70.5, the amount you must withdraw is determined by an IRS formula based on how long they think you'll live (not *you* specifically, but someone like you, based on a life expectancy table). The minimum is called a "Required Minimum Distribution" or "RMD." By the way, you have to start taking RMDs when you turn 70.5 whether you have retired or not. There is a penalty for failing to take all, or part, of your RMD.

Let's consider the pros and cons of the Traditional 401(k) defined-contribution plan.

Pros

Traditional 401(k) plans (and 403(b), 457(b), and the TSP, remember) are a mainstay retirement account with many advantages.

One huge advantage is the company match. Suppose your employer matches your contributions, up to 5% of your salary. If you make $50,000, your employer will put in up to $2,500 each year (5% of $50,000 is $2,500), provided that you contribute at least $2,500.

That's great! Not only are you putting aside money for your retirement, but your employer will actually *pay you* to do so. This is quite literally the equivalent to getting a raise. The only difference is that the raise goes into your retirement account instead of your paycheck. But it is still your money.

There are very few acceptable reasons not to contribute at least enough to your retirement plan to get the match. Even if the investment options available to aren't that great, by investing enough to get the match, you start out with an automatic 100% gain. You won't get that anywhere else, and the investment options would have to be very, very bad for you to lose enough to lose the match. It's like paying with house money.

In our example above, if you make $50,000 and contribute the $2,500 required to get the company match, you end the year with $5,000 even if the investments earn nothing. To repeat, you double your money even if the investments return nothing because your employer matched your contribution.

But what if your employer doesn't match anything? There is still a great reason to invest. Namely, every dollar you invest lowers your taxable income. In Bonus Financial Lesson One of Chapter Six, we talked about marginal tax rates, and how the last dollars you earn are taxed at a higher rate than the first dollars.

A huge tax-related advantage of 401(k) plans is that your contributions go into the account *before* federal or state taxes are taken out of your paycheck. That means you pay less taxes on your income; from the IRS' perspective, it's as if you earned less money for it to tax. Even though, in reality, you still made the money – you just put it into your retirement account.

The above paragraph sounds almost too good to be true. It almost sounds like it should be tax fraud. And it would be, if it weren't for the fact that the federal government specifically made these retirement plans legal. As it is, this tax advantage is not only legal, it's the default way 401(k) plans work. You transfer money from your paycheck to your own 401(k), and the amount you put in reduces the federal income tax you owe that year.

In our $50,000 salary example, if you put the $2,500 aside, your "taxable income" (the amount the IRS requires you to pay taxes on) suddenly becomes $47,500! That's amazing since, in reality, you still actually have the other $2,500 in your retirement account.

The news gets even better since, as we learned in Chapter Six, that $2,500 off the top of your salary would have been taxed at a higher marginal rate than the first $2,500 you earned. So, it's more valuable as a tax benefit. If the marginal tax rate on that last $2,500 were 15%, then you would pay $375 less in taxes. That income you don't pay tax on is, by definition, always the income that would have been taxed at your highest marginal tax rate.

So, to keep track of the magic of the 401(k) plan: you contributed $2,500 and your company matched that with $2,500 in free money. Then, on top of that, you were further rewarded by paying $375 less in taxes than you otherwise would have.

Not to sound like an infomercial, but wait, there's more! Just when you thought the benefits couldn't get better, there is yet another advantage. Namely, your money grows tax free while you have the account and you only pay taxes when you take it out.

A 401(k) is a tax-advantaged account. In a regular taxable account, you pay taxes every year on your earnings. With a 401(k), you do not pay taxes on any earnings (capital gains, dividends, etc.) from the account until you withdraw the money. That is another very valuable advantage. In Lesson One of Chapter Three, we discussed compound growth, and how your returns each year are based on the previous amount in your account. If you pay taxes each year, that lowers the amount in your account to be compounded the following year.

There are other advantages to 401(k) plans related to some clever methods of rolling them into other accounts, timing when you take money out based on money from other accounts, and so on. Such methods are beyond the scope of this book and based on ever-changing tax law. But, you should definitely consult a tax professional or investment advisor as you approach retirement to discuss available options. Better yet, consult experts before throughout your career to learn about things you can do to set yourself up to take advantage of the new tax laws.

Cons

Alas, even the great 401(k) plan has its drawbacks. First, there is no guarantee that your 401(k) balance will go up. Unlike a pension, there is no PBGC to insure your 401(k) balance. Remember: the 401(k) is just an account. Its balance is only as safe as the investments within it, which are usually mutual funds. In order to have a shot at meaningful returns, you will need to take risks as with any mutual fund.

Having said that, the benefits of matching contributions combined with tax advantages combined with tax-free growth give you a big cushion. You have to lose quite a bit to offset those advantages.

Another disadvantage of the 401(k) is that your investment options are limited to what the plan offers. The company you work for will likely not be the one actually administering the plan. Instead, it will hire an outside investment firm to do that for it. That firm will provide an array of investment options for you to pick from. If those options happen to be good, low-cost funds, great. If not, too bad.

When you invest on your own, you can pick and choose whatever investments you want. You can have an index fund from this basket and another one from that basket, an ETF over here and stock in a few individual companies you like from over there, and so on. Your options are almost infinitely customizable. With a 401(k) plan, you only get to choose from a few available options.

Again, the upside of the many advantages will likely outweigh this disadvantage. But it is possible that you find yourself with a 401(k) plan with investment options so poor that you would rather just invest on your own outside of it.

One thing to keep in mind, however, is that you might be able to convince your company to change its plan, especially if you work at a small company. Keep in mind that the company hires the plan administrator. If you notice that your investment options are bad, others might have noticed, too. You might be able to get enough people on your side to convince the executives who hired the plan administrators to switch.

This is not too far-fetched: 401(k) plans are a big part of how companies attract and retain talent. If management discovers that its employees and potential employees are put off by its retirement plan, they might be open to change.

Of course, if you lead the charge to lambast the plan and it happens to be run by the boss' favorite nephew, you might get fired. In which case you'll have to hope you can find another job at company with a better 401(k) plan.

Another disadvantage to 401(k) plans is that there is a maximum amount you are allowed to contribute. At the time of this writing, for instance, you can contribute up to $18,500. Most people don't put that much aside, so this is a theoretical disadvantage for a lot of people. But, it is a cap to keep in mind nonetheless.

Because a lot of people do not have nearly enough saved for retirement, 401(k) rules were changed to allow for "catch-up contributions." These contributions were designed to allow those who were approaching retirement, but who had not put enough money in their 401(k) plans, to "catch up" by contributing extra.

Specifically (as of this writing), people 50 and older can contribute an extra $6,000 to their 401(k) plans, for a total of $24,500 ($18,500 plus $6,000). For those in the 50+ category, this is a definite advantage, though the existence of a limit is still a disadvantage. You can start making catch-up contributions in the year you turn 50; you don't have to wait until your actual birthday. As with any specific numbers you read in this book, do your own research; these limits can (and do) change frequently.

By the way, these contribution limits do *not* include your employer's match; they are what *you* are allowed to contribute on your own. The employer match is extra. There is, however, a maximum overall contribution (yours plus your employers), which can come into play if you happen to have a generous employer and/ or a high enough income. If there were no maximum, you could in theory put all of your income into your 401(k) from the time you started work and never pay a dime in income taxes until 70.5 years old, when you were required to start taking distributions. Assuming you had money coming in from somewhere to live on, that is.

You can withdraw your money on certain conditions (such as turning 59.5 or meeting an exception). It turns out that you actually *can* make withdrawals even if those conditions aren't met, but it comes at a cost. You will have to pay a 10% penalty to do so. The penalty doesn't even bother going by another name. It's just a straight up 10% penalty for the right to access your own money. It is designed to prevent people from taking their money early, but is certainly a disadvantage if you really need to get to your money and an exception doesn't apply.

Another disadvantage is that, at 70.5 years old, you have to start taking required minimum distributions (RMDs). Even though the money might have might have accumulated for a long time, that's still a disadvantage. Anytime you have to do something, your options are limited. The RMD amount will be set for you, based on IRS tables and your account balance, and can have several negative consequences.

First, they will be taxable income, and you will pay tax on the entire distribution (remember, you put pre-tax money into the 401(k), so you haven't paid taxes on it yet). If you had another source of income, you might have to pay higher taxes than you had planned. Second, as soon as you get the distribution, your money is no longer in the tax-advantaged account and you lose the tax-free compounding effects. The party is over.

A big disadvantage of the 401(k) is that the penalty for not taking an RMD makes the penalty makes the early-withdrawal penalty look downright generous. Namely, if you fail to take all, or part, of your RMD, you pay a late-withdrawal penalty of **50%** of the part of the distribution you should have taken.

For example, if you were supposed to take an RMD of $2,000, but didn't take out anything, you pay a $1,000 penalty (50% of $2,000). If you were supposed to take a $3,000 RMD, but only took out $2,000, you pay a $500 penalty (50% of the $1,000 difference between the $3,000 you were supposed to withdraw and the $2,000 you actually withdrew).

The good news is that the RMDs are not a secret. The IRS publishes the tables every year and your 401(k) plan administrator will usually provide some guidance as well. There's no reason for your RMD to be a surprise if you take the time to research it, nor should you fail to take it.

Even with all the tax advantages we talked about, you still have to pay taxes eventually. When you do take your distributions, whether you take them as soon as you can at 59.5, or whether you wait as long as possible and take them at 70.5, you will pay income taxes. That's only fair. After all, remember that you didn't pay taxes on that income when you first put it into the account. You already enjoyed the tax advantages in the form of lower income taxes and tax-free compounding returns.

The key to note here is that you pay income taxes on your *entire* distribution – not just the earnings on your contributions. You didn't pay income taxes on any of your contributions, just like you didn't pay any taxes on dividends or capital gains along the way, so you are paying taxes for the first time when you take distributions.

A final note I will put in the "Cons" section is that you can take a loan from your 401(k). The "loan" isn't really a "loan" since you are taking money from yourself. And the "interest" you pay back is really money you pay into your own account. It can have some positive aspects and some might consider it an advantage. But, there can be drawbacks.

The biggest downside to a 401(k) loan is that you are taking money out of your investment portfolio. That's money that isn't compounding for you, tax-free. And, if your investments do well, you miss those gains. For those who take 401(k) loans to buy consumer goods like cars or vacations, the foregone investment gains are a high price to pay for a depreciating or short-term asset. The amount you can borrow is capped as well. On the other hand, you are borrowing money from yourself and paying it back to yourself, so there are some situations where taking a 401(k) loan can be an advantage. Just be careful.

Defined-Contribution Plans: the Roth Way

We will cover the "Roth 401(k)" in this section, separate from the above section about the "Traditional" 401(k) discussion. Now that you understand traditional 401(k) rules, the Roth version's differences will be easy to understand.

Again, this discussion will help you understand other, similar, accounts, such as the 403(b), 457(b), and TSP. The section before the "Final Word" below explains a few major differences.

A company that offers a 401(k) plan usually has both traditional and Roth options, and it's up to you to choose which kind of account you want. "Roth" is not an acronym; it is a last name – not of the famous musician, but of the senator who was a primary proponent of this savings method.

The main difference between the traditional 401(k) and the Roth 401(k) is the tax treatment. The Roth 401(k) is funded with *after-tax* income, versus the traditional 401(k), which you fund with *pre-tax* income. In other words, if you sign up for the Roth 401(k), your paycheck comes in, your company takes taxes out of it, and *then* the company puts your 401(k) contribution into your account and your chosen investments. This means that you pay taxes as usual on your income when you receive it.

There are no income limits determining whether you can participate in a Roth 401(k). The contribution limits are the same for Roth 401(k)s as they are for the traditional versions.

After the money is in your account, you invest it in various assets, usually mutual funds, just like with the traditional 401(k). Also like the traditional 401(k), your investments within the Roth 401(k) grow tax-free.

Here's the big difference: you do not pay taxes at all when you eventually take distributions from a Roth 401(k). You already paid your income taxes on your contributions up front when you first earned the money. But, not only can you take out your original contributions tax-free, any money earned is also tax-free. You don't pay taxes on either the contributions you put in or the earnings you (hopefully) made along the way. Your income tax advantage comes at the back end instead of the front end.

Tax-free earnings are an interesting advantage to the Roth 401(k) – remember that the Traditional 401(k) *does* require you to pay taxes on the earnings (and contributions, of course, since they weren't taxed initially).

One key difference to the Roth 401(k) is that you can withdraw your *contributions* early (before you are 59.5 or meet another exception) without paying taxes or a penalty. That is very unlike the traditional version, where you'd have to pay taxes and a 10% penalty. The reason for this difference is that you already paid taxes on the Roth 401(k) contributions. That is your money. Note, though, that if you withdraw more than your contributions – any of your earnings – you *will* have to pay taxes on those earnings and a 10% penalty.

Even though you are allowed to take early withdrawals of contributions from your Roth 401(k) without paying taxes and penalties, you should only do so if you have a very good reason. When you withdraw money, remember that there is still an opportunity cost. Namely, the tax-free compounding returns that your withdrawal could have earned over years or decades to come.

The Roth 401(k) has minimum distribution requirements just like traditional 401(k)s. At 70.5, you must start taking distributions (RMDs) from your account. These aren't quite as bad for the Roth version since you don't have to worry about paying taxes. But, you still have the disadvantage of losing the favorable year-over-year tax-free compounding that you get within the account. And don't forget the **50%** penalty for the portion of your RMD you fail to take – that applies with Roth 401(k)s as well.

Which one is better – a traditional 401(k) or the Roth version? The answer depends on your situation. Generally, a traditional 401(k) is better for people who will be in a lower tax bracket when they retire. That way they get the big tax advantage now, while they have higher incomes and income tax rates. When they retire, they hope to pay lower taxes on their withdrawals based on their lower income tax.

Conversely, the Roth 401(k) is generally better for those will be face *higher* tax rates in retirement. The idea is that you should pay the lower taxes now and avoid paying higher taxes later.

The inherent problem with this tax logic (for both groups) is twofold. First, those who bother estimating their retirement income sometimes misjudge how large it will be. They might end up earning more or less than they anticipated, rendering their calculations incorrect. For instance, they might underestimate how large the required minimum distributions will be, or how much they will get from Social Security.

Second, the government can change taxes anytime it wants. People who choose Roth 401(k) accounts often do so to mitigate the risk that income taxes will be much higher in the future than they are at the present. "Better the tax devil you know than the one you don't." Assuming the government honors its promise to not tax Roth 401(k) income in the future, this logic is sound.

But, it does not consider the possibility that the government will institute a separate tax, such as a "wealth tax" that isn't technically an income tax, but takes some of the money anyway. So, some like the Traditional versions because you get a definite tax break up front. "A tax bird in the hand is worth many in the distant future."

In the end, the future is always uncertain, and you don't know what will happen. But, at least you can understand the rules and make an informed decision about your best guess for the future. The good news is that you get the same tax-free growth of your investments with a Roth 401(k) as you do with a traditional 401(k), so there is no difference there.

Both traditional and Roth 401(k) accounts are much better than nothing. They both offer a perfectly legal way to lower your taxes (through deferment and avoidance) while saving for your future self.

Rolling Over (But not Playing Dead)

Another advantage of various accounts, including 401(k) accounts, is the ability to "roll them over" or "do a rollover." The advantage is important enough to merit its own section. We will discuss it here, since it naturally follows the 401(k) section, but it applies to some other types of accounts as well, such as the IRAs discussed below. You can perform a rollover with either a Traditional or Roth version.

The idea of rolling over comes into play when you transfer money from one retirement plan to another. You might do this when you switch jobs, for instance, and want your retirement money all in one place. When you switch jobs, you can roll your money from the old 401(k) account to the new one very easily. You just fill out a form or two that your HR person can provide.

The reason this is an advantage, and the reason it merits its own section, is that when money rolls over from one tax-advantaged account to another, it is always in a tax-advantaged account and you never have direct access to it. Why is that important? Remember that you have to pay any applicable taxes on 401(k) earnings when you receive them, along with a 10% early withdrawal penalty if you are younger than 59.5 and don't meet any other exceptions.

If it weren't for the rollover option, you'd have to get the money from one account and then send it to the new account. That would trigger the taxes and penalties. The rollover allows the money go seamlessly from one retirement account to another, and you avoid those taxes and penalties. So, if you are going from one job to another, think twice before just taking the money out of your account.

If you *do* somehow end up getting your 401(k) money sent directly to you (i.e. transferred into your bank account), you can undo it if you act quickly. See a tax accountant who can help you fill out the required paperwork.

Key Differences between 401(k), 403(b), and 457(b) Plans
Despite broad similarities, 401(k), 403(b), and 457(b) plans are not identical. A detailed discussion of these differences would quickly get us much further into the weeds than I plan to go. Many provisions vary from plan to plan. This section will cover some important differences to know about if you have a 403(b) or a 457(b). It will not cover the TSP for federal employees, which is very similar to 401(k) plans, and whose differences are in details too specific for this book.

As noted at the outset of the discussion of employer-sponsored plans, companies can offer 401(k) plans to their employees. Non-profit organizations (including some public schools, religious institutions, and other qualifying tax-exempt entities) can offer 403(b) plans. State and local governments can offer 457(b) plans, as well as non-government, tax-exempt entities. 457(b) plans actually come in two varieties – governmental and non-governmental.

You'll notice that both 403(b) and 457(b) plans contain wording about qualifying, non-government, tax-exempt agencies. There is some direct overlap; any entity that meets certain qualifications can offer its employees either one. Indeed, some employees have access to both a 403(b) *and* a 457(b) plan.

That overlap can be very important. If you have access to a 457(b) plan in addition to a 403(b) or 401(k) plan, you can contribute the maximum allowable to the 403(b) or 401(k), as well as the maximum allowable to the 457(b). Note that you can't contribute the maximum to all three – just the 457(b) plus the 403(b)/ 401(k) limit.

A single investment company manages a 401(k) plan for an employer. But, multiple investment companies can manage 403(b) and 457(b) plans. This can be an advantage for employees with access to those plans because they have more options when choosing where to put their money. There are more investment firms to choose from, and, consequently, more investment options.

Both Traditional and Roth versions are available for 403(b) and 457(b) plans, and the general tax differences regarding when you pay taxes are the same as with 401(k) plans. Like any plan, the employer decides what to offer. Just because both versions are *available* doesn't mean that a particular plan will have them.

Employers can offer matching contributions into 457(b) plans, but often do not. Any employer contribution counts toward the overall limit. That's a big difference from 401(k) and 403(b) plans. At current $18,500 limits, if your employer contributed $2,000 into your account, you could only contribute $16,500.

Part of the reason 457(b) plans rarely come with an employer match is that employees with these plans are more likely to have access to a pension plan to supplement their retirement income. Those with 403(b) plans are also more likely to have access to a pension plan, though employer-matching contributions are not as rare.

Governmental 457(b) plans have the usual catch-up contribution provisions that we saw with 401(k) plans, for employees fifty and older. Both governmental and non-governmental 457(b) plans also have a special catch-up provision, but it can be complicated to understand. The IRS calls this the "last 3-year catch-up," and applies if you have a minimum retirement age.

In the three years before your minimum retirement age, you can make a catch-up contribution that is twice the annual 457(b) limit (as of this writing, that's $18,500 x 2 = $37,000), *or* your annual 457(b) limit plus amounts that you were allowed to contribute in prior years, but that you didn't. You can only use this special catch-up provision if you are not taking the standard catch-up for being fifty or older (recall that the standard catch-up is only available for the government version of a 457(b)).

I told you it was complicated. Your plan will help you calculate your catch-up if you have it; the important thing is to remember that 457(b) plans have a special catch-up limit that can apply.

Some 403(b) plans offer an extra catch-up on top of the standard fifty-and-older catch-up. This additional catch-up provision is available for people with 15 years or more of eligible service (it's called a "15-year catch-up"), and whose plans allow it. As of this writing, the 15-year catch-up is capped at $3,000, but it's on top of the regular $6,000 catch-up for those fifty years old and older.

Distribution rules are different for 457(b) plans. Unlike 401(k) and 403(b) plans, 457(b) plans do *not* have early-withdrawal penalties if you leave your job. You still pay any applicable taxes, of course, but you don't pay an extra penalty, even if you're younger than 59.5. That's a nice advantage. On the downside, some tax-free early-withdrawal provisions (such as "hardship withdrawals") are harder to get in 457(b) plans.

If you still work for the employer that offered you the 457(b) plan, you can't take distributions until age 70.5 without paying a penalty. But, as noted above, you can take distributions without penalty at any age if you leave the employer.

There are various other differences between 403(b), 457(b), and 401(k) plans as well, but they are too involved for an overview discussion like this. The primary point, regardless of what kind of plan you have, is to familiarize yourself with its rules, terms, and provisions. You want to know the advantages so you can capitalize on them, as well as the disadvantages so you can avoid, or mitigate, them.

Final Word

Employer-sponsored retirement plans are the foundation of many people's retirement planning. While pension plans are on the decline, 401(k) (and equivalent) plans have become a cornerstone of retirement planning. If you are fortunate enough to work for an employer that offers a 401(k) plan, you should almost always take advantage of it, at least contributing enough to get any matching contributions from your employer. There are virtually no scenarios where it is to your advantage to contribute less than the company match to a 401(k) plan.

401(k) plans are just tax-advantaged accounts into which you put investments, and those investments will be limited to your particular plan's offerings. All of the pros and cons specific to those types of investments (usually mutual funds) apply, particularly the risk of loss.

403(b) and, to a greater extent, 457(b) plans, have different provisions from 401(k) plans. But, an understanding of how 401(k) plans work, and the differences between Traditional and Roth versions will make you much more equipped to understand the specifics of such a plan, if you have access to one.

For all the bad press it gets, you should at least factor Social Security into your retirement planning, if only to discount its value, explicitly assume it away, or use your concerns about it as motivation to create your own future income stream.

IRAs: The Do-it-Yourself Retirement Plan

What are they?

Now that we have discussed 401(k) plans in the previous section, Individual Retirement Accounts (IRAs) will be easier to understand.

First, remember that we are in the "Accounts" section of the Appendix, so IRAs are accounts into which you put investments. Rather than opening these accounts through your employer, however, you open them on your own (as the "I" in "IRA" suggests) through an investment company (a brokerage or the investment side of a bank, for instance).

Like 401(k) plans, IRAs come in two flavors — Traditional and Roth. Since they are similar to their 401(k) counterparts that we talked about in the previous section, let's compare and contrast both in one section rather than devote a section to each.

The traditional IRA works like the traditional 401(k): you get a tax deduction up front on the money you contribute, but pay taxes when you take it out. The Roth IRA works like the Roth 401(k): you put after-tax money into the account, but then the withdrawals are tax-free (assuming you meet the age requirements, or an exception). Also like the Roth 401(k), you can withdraw your *contributions* early from a Roth IRA without penalty or paying taxes.

One difference between a Traditional IRA and a Traditional 401(k) is the logistics for getting your up-front tax advantage. With a 401(k), your employer takes your contributions out of your paycheck before applying taxes. So, when you file your federal and state taxes, your taxable income is already lowered to reflect the pre-tax contributions.

But, with a traditional IRA, there's no employer to take the money out up front, so you have to enter your contributions as a line item on your taxes and deduct them from your gross income. This is an "above-the-line deduction," which just means it applies whether you itemize your deductions or claim the standard deduction. The effect is the same as with the 401(k); the IRA just requires you (or your accountant) to do the work. Remember, the "I" in IRA means you're responsible, not an employer.

Within both IRA types, you can invest your money into mutual funds and so forth, and, like with 401(k)s, those investments grow tax-free in your account until you withdraw them.

You can start taking distributions from both types of IRA, tax and penalty-free, at 59.5 years old (or when certain exceptions apply to you). With the Traditional IRA, you will then pay taxes on your withdrawals (the entire amount). With a Roth IRA, you will pay no taxes on your withdrawals at all (neither your original contributions nor the earnings).

One wrinkle for the Roth IRA is that your first contribution to the account must have been at least five years before your first distribution. If you haven't held the Roth IRA account for five years, but are 59.5 or older, you pay taxes on the earnings (but not penalties). If you've had the account less than five years and are under 59.5, you'll pay both a 10% penalty and taxes on the earnings, unless an exception applies to you.

You must take at least the required minimum distributions (RMDs) from a *Traditional* IRA beginning at age 70.5. And, the same **50%** late-withdrawal penalty that applied to 401(k)s applies to the amount of a traditional IRA's RMD you fail to take.

The Roth IRA does *not* require you to take distributions within your lifetime and your heirs can take the distributions over the course of many years. The Roth IRA is the only one of the four types of plans we are talking about (Traditional 401(k), Roth 401(k), Traditional IRA, and Roth IRAs) that does *not* require you to take required minimum distributions. Because there are no RMDs, there are no late-withdrawal penalties.

The same wrinkle related to the five-year account age we talked about above applies to the Roth IRA even if you are 70.5. If you take distributions at 70.5 or older from a Roth IRA, but the account is less than five years old, you pay taxes (but not penalties) on the earnings. If you're over 70.5 and you've held the account for five or more years, you pay no taxes at all on the Roth IRA (which should be obvious, since if you're over 70.5, you are also over 59.5, which is when you can start taking tax-free withdrawals).

A big difference between 401(k) plans and IRAs (both traditional and Roth) is the contribution limit. You can put much smaller amounts into

IRAs. At the time of this writing, the maximum contribution for each is $5,500, with an additional $1,000 catch-up contribution for those 50 and over. As with any specific numbers in this book, the amounts change from time to time, though, so be sure to check before you contribute.

Although you can contribute to both a Roth and a Traditional IRA, your total overall contribution cannot be more than the single limit. Given a $5,500 limit; you'd have to divide the $5,500 up between the two. There are some restrictions on whether you can contribute as well, discussed below.

Pros and Cons

Because IRAs are so similar to 401(k) plans, we've already covered many of the general pros and cons of each above. Rather than reiterate, let's just look at some specific differences and pros and cons. Remember, the rules and numbers I cite here can (and do) change over time, do some research for yourself to make sure you act with current information.

You can contribute to both a 401(k) and an IRA, and you can combine those two amounts. So, at the time of this writing, those under 50 can contribute a maximum of $18,500 to a 401(k) and $5,500 to an IRA, for a total of $24,000 for that year. Catch-up contributions for those over 50 for each plan raise the total even higher: as of this writing, an extra $6,000 catch-up for 401(k) plans and an extra $1,000 catch-up for IRAs brings the total annual contribution limit to $31,000).

There are some caveats.

Anyone younger than 70.5 years old can contribute to traditional IRA, but your ability to take an income tax deduction on those contributions depends on how large your income is, and whether you have access to a 401(k) account. If you (and your spouse) do *not* have access to a 401(k), then you can contribute the maximum to a traditional IRA and take the full tax deduction, regardless of your income.

If you or your spouse *do* have access to a 401(k), then there are income limits that determine whether you can contribute to a traditional IRA. The limits are fairly high, but are definitely something to watch out for. I won't bother listing the current limits here, because they not only change each year, but also depend on your tax filing status (single, married, married filing jointly). They are very easy to look up, though. Even if your income is on the high side, the amount you can contribute to a traditional IRA doesn't suddenly drop from the maximum to $0. Instead, it gradually "phases out," so you might still be able to contribute something.

An important, but often overlooked, feature of the traditional IRA is that you can *contribute* the maximum amount to it and get the advantage of tax-free growth regardless of your income. It's the ability to *deduct the contributions* on your taxes that phases out with income. Some people mistakenly believe that their ability to contribute disappears as income increases.

Roth IRAs have no age restrictions on contributions, but there *are* income restrictions. You can only contribute to a Roth IRA if your income is below certain limits. Your ability to contribute to a Roth IRA gradually "phases out" as your income rises above a certain threshold, until it goes away.

As noted above, you must have owned a Roth IRA for at least five years before you get the advantage of tax-free Roth IRA withdrawals. That is an odd rule, but it means that, even if you are 59.5 years old (making you eligible for tax-free withdrawals), your first contributions to the Roth IRA must have been at least five years before your first withdrawal. The same rule applies even if you are 70.5.

If you do not have an employer that offers a 401(k) plan, an IRA is a substitute. Granted, it is not a perfect substitute, given the lower contribution maximums, but it is much better than nothing. Note that you must have "earned income" to contribute. If you have a job, that's earned income. The IRS uses the phrase to distinguish job income from things like dividends, interest, and income from other investments.

There are also many clever strategies related to IRAs and Roth IRAs, some of which can include what to do with your 401(k) account when you retire. Particular strategies like the ones I refer to are a definite advantage of IRAs, but are too intricate to discuss in an overview-style book like this one, though I encourage you to look into the possibilities. Creativity in investing often relies on the account structure you build (along with the ownership structure, as discussed in the Trusts section in Chapter One), and can greatly improve your financial picture (assuming you stay on the right side of the IRS). This is the type of area where proactive discussions with tax professionals can be very valuable.

An advantage of IRAs is that you are not limited by the investments offered by a company's plan administrator. You can pick and choose your investments and enjoy all of the tax advantages provided by the IRA (provided all activity takes place within the account; the moment you take money out of the account, it counts as a distribution and relevant taxes and penalties apply).

Because they aren't limited to company offerings, some people try to put very unusual things into IRAs. Remember, an IRA is simply an account – a container for investments. Thinking outside the box can be a good idea, but if you plan to put unusual (i.e. investments other than stocks, bonds, mutual and index funds, ETFs) into an IRA, you should run it by an accountant or tax attorney first, for two reasons.

First, the unusual circumstances often raise red flags for the IRS (worried that you might be pushing the bounds of the law too far). It's never good to be on the IRS' radar. Second, even if your idea is legal, it might not be as advantageous as you think, and could even have negative consequences (i.e. if you put an asset into an IRA and then are unable to sell it to someone else without triggering an unplanned tax bill).

Another big advantage to IRAs is that they qualify for the same rollover options discussed in the previous section about 401(k) accounts. Namely, you can roll money from one IRA into a different one. That is an advantage because it means you are not locked into doing business with any one company that happens to have your IRA. If you have an account with a company, but don't like their customer service or fees, you can roll your account over into an account with a different company without being subject to early withdrawal penalties and income taxes.

In addition, you can roll money over from a 401(k) into an IRA. That might make sense if you are leaving your company to work for yourself, or leaving a company with a 401(k) to work for a company without a 401(k), and don't want to leave your money with the old company. Or, you could just be retiring and want to move your money into an account that you have more control over. Rather than needing to take the money out of your 401(k), you can fill out a form or two and have the money sent directly into an IRA, avoiding taxes and penalties.

IRAs for Non-Traditional Employment
Let me very briefly discuss one final type of IRA for those who are self-employed and/ or small business owners. This is worth mentioning due to the growing number of people who own their own business or have non-traditional employment like freelance work.

There are two IRA account types you might want to consider. One is a "SIMPLE IRA" ("SIMPLE" is an acronym; I'm not yelling at you) and the other is as "Self-Employed Pension IRA" or (SEP-IRA).

Either of those types of accounts can potentially be beneficial, depending on factors like your expenses and whether your business employs other people. Either of these can potentially offer you some tax benefits for things you are doing, or planning to do, anyway, and are worth looking into.

Final Word
IRAs have much in common with 401(k) accounts. You can invest in IRAs in addition to, or instead of, a 401(k) plan, and they can also serve as a partial substitute for a 401(k) plan. Although the contribution limits are lower and there are income limits that determine whether you can even invest in IRAs, you have much more flexibility in determining what to invest in.

Health Savings Accounts: Stealth-Mode, Tax-Free Retirement Accounts

What are they?
Health Savings Accounts (HSAs) are an interesting type of account that more and more people are starting to use. HSAs, as the name suggests, are designed to help people save for health care. This isn't a book about health insurance, and I wouldn't go into much detail about these plans except for the fact that they provide unique tax advantages and can be used as "stealth" retirement accounts that let you legally avoid paying taxes altogether.

I also simply must cover this account type because it offers the absolute best of all worlds that we will discuss. HSAs let you put aside tax-free income, compound it tax-free, and then use it tax-free. To reiterate: HSAs are a perfectly legal way to avoid ever paying any taxes whatsoever on a portion of your income.

In order to have an HSA, you must first have a high-deductible health insurance plan (HDHP). In order to qualify as a HDHP, the health insurance plan must meet certain "deductible" and "out-of-pocket maximum" requirements.

We talked a bit about insurance in Chapter One, and how a deductible is the amount you pay before your insurance starts to pay. Once insurance starts to pay, you might be responsible for a certain amount, or percentage, of future additional costs, up until you hit a maximum amount. That maximum amount you can be required to pay is called the "out-of-pocket maximum." If a health insurance plan has sufficiently-high deductibles and out-of-pocket maximum amounts, it qualifies as a high-deductible health plan (HDHP).

The qualifying amounts change each year, and depend on whether you have a plan that covers a single person or a family.

HDHPs usually cost less than traditional insurance policies, but that's because you are responsible for a lot more of your health insurance costs each year before insurance pays. People generally use HDHPs when they plan to pay for their own medical needs unless something really bad happens. Sometimes these are called "catastrophic plans."

So, for a typical HDHP, you pay quite a bit for doctors' visits, medicines, procedures, and other medical costs each year, until you hit the deductible. Once you hit that deductible, the insurance company will help pay a certain percentage of the next amount of costs, until you hit a still-higher amount (the out-of-pocket maximum). At that point, the insurance company pays for the rest of your covered costs for the remainder of the year.

Having explained what HDHPs are, we can now get on to how they relate to HSAs and why we're talking about them in a personal finance book.

Once you have an HDHP, you can open an HSA. An HSA is an account – we're still in the Accounts section of this Appendix. An HSA can either be employer-sponsored (you open it through your job) or individual (you open it on your own).

An HSA starts out working very much like the Traditional IRA we discussed earlier. You start out by putting aside pre-tax (federal and state) income into the HSA account. If you have an employer-sponsored HSA, your company will automatically deduct your contributions from your income for tax-reporting purposes. If you have an individual HSA, you will enter your contributions as an above-the-line deduction when you do your taxes.

Unlike 401(k) plans and IRAs, you aren't even required to have "earned income" as defined by the IRS to contribute. In other words, even if all your money comes from things like interest, dividends, or investment income, you can still contribute to an HSA.

The maximum amount you are allowed to contribute is set by law and can change each year. But, those 55 and older can make catch-up contributions in addition to their regular contributions. This is just like 401(k)s and IRAs, too, except you'll find that the contribution limits are lower. You can contribute to an HSA in addition to a 401(k) and an IRA.

You contribute cash to your HSA. After that, it depends on your plan. Many plans let you invest the cash into various things, such as mutual funds, just like an IRA or 401(k). Also like an IRA or 401(k), the money in your HSA grows, tax-free, until you withdraw it.

Here's where things get interesting.

If your withdrawals are used for medical expenses, regardless of your age or when you withdraw them, you don't pay taxes on the contributions or the investment gains. The list of qualified medical expenses changes each year (they are described in section 213(d) of the Internal Revenue Code), but the plan itself usually maintains an updated list you can refer to.

You get a card – like a debit card – or a checkbook with your account. When you have medical expenses, you can use this debit card or checkbook to pay for them. These payments are sort of like making a withdrawal or taking a distribution from your account, but you don't pay taxes on them.

If you withdraw money for non-medical expenses before turning 65, you will pay taxes on it, plus a 20% penalty. If you are 65 or older when you withdraw money for non-medical expenses, you don't pay a penalty, but you still owe taxes.

There is no minimum age at which you have to take HSA distributions, and you don't have to get it at all. You can instead leave it to your heirs.

Pros

Where to start? The HSA offers almost unbelievable advantages. When I first learned of about it, I assumed I had misunderstood something. Further research verified that they are not too good to be true. They are so good that I assumed the federal government would quickly rescind the law that made them legal, once it realized the loophole it had created. So far so good, though (at the time of this writing).

First of all, this section referred to HSAs as a "stealth" retirement account that lets you avoid taxes altogether. The stealthy part stems from the fact that your contributions can stay in your account year-over-year, and that some plans let you invest that money in mutual funds until you use it. So, even though it is an account for *medical* expenses, it works exactly like an account you might invest in for retirement.

The tax-free part is threefold. First, you put tax-free money into the account. Second, it grows tax-free. Both of those are just like a traditional IRA. Third, when you take money out for medical expenses, it is *also* tax-free – like the *Roth* IRA. That's the big difference. With every other retirement account, you eventually have to pay the piper (the IRS is the piper in my metaphor). With Roth 401(k)s and Roth IRAs, you pay taxes up front. With traditional 401(k)s and traditional IRAs, you pay taxes on withdrawals. With HSAs, you *never* pay taxes, as long as you withdraw money for medical expenses.

That's huge. Note one important detail. To serve as a stealth retirement account, you need to use an HSA that allows for investments, rather than simply cash or low-rate interest.

If you are in relatively good health, you can put money into an HSA, invest it, and let it compound year over year, paying for your health needs out-of-pocket. Then, in retirement you can use the HSA balance, which has (hopefully) grown to a much larger amount, to pay for medical expenses you would be paying for anyway. I have seen various estimates, but the general consensus seems to be that the average retiree will spend over $200,000 on medical expenses in retirement.

So, think of an HSA as a retirement account for a specific *part* of your retirement. You can spend your HSA money on the inevitably-large medical expenses that come with aging, while spending money from your other retirement savings accounts on non-medical expenses (vacations, exotic teas, components for the doomsday device you're building in your basement, etc.).

Another advantage of HSAs is that a lot of expenses qualify as medical expenses for purposes of tax-free withdrawals. The list of what qualifies changes each year, though it seems to become ever more expansive, not less. As mentioned above, your plan will probably provide you with an updated list of expenses each year, but even things like nursing homes are now covered. Given the high costs of nursing homes, you can imagine using this as a way to provide your own long-term care insurance.

HSAs can be individual or employer-sponsored. That advantage gives you flexibility. If your employer does not offer one, or if you don't like the one it offers, you can find a different provider with terms you like better.

There are no income limits on an HSA, which is an advantage for those whose incomes are too high for tax advantages on IRAs.

Finally, you can choose a beneficiary to inherit the funds in your HSA when you die. If you happen to choose your spouse as your beneficiary, your spouse can continue using the account as an HSA and the same rules apply to him or her that apply to you. Your spouse can use the funds, tax-free, for medical expenses (and is subject to the same penalties and taxes for non-medical withdrawals).

You can name a beneficiary other than your spouse on the HSA if you want. If you do, though, the account is essentially liquidated as soon as you die, and the beneficiary gets whatever its worth. And they have to pay taxes on it. They can pay for your final medical expenses out of the balance, tax-free, though.

You might have heard of a "Flexible Spending Account" (FSA) and wonder how they compare to HSAs. FSAs let you put money aside, tax-free, to pay for medical expense. But, the key difference is that the balance of an FSA does *not* roll over from year to year, and you can't invest it in anything. An FSA is certainly a weapon in your retirement arsenal; it does let you reduce your taxes for medical expenses. But if an FSA is a slingshot, an HSA is a bazooka.

Cons

The main drawback to an HSA is that you have to use it for health-related reasons in order to get the full tax benefits. So, if you have the "bad luck" to be in good health in your old age, you might not have enough medical expenses to use the balance.

Even this negative aspect has a silver lining. As described above, if you die and leave the plan to your spouse (i.e. in your Will, described in Chapter One), your spouse gets the balance tax-free to use for medical expenses. Anyone else who gets it will have to pay taxes.

Another important drawback to HSAs is that they can be expensive. That is true in two ways. First, they can have relatively high fees. A more notable and practical expense, though, is that you need a high-deductible health insurance plan (HDHP) to qualify for an HSA, The key word being "high." By signing up for an HDHP, you do so with the understanding that you must pay for quite a bit of your medical expenses out of pocket before you can use the HSA's funds.

What qualifies as "high" changes each year, but it's on the order of several thousand dollars as of this writing. That means you will potentially be liable for thousands of dollars each year while building up your HSA. You might be in good health when you start it, thinking how smart you are, only to be unexpectedly hospitalized and get a crash course of how fast medical expenses add up.

Of course, many people sign up for HSAs in order to use them as stealth retirement accounts. If you're in that group, you have no intention of using HSA funds for medical expenses until you are in retirement and have accrued a large balance. After all, you want the HSA money to roll over year after year, compounding tax-free.

If you use the HSA as a stealth retirement account, you already plan to pay for your medical expenses out of pocket anyway and aren't bothered by the high costs. You're essentially trading potentially-high medical costs now for the compounding and tax advantages of the HSA that will benefit you later.

Having read the above paragraphs, you will understand a common criticism of the HSA: namely, that they benefit young, healthy, high-earners the most. The underlying facts of that are certainly true. Young people are more likely to be healthy than older people, and will have longer for HSA funds to compound until they need them. Healthy people of any age will also benefit more because they will not be paying the high deductibles and high out-of-pocket expenses that sicker people will pay. And, those with higher incomes are more likely to be able to take advantage of HSAs because they are better able to afford both the higher medical expenses associated with HDHPs, and to make contributions to HSAs in the first place.

My main response to the above would be to say that all retirement accounts, and most aspects of personal finance (even the mathematics of compounding, and life in general), benefit young, healthy high-earners. This is not a book about social commentary or subjectivity on what rules should apply. Rather, it is a book of facts. And, as of now, HSAs are an excellent, legal investment account.

The relatively low contribution limits are a disadvantage. As of this writing, you can't contribute as much to an HSA as you can to an IRA or a 401(k). But, the tax advantages help make up for that, along with the lack of income limitations and the fact that you can have an HSA in addition to 401(k)s and IRAs. In fact, given the tax advantages, some people *prefer* funding an HSA before an IRA. Again, this goes back to the idea of using the HSA as a "stealth" retirement plan, rather than as a vehicle to pay for medical expenses early on.

Penalties and taxes are always negatives, but even these have an advantageous aspect with HSAs. Recall that there's a 20% penalty for non-medical-related withdrawals before you're 65, plus you have to pay taxes. That sounds tough – 401(k)s and IRAs only have a 10% early-withdrawal penalty. But, with HSAs, the 20% penalty disappears after you turn 65, and you only have to pay taxes on non-medical withdrawals. In other words, it operates just like a traditional IRA after you're 65, so the "H" in the HSA is no longer that big of a deal.

Another drawback is that HSAs have some state-specific tax problems. All of the tax benefits discussed in this section are true at the federal level. They are also true at the state level for *almost all* states. However, a few states tax HSA contributions, and few states tax HSA withdrawals. There aren't many, and the list can change, but check your state's laws so there are no surprises.

More Number-Names: 529 Plans

What are they?

If you thought we had left behind accounts whose names consisted of seemingly-random numbers and letters, think again! Let's look at the "529 Plan," which I promise will be the last account type we discuss whose name is an acronym or a number. This account is sometimes referred to as a "College Savings Plan," though that is something of a misnomer as we will see.

Like 401(k), 403(b), and 457(b) plans, 529 plans are named after the section of law that creates them. Like 401(k) plans, the 529 comes from Title 26 of the Internal Revenue Code. Also like the other retirement accounts we have discussed, their benefits would amount to tax evasion if the federal government didn't explicitly make them legal. These plans have been around since 1996, so they are relatively newer than most of the other account types we discussed (the HSA from the last section is newer, and the only one from the new millennium).

Although the federal government enables 529 plans in the tax code, states and educational institutions actually administer them. Recall that your *employer* administers your 401(k) plan.

Remember: the 529 is a type of account into which you can put various investments; it is not itself an investment. The account/ plan is the container; the investments are what you put in.

IRAs and 401(k)s are actually very similar to 529 plans. A key difference is that IRAs and 401(k)s help you save for *retirement*, and 529 plans help you save for *education*. In fact, the tax code calls 529 plans "Qualified Tuition Programs."

There are two types of 529 plans: "Savings Plans" and "Prepaid Tuition Plans." We will consider each one below, in its own section.

529 Savings Plans

First, let's look at how 529 "Savings Plans" work. When you read "529 plan" in this section, I am talking about the "Savings Plan" version; the Prepaid Tuition type is covered separately.

You open a 529 Savings Plan through your state. But, you don't open the account for yourself. Instead, you open it for a beneficiary. This can be your child, grandchild, nephew, a friend of the family, or some random person you want to be generous with.

After opening the account, you contribute money and buy various investments, likely mutual funds. Those investments grow, tax-free, until you withdraw them for the beneficiary to use to pay for education expenses.

With the 529 Savings Plan, you contribute *after-tax income*. So, there's no up-front tax advantage. Your investments grow, tax-free, and you pay no taxes when you take them out for education. The two key differences between 529 Savings Plans and the Roth IRA and Roth 401(k) are that someone *else* gets the money and they only get it to use for *education* expenses. Note that this is very unlike the HSA we talked about in the previous section, because you pay taxes on the income before you contribute it.

The pros and cons of these plans, like the Devil, lurk in the details.

Pros

As you read through this section, bear in mind that each plan's details are specific to the state that administers them. Federal law sets out the basic principles, but the state-by-state details can vary quite a bit. And both federal and state rules can change at any time. So, while the advantages laid out in this section are generally true, verify the particulars of the plan you are looking at before opening an account.

The most obvious advantages of 529 plans are the tax benefits. After all, like the 401(k), it was created by the Internal Revenue Code specifically to give you tax breaks. Your investments grow tax-free until you take them out. Then, the investment gains are themselves tax-free when you use them for education expenses. Those are two distinct tax advantages, each of which works in your favor. Withdrawals are always free of federal tax and are almost always free of state and local taxes as well.

If you have children and plan to help pay for their education, you are (hopefully) already saving anyway. A 529 plan is simply a more tax efficient way to save. The types of available investments within the plan vary, but most have a low-risk version that is essentially like a savings account.

So, if you were just planning to save money for your child's college fund through a low-risk investment like bonds, why not do it within a 529 plan so the interest is tax free? If you were planning to invest your savings in something riskier, but with a higher return (i.e. if your children are younger and you have a longer time horizon), why not just invest in riskier things within the 529 plan's tax-advantaged bubble?

Another advantage is that you can save for anyone's education, not just your children. You can save for your grandchildren, nieces and nephews, random people you happen to take a liking to, and so on. This is an important advantage because it opens up a new avenue for giving gifts. If you want to give someone routine monetary gifts over many years, this might be something to consider. It is a way to give money, let your gift money compound, and avoid anyone paying taxes on it (as long as it's used for education). The recipient might not initially thank you for a check she can't spend, but will probably reconsider when her friends are paying off student loans and she has disposable income (to invest, hopefully).

Speaking of gifts, note that there is no federally-specified limit on how much you can put into a 529 plan. This is very distinct from 401(k) plans, IRAs, and HSAs, where your annual contributions are capped by federal law. However, check the plan you're looking at; while *federal* law doesn't set a maximum, most states do. The real key to this advantage is that, because states can set their own maximums, you can shop around and find higher maximums if that's important to you.

The above paragraph implies advantage: you are not limited to the plan administered by the state you happen to live in. Every state, plus DC, has a 529 Savings Plan available, and you are free to sign up for whichever one you want.

That means you can shop around for the state plan that works best for you. Some states have better (i.e. better variety, lower-fee) investment options than others, some states have higher contribution limits, and so forth. Just remember that this works in reverse, too, and you need to look out for any downsides. For example, most states' plans let you use the money for out-of-state education, but be sure to check.

There is little need to worry about what type of schooling you want to pay for. Another advantage of 529 plans is that they are pretty expansive in terms of where you can use the money. It can pay for college and (usually) graduate school, as well as secondary and elementary schools. There are a few qualifications as to which schools qualify, but it is not very limiting.

Qualifying schools can be public or private. Private schools were initially excluded, a fact that underscores the point that the rules are always changing and you need to do your research before jumping in.

In addition to a generous interpretation of what kind of school qualifies, another advantage is that quite a few expenses qualify for 529 plan money. Most obviously, the money can pay for tuition. But, it can also pay for other education-related items like fees, books, room and board, and even required computers and Internet service if it's required for school.

You should verify what counts and what doesn't. "Room and board," for instance, is only what a school charges for its living quarters – not a penthouse apartment downtown so your little Princess can throw classy and memorable soirees to impress her new besties.

Don't try any nonsense with this, either, like trying to use 529 plan funds to pay for the mortgage on a house for the student to "live in while in school," but that you happen to turn into an investment property or a gift to her once she graduates. Those sorts of shenanigans can quickly earn you an education in how tax courts and the prison system operate.

Another advantage of 529 plans is that you control the account. Remember, the student who eventually uses the money is the *beneficiary* – not the owner. You're the owner and control the account and the money until it's withdrawn.

That control is actually a big advantage because it gives you flexibility. Imagine the beneficiary ends up stealing your jewelry to sell for black market oxycodone, for instance. You might decide that you have funded her quite enough already, and that you don't want to fund her school as well.

A related advantage of 529 plans is that you can *change* the beneficiary. Maybe the original beneficiary decides not to go to school (or is otherwise engaged in rehab), but she has a cousin who shows some promise and could use the money. You can substitute one for the other.

There are more mundane reasons for changing a beneficiary, of course. Maybe the first beneficiary gets and unexpected inheritance or decides not to go to school and doesn't need the money. You could always change the beneficiary to someone else.

Another advantage that helps with similar situations is the ability to roll the account over into someone else's name, as long as the new person is a family member. We talked about "rolling over" retirement accounts in the 401(k) and IRA sections. There, the rollover prevented you from ever taking possession of the money, triggering a tax bill.

A 529 rollover has similar benefits. You can roll over one beneficiary's 529 account into another's account, assuming both beneficiaries are in the same family. There are a number of instances where a rollover might prove useful. For example, if you are funding a 529 plan for two grandchildren, and one ends up not going to college, you can roll that child's money into the other child's account to save the tax benefits.

Finally, 529 plans aren't limited to children. Children are often named as beneficiaries, but there is no age requirement. This can be an advantage if you want to save for someone's education later in life.

Cons

As beneficial as they are, 529 Savings Plans have drawbacks.

First, their balances are not guaranteed. That might be obvious, but it is worth saying. Like other account types we have talked about, the money in the account is only as safe as the underlying investments. If you invest Junior's college savings in a mutual fund that suddenly takes a nosedive right before he's scheduled to go to school, he might need to make an emergency trip to the student loan office.

Many 529 plans have built-in options designed to gradually go from higher-risk to lower-risk investments based on when the beneficiary will need the money (like the "Lifecycle Funds" we discussed in the 401(k) section), but they are not guaranteed.

These plans don't lower your taxable earnings, either. You can't deduct your 529 plan contributions on your income taxes. In this way, 529 plans are very similar to the *Roth* 401(k) and the *Roth* IRA. You contribute after-tax money, but don't pay taxes on the earnings when you take withdrawals. There is no current version that mimics the up-front tax advantages of the traditional 401(k). That means that, as of this writing, you have less control over the tax advantages, unlike 401(k) and IRAs, where you can choose whether to pay taxes now or later by selecting either a Roth or Traditional version.

We discussed the advantage of there being no (federal) contribution limits. But, there are withdrawal limits for money you get the tax deduction on – namely, the tax-free withdrawals are limited to the beneficiary's qualified education expenses. Even if you find a state with no contribution limit, and put in a huge amount of money, the tax advantages would only apply to the education's actual costs.

"Fortunately," given the trend in education prices, you would have to contribute a lot of money, and/ or your contributions would have to grow quite a bit before you would have trouble spending it all.

Another disadvantage to 529 plans, relative to other accounts, is that you generally have less time for the money to compound. With some of the other accounts we've talked about, you either don't *have* to take withdrawals until you are 70.5 years old, or never have to take withdrawals at all. Those accounts potentially give you many, many decades of compounding returns before you have to take the money out or bequeath it. With a 529 plan, you're funding someone's education, which usually means the money is in the account for less time.

If you start funding Junior's account when he's born, and use it for college, the funds compound for 18 years. That's still very good. Just remember from Chapter Two's financial lesson about the magic of compounding that each additional year of compounding can have a huge impact on the eventual account balance. In an example from that section, the compounded returns from the last 10 years of a 30-year investment were higher than the returns from the entire first 20 years. That's not a reason to ask Junior to wait until he's 30 or 40 to attend college; it's just an observation about the practical limits of compounding since 529 account money is used for education.

Relatedly, we noted that an advantage of 529 plans is that you can now use them for secondary and even elementary schools. In reality, the advantages diminish rapidly when you use money for early education because it doesn't have very long to compound. That's true even if you put a very large amount into the account for a few years.

Remember: you are putting in after-tax money, so your contributions do not lower your taxable income. You get your tax benefit at the end, when you don't pay taxes on the compounded *earnings* (you already paid taxes on your contributions). Unless you happen to hit the market at a lucky time, even large contributions over a short time probably won't generate enough earnings to give you a big tax benefit.

There are also tax disadvantages. If you contribute to a 529 plan and the beneficiary doesn't go to school, or if you need the money early, you not only pay taxes on the earnings, but you also pay a 10% penalty. Again, you hear echoes of 401(k)s and IRAs with 529 plans. There are few instances where you would not have to pay the taxes and penalties – mainly if the beneficiary gets a scholarship, dies, or is disabled such that she cannot attend school.

Finally, 529 Savings Plans are state-specific. A related disadvantage is that there are (at the time of this writing) 50 states (plus DC). That means you have 51 potential plans and the rules for each are slightly different. There are some resources available in print and online that can help you narrow your search down to a few plans. You definitely want to look over at least a few options, though, and make sure there's nothing in the plan that would exclude your intended use.

Prepaid Tuition Plans

Now that we have talked about the "529 Savings Plan," we're better equipped to understand the other type of 529 plan: the "529 Prepaid Tuition Plan." For brevity, I will distinguish the two in this section by calling them "Savings Plans" and "Prepaid Plans."

Let's look at some key differences between the plans, leading to a discussion of Pros and Cons.

Prepaid Plans can be offered by both states and educational institutions, like schools (as of this writing, Savings Plans can *only* be offered by states). Individual schools can offer them, as well as groups of schools.

The key to Prepaid Plans is that (as the name suggests), you prepay tuition. It is essentially like putting aside money that grows at the same pace as tuition increases. Suppose you just had a baby. Looking down at her cherubic face in the crib, you dream of sending your little Princess to your alma mater to study in the same classroom where you studied, cheer for the same team you cheered for, and be chased by the same campus police department that chased you. You get misty-eyed at the nostalgia.

When you attended the school ("not that long ago," you tell yourself), it only cost $5,000 per year. But you peruse your alma mater's website and discover that one year of tuition now costs $20,000. The next year, you look it up again and it's $23,000. That's a 15% increase in one year!

A Prepaid Plan is a way to lock in future tuition at today's prices. It would be like if you gave the school $23,000 now (the cost of one year's tuition), and then, 17 years from now when your daughter enrolls, one year of tuition is already paid for, even if the going rate is $290,000 per year.

Don't laugh. I didn't just make that number up out of thin air. $23,000, compounded for 17 years at 15% is almost exactly $290,000.

Prepaid Plans let you put money into an account that is essentially guaranteed to grow at the rate of inflation *of education* for the school. The moment you put your money into the Prepaid Plan, you lock in however much tuition that buys, whenever your daughter goes to school, regardless of how fast education prices rise.

Note: this is *not* the same rate of inflation we talked about earlier in this book (the "Consumer Price Index," or CPI). Which is good, because for a long time tuition inflation has been much, much higher than inflation given by the CPI. The inflation we're talking about is not a standard amount – it is calculated on a plan-by-plan basis, according to a formula designed to replicate the rate at which the tuition in question is increasing.

While *Savings Plans* consist of money invested in things like mutual funds that can lose value, *Prepaid Plans* are investments in shares, or units, of tuition. Unlike Savings Plans, Prepaid Plans are guaranteed.

Of course, you don't have to pay for one full year at a time. You invest your money along, putting in whatever you are willing and able to contribute. Each contribution buys a certain number of educational units (think of the units like hours), based on the price when you made your contribution.

The main advantage Prepaid Plans have over Savings Plans is your peace of mind. Once you contribute enough to buy a semester of school, that is locked in – your Princess gets to go to school for at least one semester.

I used to have a friend that I visited frequently. Mary was in her late 90s when I knew her, and she often mentioned that she had prepaid her funeral expenses when she was younger. It gave her tremendous peace of mind knowing that, when she died, her grandson (she had long since outlived her children) would not have to worry about paying for her funeral.

A Prepaid Plan is like that, only for education.

Prepaid Plans are also fairly simple, in that there are no investment choices to make, keep track of, or change. It's like putting money into an investment that is guaranteed to increase in value at a specified rate –

namely, the rate at which tuition increases. This might remind you a bit of the "Treasury Inflation Protected Securities," or TIPS we talked about in the section on government bonds in first part of this Appendix. Those bond-like investments increased at a given percentage plus the rate of (CPI-based) inflation. Prepaid Plans are similar, and offer simplicity and a guarantee.

If the Prepaid Plan is administered by the state, it is usually guaranteed by the state just like a state bond. Because the beneficiary can go to various different schools, the rate of education inflation is usually tied to average tuitions at a given set of schools. That is an important point: be sure to research how the plan determines the number of education units your money buys at any particular time.

The advice to carefully review details of any plan you are considering is even more important now that educational institutions are allowed to offer Prepaid Plans. As noted earlier, the Devil is in the details, and lots of little things can trip you up. A particular institution's plan might only be valid for tuition at its school. A group of schools offering a plan will likely require the beneficiary to go to a school within that group. Other details, such as whether the Prepaid Plan covers room and board or just tuition, whether it applies to out-of-state tuition as well as in-state, what type of fees (if any) are covered, what happens if the student transfers, and so on, are very important to research.

Many other features of Prepaid Plans are generally the same as Savings Plans. You can contribute to the account for anyone, they can be transferred from one beneficiary to another, and the account owner still controls the account. Many cover room and board in addition to tuition, but that is less common for Prepaid Plans than Savings Plans.

Final Word
By carving out a section of the Internal Revenue Code for 529 Plans, the federal government created a vehicle to help people save for a beneficiary's education. One type, the 529 Savings Plan, gives savers many of the tax advantages of Roth 401(k) plans and Roth IRAs, only for education purposes instead of retirement purposes. Parents, grandparents, and others can leverage the advantages of mutual funds'

potential returns, combined with tax savings, to pay for certain education expenses at a wide range of schools.

The less-risky 529 Prepaid Plan allows savers to lock in units (hours) of education at the time of their contribution and then rest easy knowing the account's beneficiary has at least that amount of school paid for, regardless of how expensive tuition becomes in the future.

Taxable Accounts
What are they?
This bulk of the "Accounts" section of this appendix has focused on accounts with tax advantages. Employer-sponsored retirement accounts, IRAs, HSAs, and 529 Qualified Tuition Programs all allow some form of tax *deferment* (putting off paying taxes until later) or tax *avoidance* (lowering the amount of income you pay taxes on).

This final section focuses on "un-fancy" taxable accounts. We're still in the accounts section, so we're still talking about a container for your investments. The difference is that many of the previous containers we've talked about had fancy lids or special compartments to put things in. The containers in this section are just plain old containers with regular lids. They hold your investments just fine – they're much simpler, actually – but they don't come with many tax advantages.

If there are no tax advantages, why would you want these containers? There can be many reasons. One reason might be that you have already put the maximum amount you're allowed into the other containers. Or, maybe you noticed that tax advantages come with strings attached. Actually, more like ropes. Namely, you can't get to your own money for a long time without paying a penalty, you have to use the money for specific purposes, or the money is for someone else. Maybe you would like to have some money that you can invest, but can also, you know, *get to and use for whatever you want, whenever you want, without paying a penalty*.

That's where taxable accounts come in. These are places where you can deposit cash to buy and sell investments and move money around without worrying about attached strings.

We have already talked about one kind of taxable account – deposit accounts at a bank or credit union. You likely already know about this type of taxable account; you go to the bank (in person or online), fill out some forms, and then you have an account. Of course, the only investment these accounts can hold is cash. Any interest you earn on money deposited into a checking, saving, or money market account will be taxable.

The same is true of an investment account you set up through a financial institution like a brokerage firm or mutual fund company, which can hold assets besides cash. With a taxable investment account, whatever earnings you make, on whatever investments the account holds, will be taxed in the tax year that you accrue those earnings.

An investment account can be just for you (an "individual" account), one you own with someone (a "joint" account), or a few other types that relate to how and when other account owners can access the account). The various versions of investment accounts you can hold with other people ("joint" versus "joint tenants with rights of survivorship" versus "tenants in common" versus "tenants by the entireties," for instance) is a bit beyond the scope of this Appendix, since that is about *who* can access the account *when*, instead of features of the account itself. The idea is that there are different ways you can hold an investment account with other people, each of which has its own pros and cons. If you plan to hold investments in an account with someone else, you should know that there are options besides simply "joint" ownership.

After depositing money into your investment account, you can leave it in cash or buy stocks, bonds, mutual funds, ETFs, complicated commodities options contracts, and so forth.

The key difference between a taxable investment account and, say, an IRA, is that you can sell the investments in the taxable account and take the cash out at any time, without penalty. You pay *taxes* on any gains, but no *penalty*.

In fact, you can open an IRA and a taxable account with the same institution. The account setup will look very similar (just an extra box or two to check in order to establish the account as an IRA), and once you log into the account, it will also look very similar. This underscores the idea that the tax advantages with other accounts we discussed are simply legal constructs – there's nothing magical about those accounts themselves, other than the fact that they have special approval from the IRS to be taxed differently.

The main difference you will see between a taxable account and an IRA is when depositing money. An IRA will tell you how much more you can contribute before you hit the legal maximum, but you can deposit as much money as you want into a taxable account. Note the subtle word difference – you "contribute" money to a tax-advantaged account, while you "deposit" money into a taxable account. It's the same action and effect, just a matter of semantics.

If you go down to your bank and ask for an investment account, the odds are very good that they will send you over to somebody to set one up for you. That person might even sit in an office right down the hall from the bank manager. But, the bank that holds your deposits is not the same bank that you open your investment account with.

It might look the same. It might be in the same building. But it will have a different name, and, more importantly, its accounts will *not* be FDIC (or NCUA, for credit unions) insured. Look and see for yourself – there will be a note on every page of its pamphlets saying there is no FDIC insurance. Some representatives even have it on their business cards (which often have the same logo as the bank, only with a slightly different name – like "Megabank *Investments*" versus "Megabank").

I bring that up because, if you open anything other than a deposit account or CD with your bank, it will not be insured. It's the Federal *Deposit* Insurance Corporation, after all, not the Federal *Investment* Insurance Corporation. That is an important point to know since many people do their investing business with the "same" bank that holds their regular deposit accounts. It would be easy to assume the same federal insurance applied to both.

You open taxable accounts, you put your money in, and buy and sell investments at your leisure. You incur "trading costs" – a fee for buying and selling.

Pros

Taxable accounts are great for getting your money out, penalty-free. If you want to go to Aruba and have a couple of thousand dollars in the account, you can take it out and use it for your vacation without paying any 10% or 20% or – I'm feeling faint – 50% penalties.

There are no maximum contribution limits. If you inherit $100,000 that you want to invest, you can put it right into your investment account and buy whatever investments you please. An IRA would wag a scolding finger at you and remind you that you can only put in a certain amount each year. In fact, at current contribution limits you'd have to put your $100,000 inheritance into an IRA over the course of almost 20 years' worth of contributions.

You can put many different types of investments into a taxable account. There are some exceptions (like real estate), but you'll have enough options to keep you busy for a long time.

Another advantage to taxable accounts is that they provide a place for you to invest if you are in the happy position of having more money to invest after funding all of your other, tax-advantaged, investment accounts. Even though you have to pay taxes, more money is generally better than less, and taxable accounts are sort of a last resort investment account for those who have a lot to invest, but who have exhausted other account options.

Cons

The main drawback to taxable accounts is that they are, well, taxable. If you get an interest payment or dividend payment, you have to pay taxes on it that year. If you sell a mutual fund or stock at a profit, you have to pay taxes on it that year.

I explicitly say "that year" in the above paragraph to underscore the idea that you have to pay taxes on your earnings *in the year that you get them*. Unlike some other account types we discussed earlier, you do not get the advantage of tax-free compounding within the account. That advantage is called "tax deferment," where you defer, or put off, paying taxes until later.

With the tax-advantaged accounts we talked about, your earnings grow, tax-free, over the life of your account. You can invest those earnings to earn more money in subsequent years. With a taxable account, taxes reduce your earnings each year, such that you have less money available to buy additional investments. Tax deferment has a tremendous effect on your overall compounded returns over long time periods.

Of course, any stock you own *does* grow tax free until you sell it. If you own shares of stock that double in value over the course of a year, you don't pay taxes unless you sell. If it doubles again the next year, you again pay no taxes unless you sell. We discussed this in terms of "price appreciation" and "capital gains." Price appreciation just means the price of your investment has gone up; you don't actually realize ("get") that money until you sell.

But, you eventually have to pay the piper. The only way to get to that money is to sell it, and when you do, you will have to pay capital gains taxes. And, you have to pay taxes on any dividends you earn each year.

Mutual funds owned in a taxable account are similar, but you don't control when the mutual fund manager buys and sells. So, you will pay taxes on any capital gains that the mutual fund reports, as well as any dividends you earn.

One tax-related matter that can work in your favor is that, at the time of this writing, money you earn from capital gains (i.e. selling an investment like stock) is often be taxed at a lower rate than your regular income (it could be the same, depending on your tax bracket). That's not so much as an advantage as a mitigated disadvantage. But, for most people, capital gains are taxed more favorably than income, so that's something.

In addition, current tax rates penalize you for short-term (less than one year) capital gains in a taxable account by applying a higher tax rate than you would face for long-term gains. Suppose you turn out to be a very good (or lucky) stock trader and are able to buy stocks shortly before they go up in price, when you sell for quick profits. That's good, but your tax bill would be higher than if you had held them for more than a year. It's just a disadvantage to keep in mind if you plan to make your money as a day-trader (someone who buys investments to quickly resell for a profit).

Final Word

Taxable accounts, particularly investment accounts, are easy to open and provide a vehicle through which you can invest your money in stocks, bonds, mutual funds, and many other investments. You can easily liquidate your investments for cash at any time without paying penalties for accessing your own money. There are no age limits determining when you *may* withdraw your money or when you *must* withdraw your money. Consequently, there are no early- or late-withdrawal penalties for taxable accounts like there were for tax-advantaged accounts.

The main drawback to taxable accounts is obviously their taxable nature. You will not only pay taxes on your earnings each year, but the taxes you pay represent money that will not be available to compound year after year.

Because of the availability and benefits of tax-advantaged accounts like 401(k)s, IRAs, HSAs, and 529 Plans, many people choose to invest in taxable accounts only after exhausting tax-advantaged account options.

Conclusion

I hope you have a better sense of the investments and investment account types available to you after reading over this Appendix. Specifically, I hope you don't confuse an *investment* with an investment *account*, as many people do, and that you have a basic understanding of some options available to you, along with some advantages and disadvantages of each.

The investing landscape is constantly changing. Laws governing investments and accounts change. Some options disappear entirely, while others spring up overnight and offer new choices. Although the lessons derived from the biblical parables and stories in this book itself are timeless, the rules about specific investments and account types in the Appendix are ever-changing.

The point of this Appendix is to arm you with enough information to know what to look for when examining a potential investment or account type, and to ask good questions of your financial, tax, and legal advisors. Even if the rules have changed dramatically by the time you read this, you will know to do your own research and to think for yourself before committing your hard-earned money.

www.ingramcontent.com/pod-product-compliance
Lightning Source LLC
Chambersburg PA
CBHW031611210526
45464CB00004B/1523